The Political Theory of Che Guevara

The Political Theory of Che Guevara

Renzo Llorente

ROWMAN &
LITTLEFIELD
INTERNATIONAL
London • New York

Published by Rowman & Littlefield International Ltd.
Unit A, Whitacre Mews, 26-34 Stannary Street, London SE11 4AB
www.rowmaninternational.com

Rowman & Littlefield International Ltd. is an affiliate of Rowman & Littlefield
4501 Forbes Boulevard, Suite 200, Lanham, Maryland 20706, USA
With additional offices in Boulder, New York, Toronto (Canada), and Plymouth (UK)
www.rowman.com

British Library Cataloguing-in-Publication Data
A catalogue record for this book is available from the British Library.

ISBN: HB

Library of Congress Cataloging-in-Publication Data
978-1-78348-716-5 (cloth)
978-1-78348-717-2 (paperback)
978-1-78348-718-9 (electronic)

Contents

Acknowledgments

I wish to thank my editors at Rowman & Littlefield International—Anna Reeve, Dhara Snowden, Rebecca Anastasi and Elaine McGarraugh—for their patience, encouragement, and guidance. I would also like to thank Saint Louis University–Madrid Campus for providing the financial support for my research in Cuba.

Timeline

June 14, 1928	Ernesto Guevara de la Serna is born in Rosario, Argentina. He is the first of the five children of Ernesto Guevara Lynch and Celia de la Serna.
May 1930	Guevara endures his first asthma attack. He will continue to suffer from asthma for the rest of his life.
1947–1953	Guevara studies medicine at the University of Buenos Aires.
January 1950	Using a motorized bicycle, Guevara journeys to various provinces in northern Argentina.
December 1951– August 1952	Accompanied by his friend Alberto Granado, Guevara travels throughout Latin America, including visits to Chile, Peru, and Colombia.
June 1953	Guevara receives his medical degree.
July 1953	Guevara begins a second trip to Latin American countries with his friend Carlos (Calica) Ferrer. The trip includes visits to Bolivia, Ecuador, and Guatemala.
December 1953	Guevara arrives in Guatemala, where he meets exiled Cuban revolutionaries.
June 1954	Guatemala's democratically elected government, headed by president Jacobo Arbenz, is overthrown by reactionary forces supported by the United States. Guevara joins the resistance fighting against the coup d'état.
August 1954	Guevara takes refuge in the Argentine embassy in Guatemala City.
September 1954	Guevara arrives in Mexico City.

July 1955	Guevara meets Fidel Castro in Mexico City and joins Castro's group of expeditionaries.
August 1955	Guevara marries Hilda Gadea, an exiled Peruvian economist and political activist.
February 1956	Guevara's first child, Hildita, is born.
June 1956	Guevara is arrested by Mexican police, along with more than two dozen of the future expeditionaries, including Fidel Castro. Guevara spends several weeks in jail.
November 25, 1956	Guevara is one of the eighty-two revolutionaries aboard the *Granma* yacht as it leaves Tuxpan, Mexico, for Cuba.
December 2, 1956	Castro's revolutionaries land in southeastern Cuba.
July 1957	Guevara is put in charge of the Rebel Army's Fourth Column and promoted to *comandante* ("major," but also "commander"), the Rebel Army's highest rank.
August–December 1958	Guevara leads the invasion of the province of Las Villas and the conquest of central Cuba.
December 28, 1958	Guevara commands the Rebel Army's forces in the decisive Battle of Santa Clara, part of the Rebels' final offensive.
January 1, 1959	Guevara achieves victory in the Battle of Santa Clara. Dictator Fulgencio Batista flees Cuba.
January 3, 1959	Guevara assumes control of Havana's La Cabaña military fortress.
February 9, 1959	The Council of Ministers grants Guevara Cuban citizenship.
May 1959	Guevara divorces Hilda Gadea.
June 2, 1959	Guevara marries Aleida March, whom he had met in 1958 and who had been one of his collaborators during the revolutionary war. Guevara goes on to have four children with March—Aleida, Camilo, Celia, and Ernesto.
June–September 1959	Guevara visits the Middle East, Africa, Asia, and Europe and signs trade and cultural agreements on behalf of Cuba.
October 7, 1959	Guevara is chosen to head the Department of Industrialization at the National Institute for Agrarian Reform.
November 26, 1959	The Council of Ministers appoints Guevara president of the National Bank of Cuba.
March 4, 1960	A French ship carrying Belgian arms explodes in Havana Harbor. Apparently caused by sabotage, the explosion kills around one hundred people.
March 5, 1960	At a memorial service for the victims of the explosion the previous day, photographer Alberto Korda takes the picture that will become the single most famous photo—and image—of Guevara.
Spring 1960[1]	Guevara publishes *Guerrilla Warfare* (*La guerra de guerrillas*).

October–December 1960	Guevara travels to various socialist countries: Czechoslovakia, the Soviet Union, China, North Korea, and the German Democratic Republic.
February 23, 1961	The Ministry of Industries is created, and Guevara is appointed minister.
April 16, 1961	Fidel Castro publicly declares that the Cuban Revolution is a socialist revolution.
April 17, 1961	The Bay of Pigs Invasion commences, as 1,500 mercenaries attack Cuba with US backing. Guevara is put in charge of the military in the province of Pinar del Río, in western Cuba.
April 19, 1961	The mercenaries are defeated.
August 1961	Guevara leads the Cuban delegation to the Organization of American States' Inter-American Economic and Social Council conference held in Punta del Este, Uruguay.
August–September 1962	Guevara visits the Soviet Union and Czechoslovakia.
October 22–28, 1962	The "Cuban Missile Crisis": In response to Cuba's acquisition of Soviet nuclear missiles, US president Kennedy orders a naval blockade of Cuba. In preparation for a possible US invasion, Guevara once again assumes military command of the Pinar del Río province. The crisis ends when Soviet premier Nikita Khrushchev agrees to the withdrawal of the missiles and the United States promises not to invade Cuba.
July 1963	Guevara visits Algeria.
1963–1964	Guevara contributes several articles to an important theoretical discussion on the political economy of socialism, a discussion that would later be dubbed "the Great Debate."
March 1964	Guevara heads the Cuban delegation to the United Nations Conference on Trade and Development in Geneva.
Spring 1964[2]	Guevara publishes *Reminiscences of the Cuban Revolutionary War* (*Pasajes de la guerra revolucionaria*).
November 1964	Guevara visits the Soviet Union.
December 11, 1964	Guevara addresses the United Nations General Assembly.
December 1964	Guevara leaves New York for Africa. His nearly three-month trip will include stops in Algeria, Egypt, Ghana, Tanzania, and Mali.
February 24, 1965	Guevara delivers a speech at the Second Economic Seminar of the Organization of Afro-Asian Solidarity.
March 1965	Guevara's essay "Socialism and Man in Cuba" ("El socialismo y el hombre en Cuba") is published.

March 15, 1965   Guevara returns to Cuba.

April 1, 1965   Guevara leaves Cuba for the Congo.

April 24, 1965   Guevara arrives in the Congo, where he joins rebels fight-
                        ing against the government.

October 3, 1965   Fidel Castro reads Guevara's "farewell" letter, written by
                        Guevara six months earlier, in the course of introducing
                        the members of the Central Committee of the newly
                        founded Cuban Communist Party.

November 21, 1965   Guevara abandons the Congo.

November 1965–   Guevara lives, in secret, at the Cuban embassy in Dar es
  February 1966[3]   Salaam, Tanzania. During this period he prepares an ac-
                        count of his experience in the Congo, which would be
                        published more than three decades later as *Congo Diary:*
                        Episodes of the Revolutionary War in the Congo (*Pasajes de*
                        la guerra revolucionaria: Congo).

March–July 1966   Guevara lives, in secret, in Prague, where he continues to
                        work on the notes that would eventually be published as
                        Apuntes críticos a la economía política (*Critical Notes on*
                        Political Economy).

July 1966   Guevara secretly returns to Cuba and goes to Pinar del
                        Río, the location in which the volunteers who will be
                        fighting with him in Bolivia are to undergo training.

October 23, 1966   A disguised Guevara leaves Cuba for Bolivia.

November 3, 1965   Guevara arrives in Bolivia.

March 1967   Guevara's National Liberation Army of Bolivia (Ejército de
                        Liberación Nacional de Bolivia) has its first engagement
                        with the Bolivian Army.

April 1967   Guevara's essay "Mensaje a los pueblos del mundo," gener-
                        ally known in English as "Message to the Tricontinen-
                        tal," is published.

October 8, 1967   During a battle at Quebrada del Yuro, a wounded Gue-
                        vara is captured by the Bolivian Army.

October 9, 1967   The Bolivian Army executes Guevara in the small village
                        of La Higuera.

October 18, 1967   Fidel Castro delivers a tribute to Guevara at a mass me-
                        morial meeting held in Havana's Plaza de la Revolución
                        (Revolution Square).

June 1997   A mass grave containing Guevara's remains is discovered in
                        Vallegrande, Bolivia.

July 1997   Guevara's remains are repatriated to Cuba.

Introduction

Half a century after his death, Ernesto Che Guevara[1] (1928–1967) remains a compelling and controversial figure, as is evident in both the steady stream of books and articles devoted to the revolutionary's life and legacy and the perennial popularity of T-shirts, posters, decals, and so on bearing his image. The enduring interest in Guevara is not hard to understand. After all, people tend to associate Guevara, not without good reason, with a decade that was, at least on a cultural level, one of the most memorable periods of the twentieth century—namely, the 1960s. Indeed, if, as Ambrosio Fornet has suggested, the 1960s effectively "began" with the triumph of the Cuban Revolution in 1959[2] and, as Rafael Hernández has suggested, 1968 effectively "began" with Guevara's execution in October 1967,[3] then it turns out that Guevara was one of the central figures in the event that ushered in that decade as well as *the* central figure in the event that ushered in that decade's most momentous year. It is therefore probably fair to say that Guevara was "the supreme expression of the sixties," the image of that decade par excellence.[4]

Of course, both of these events—the triumph of the Cuban Revolution and Guevara's murder—immediately followed periods in which Guevara formed part of armed insurrections fighting against regular armies, and hence it is no surprise that Guevara tends to be thought of primarily and above all as a guerrilla soldier.[5] This association of Guevara with guerrilla warfare and armed resistance to injustice more generally is, to be sure, perfectly justified, as is the attention paid to his accomplishments in this regard, whether as a soldier or as a theorist. For these reasons it also seems appropriate, in proposing a general "classification" of Guevara, to use the label "Latin American revolutionary," as does one well-known encyclopedia.[6] At the same time, this label, "revolutionary," which denotes "one engaged in a revolution" or "an advocate or adherent of revolutionary doctrines,"[7] may prove inadequate and misleading in Guevara's case, even if we construe the term in such a way as to

1

encompass Guevara's accomplishments as, say, president of the National Bank of Cuba, Minister of Industries, or Cuba's sometime-roving envoy—just three of the roles that he assumed as a participant in the Cuban Revolution. The problem is that the term "revolutionary" may well obscure the fact that Guevara was actually, as Margaret Randall puts it, an "unusual combination of theoretician and warrior."[8] That is, Guevara was also an original, creative political thinker whose abundant writings, speeches, lectures, and talks attest to an innovative interpretation and development of various concepts, principles, and commitments central to Marxist political theory. Indeed, Guevara—who was well versed in both the Marxist classics (Marx, Engels, and Lenin) and contemporary Marxist theory (including Althusser, Mao, and Paul Baran)—produced a body of work that should be of interest to anyone concerned with fundamental questions in radical social theory, for his books, essays, speeches, and so on address questions that have shaped some of the most important debates in this theoretical tradition. For example: Is it possible for revolutionaries to take power without recourse to armed struggle? How should work be organized in a liberated society? How should we conceive of—and undertake—the transition from capitalism to socialism in an underdeveloped country? What role should moral incentives and motivations play in this transition? What are its preconditions? What mechanisms or practices promote equality and social solidarity? How should revolutionaries deal with resistance to their initiatives and with the opposition from imperialism? What are the appropriate methods of management and administration in a socialist economy? What role should the peasantry play in the struggle for national liberation? Do we need to transform human beings in order to realize communism, and, if so, how?

Yet, despite the fact that Guevara's works address such questions, along with many others of central importance to radical social theory, his contributions to this body of thought have not received the attention that they deserve, with the result that Guevara has not been given his due as an analyst and theorist, at least outside of Spanish-speaking countries. There would seem to be two basic reasons for this neglect of Guevara's contributions to radical social thought. First of all, the extraordinary interest and drama of Guevara's exploits as a "man of action," from his youthful travels throughout Latin America to his final attempt at kindling an insurrectionary struggle in Bolivia, tend to overshadow, or deflect attention from, the rest of his accomplishments. Second, much of what Guevara wrote and said has yet to be translated into English. This is the case with many of the texts included in *Escritos y discursos*, the standard, nine-volume edition of Guevara's works; and it is true to an even greater extent in the case of *El Che en la Revolución cubana*, whose seven volumes run to well over 3,500 pages and comprise the single most comprehensive—yet still highly incomplete—collection of Guevara's articles, lectures, speeches, addresses, interviews, talks, meeting transcripts, reports, and letters. Nor are there, at present, English-language versions of the recently published *Apuntes filosóficos* (Philosophical notes) and *Apuntes críticos a la economía política* (Critical notes on political economy), which include countless fragments and notes on various works in Marxist theory, ranging from an influential Soviet manual of political economy to writings by Engels, Lenin, and other notable Marxist authors. (By contrast, Guevara's writings dealing with his youthful trips across Latin America and guerrilla campaigns in Cuba, the Congo, and Bolivia, as well as his treatise on guerrilla warfare, are all readily available in English translations.) With so much of Guevara's prodigious output unavailable in English, and still largely unknown even to those who read Spanish,[9] it is not surprising that so many people are quite unaware of the full extent of Guevara's engagement with the central problems in radical social theory or the key figures and writings from the Marxist tradition.

In any event, the upshot of this neglect of Guevara's thought is that English-language scholarship has barely registered his valuable contributions to radical social thought in general and Marxist theory in particular. For example, Guevara does not merit an entry in either the *Blackwell Encyclopaedia of Political Thought* or, even more inexplicably, the authoritative *Dictionary of Marxist Thought*.[10] These omissions are plainly unjustifiable, considering that Guevara's ideas exercised a profound influence on the Cuban Revolution and the political history of Latin America after 1959 (and considering the other topics and figures included in these works). The small number of volumes in English that do aim to analyze Guevara's political thought— as opposed to the innumerable books that address other themes connected with Guevara, ranging from straightforward biographies to meditations on his cultural significance—tend to be of a very introductory nature[11] or else prove rather superficial because of a desire to cover aspects of Guevara's life and/or historical context along with his thought.[12] In short, none of the existing works provides an analysis and assessment of Guevara's overall contribution to radical social thought in general and Marxist theory in particular.

The main aim of the present book is to remedy this neglect of Guevara's achievements in this regard through a careful study of his political thought. Accordingly, it seeks to provide reliable accounts of the theses, concepts, and commitments that lend Guevara's theoretical and political orientation its distinctive, original character. But this study also aims to situate Guevara's ideas within the context of the Marxist theoretical tradition, for Guevara regarded himself as a Marxist,[13] includes many references to Marx and Marxist ideas in his writings, speeches, lectures, and so forth, and plainly viewed his contributions to political and economic debates in the early 1960s as contributions to the development of Marxism. In addition, the present study also furnishes critical assessments of Guevara's key ideas and argues that several of them are defensible today and remain relevant to contemporary debates in socialist theory (and not merely debates within Marxism). In other words, I reject the view that Guevara's thought is of merely historical interest. To the contrary, I believe that John Gerassi was correct in claiming, in the introduction to his 1968 anthology of Guevara's speeches and writings, that "In the history books he [Guevara] will, in due course, be recorded as one of the great contributors to Marxist-Leninism [*sic*]"[14] and that some of Guevara's contributions to this tradition constitute a valuable resource for the regeneration of left-wing social theory and the political project that has come to be known as twenty-first-century socialism, even if one eschews "Marxism-Leninism."

The following chapters examine what are, in my view, the most important components of Guevara's political thought. Chapters 1 and 2 consider two of Guevara's
most distinctive contributions to radical social theory, namely his conception of the
"new man"—which I shall be calling the "new person"[15] or "new human being"—
and his views on the need to transform our attitude toward, and experience of, work.
As we shall see, Guevara's interest in the creation of a new human being and his
concern with the transformation of work occupy a preeminent place in his political
thought and vision of social renewal and are, moreover, closely connected with one
another. However, each of these two topics merits a chapter-length treatment, given
their importance in Guevara's thought and given the fact that Guevara's proposals
and vision are often misunderstood, when not deliberately distorted and caricatured.
Chapter 3 examines Guevara's views on internationalism and imperialism. Chapters
4 and 5 then consider various aspects of Guevara's ideas on socialism, communism,
and revolution, including his views on economic management and organization in
the transition to socialism. In the final chapter, 6, I discuss a few dimensions of Guevara's legacy as a political thinker in general and as a Marxist theorist in particular.

Practically all of the essays, speeches, books, and so on in which Guevara develops
his political ideas—that is, all of the works that, taken together, reflect and register
his political outlook—were written or presented between the beginning of 1959
and late 1967. (This span of time excludes the letters and diaries from Guevara's
trips throughout Latin America prior to joining Fidel Castro's rebels, as well as those
that he wrote during the Cuban Revolutionary War.) However, while amounting
to less than a decade, these were years of frenetic activity and successive, dramatic
transformations for both the revolution as a whole—it passed through several phases,
confronted a variety of challenges, survived several crises (including the Bay of Pigs
Invasion and the October 1962 missile crisis)—and for Guevara himself, who was
variously, and among other things, president of the National Bank, a minister in the
government, Cuba's preeminent envoy, and a leader of guerrilla operations on two
different continents. Given the pace and scope of these social and political changes
and the dizzying array of questions that Guevara had to address in these different
roles, one might reasonably assume that Guevara's thought likewise underwent
significant changes between January 1, 1959,[16] the day of the rebel army's triumph
over the Batista dictatorship, and October 7, 1967, when Guevara jotted down his
final diary entries before being captured and murdered by the Bolivian Army. As
it turns out, however, Guevara's thought is remarkably consistent over the course
of this period: while there is plainly a great deal of development and evolution in
his thinking on the questions that most concerned him, what we find above all is
remarkable continuity and coherence in his outlook[17] and the absence of any major
inconsistencies, contradictions, or tensions. It is worth pointing out, in this connection, that Guevara was already developing two of his most characteristic ideas—the
need to create a "new man" and the value of "voluntary labor"—in 1959 and 1960:
the first experiment with the latter took place in November 1959,[18] while in a lecture
delivered in August of the following year Guevara was already defending the need to

create a "new type of human" and declaring that it was starting to come into being in Cuba.[19] This continuity of thought is due, in my view, to the fact that Guevara would never really modify, let alone abandon, the fundamental ethicopolitical commitments that he had acquired by the time the revolution triumphed and that all of his specific proposals, initiatives, policies, and so on flow from these basic commitments. Indeed, even one of the few unmistakable changes in Guevara's outlook—his shift from a more or less acritical enthusiasm for Soviet-style socialism in the early years of the Revolution to an attitude combining solidarity with the Soviet Bloc countries with criticism of their economic doctrines and approach to supporting Third World liberation movements[20]—represents, in the last analysis, an adjustment of his views in light of the same ethicopolitical commitments, an adjustment prompted by more extensive knowledge of, and reflection on, the socialist nations' economic and political policies.

Thus, in contrast to the striking discontinuities in Guevara's life from 1959 to 1967—after several years of performing a variety of functions within the Cuban government (and Cuban society), Guevara would join an uprising in the Congo, subsequently spend a number of months in Czechoslovakia, briefly return to Cuba, and end his life leading a guerrilla insurgency in Bolivia—Guevara's basic political outlook over the same period is characterized by continuity. Accordingly, I make no attempt to periodize Guevara's thought. Nor do I distinguish between materials published during Guevara's lifetime and those that only appeared posthumously, since here, too, we find no significant contradictions or discontinuities in Guevara's thought.

But while there is little justification, in my opinion, for holding that the content of Guevara's political thought underwent important modifications during this period, there was one notable change with respect to the transparency and explicitness with which he articulated his fundamental political beliefs, commitments, and objectives. On April 16, 1961, during the funeral service for victims of US–backed bombing raids over Cuba and on the eve of the Bay of Pigs Invasion (likewise backed by the United States), Fidel Castro publicly proclaimed, for the first time, that the Cuban revolutionaries were carrying out a "socialist" revolution. Until this time, the leaders of the Revolution had studiously avoided using the words "socialist" and "socialism," even though many of the measures enacted by the revolutionary government, such as the nationalization of key industries and the passage of laws increasing state intervention in the economy, along with the expanding economic relations with the socialist countries, suggested that the revolution was indeed following a socialist course. Guevara was no exception in this regard: prior to Castro's announcement, Guevara had eschewed such terms as "socialist," "Marxist," "socialism," and "communism,"[21] even when presenting ideas, defending policies, or invoking concepts that were either of Marxist provenance or typical of socialist thought. For example, in a June 18, 1960, speech whose main topics are the problems, role, and duties of the working class, Guevara uses the term free enterprise rather than "capitalism," refers to "employers" (*clase patronal*) rather than "capitalist" or "ruling" class, and, most significantly, contrasts the "free-enterprise"-type of development not with a "socialist" type of development but with "revolutionary development."[22] Likewise, Guevara's book *Guerrilla Warfare*, published in 1960, is devoid of references to the Marxist tradition, whereas a 1963 essay dealing with similar topics, "Guerrilla Warfare: A Method," includes quotations from Engels and Lenin and refers to "Marxist-Leninist parties" in an unmistakably favorable manner.[23] Indeed, in a lecture from March 1961 Guevara could still discuss at length, and with gratitude, the scope of the aid received from the socialist countries without expressing any explicit identification with those countries' doctrinal orientation.[24] (The belief that Guevara did not become a committed Marxist until around the time of Castro's declaration is untenable, even though he himself stated on occasion that it was during, and as a result of, the revolutionary process that he, along with other leaders of the Cuban Revolution, came to embrace Marxism and communism. I discuss the relevant passages, as well as the reasons for doubting their reliability, in chapter 4.)

In fact, prior to Castro's declaration that the Cuban Revolution was a socialist revolution there seem to be only two occasions on which Guevara hints at his own political outlook, but on both occasions his language is highly ambiguous. The first occasion involves a July 1960 address to a Latin American Youth Congress, in which Guevara rather evasively grants that the revolution *might* be taking roads that Marx had pointed out and suggests, furthermore, that if the Cuban revolutionaries are practicing "that which is called Marxism," it is in the form of the Maoist military theory that they learned when one of Mao's pamphlets happened to fall into their hands during the final phase of the Revolutionary War. The second occasion is Guevara's October 1960 article "Notes for the Study of the Ideology of the Cuban Revolution." This piece includes favorable, relatively lengthy references to Marx and Marxism, but the essay's almost academic detachment leaves Guevara's own relationship to the Marxist tradition rather unclear: "We recognize," he wrote, "the essential truths of Marxism as part of humanity's body of cultural and scientific knowledge," and "the laws of Marxism are present in the events of the Cuban Revolution," but they are present "independently of whether its leaders profess or fully know those laws from a theoretical point of view."[25]

Guevara would not abandon his discretion until after Fidel Castro's public acknowledgment of the Cuban Revolution's socialist orientation,[26] even though Guevara claims in a 1962 report to the Council of Ministers that by the "second semester of 1960"—that is, several months before Castro's announcement—Cuba was already entering the "period of transition from capitalism to socialism"[27] (and so, one would think, it would have been reasonable and appropriate to begin using the "language" of socialism publicly). But once Castro made his announcement, Guevara's terminology underwent an immediate and dramatic change: in his April 30, 1961, lecture ("On Economic Planning in Cuba"), delivered a mere two weeks after Castro's announcement, Guevara refers to the revolution as "socialist" on several occasions and is less inhibited in his use of characteristically Marxist language and concepts, such as "petit bourgeoisie" and "the capitalist system."[28] Thereafter,

Guevara would consistently invoke Marxist concepts and regularly use Marxist language, explicitly identify the measures he defends with policies aimed at establishing socialism and communism, and unhesitatingly proclaim his adherence to Marxism and Marxism-Leninism.[29]

This ideological candor in Guevara's texts (including his speeches, lectures, and other works) after mid-April 1961 makes these documents far more illuminating and reliable than Guevara's output in the period preceding Castro's historic announcement. But the postannouncement period also roughly coincides with Guevara's tenure as Minister of Industries, as his appointment to this position had occurred less than two months earlier, at end of February 1961, and would not end until his departure for the Congo at the end of March 1965. During these years as minister, Guevara was actively engaged in economic planning—besides heading the Ministry of Industries, Guevara was a member of the revolution's organ for central planning (JUCEPLAN)—and this experience, which involved the attempt to undertake the transition to socialism in a country that was both underdeveloped and under siege (and so also involved constant improvisation, experimentation, and innovation), enriched, and is registered in, Guevara's works from this period. Guevara also contributed to the general political orientation of the Cuban Revolution during these same years, especially with regard to its international outlook, and Guevara's texts from this time also reflect this dimension of his activity in Cuba. This extraordinary period culminates in Guevara's speech at the Second Economic Seminar of Afro-Asian Solidarity in Algiers on February 24, 1965, and his best-known text, "Socialism and Man in Cuba," which he wrote at approximately the same time and published in the March 12, 1965, issue of the Uruguayan weekly newspaper *Marcha*; the latter text was, as Fernando Martínez Heredia points out, the last piece of work that Guevara wrote for immediate publication.[30] Guevara's last recorded talk as minister likewise took place in March of that year. His last published interview, apparently also conducted in March, appeared in April, which is also the month in which he sent an illuminating letter to Fidel Castro summarizing his considered views on the transition to socialism in Cuba.[31] By contrast, after April 1965 Guevara would prepare but one major essay for publication, the text usually referred to as the "Message to the Tricontinental"; Guevara's only other writings from the final years of his life were, apart from letters, a lengthy report on his guerrilla campaign in the Congo, a series of brief communiqués in the name of his Bolivian guerrilla army, a document with instructions for his urban collaborators in Bolivia, the diary he kept while in Bolivia, and the highly suggestive yet fragmentary comments and notes on his readings in political economy and Marxist theory.[32]

Thus, the four-year period that stretches from April 1961 to April 1965 is of particular importance for the crystallization and expression of Guevara's mature political thought: from mid-April 1961 on, circumstances no longer obliged Guevara to articulate his ideas in guarded, somewhat equivocal language, and, on the other hand, what he wrote after April 1965 is—with the notable exception of his "Message to the Tricontinental"—either of little interest as regards the central ideas of his political thought or simply restates what he said and wrote earlier. For all of these reasons, I devote particular attention to the texts dating from this period in expounding and analyzing Guevara's political thought, without neglecting in the least what Guevara said and wrote during the first years of the revolution (or, for that matter, prior to the revolution) or after leaving Cuba in the spring of 1965. For by January 1959 Guevara was, to borrow Engels's description of Marx at the latter's graveside, "before all else a revolutionist,"[33] and, as we shall see, a revolutionary outlook characterizes Guevara's political thought from beginning to end.

1

The New Human Being

Whatever other differences may separate them, radical (left-wing) thinkers typically are at one in assuming that major social progress requires some sort of transformation of human nature. This is certainly true of Marxist thinkers on the whole, the more specific radical tradition within which Guevara's thought should be situated. But what exactly do radical social theorists have in mind when they assert that it is necessary to transform human nature?

THE TRANSFORMATION OF HUMAN NATURE

To begin with, it should be noted that the "nature"—that is, that dimension of our nature—that is to undergo a transformation is not our *physical* nature but rather a part of our psychological nature.[1] More specifically, what radical social thinkers have in mind is an array of motivations, aspirations, values, preferences, and dispositions common to the immense majority of people, and that consequently define their society's prevailing ethos. The transformation in question refers to a substantial modification of these values, preferences, motivations, and so on, either by heightening, expanding, and intensifying them or by tempering, reducing, or eliminating them.

Of course, the insistence on the need to transform human nature presupposes that at least certain aspects of human nature are indeed susceptible to change, but this premise, which, following the philosopher Joseph H. Carens, we may call the "plasticity" view of human nature, is widely accepted by social scientists.[2] Everyday experience should also incline us to accept this premise, since it is not uncommon to have friends or acquaintances at least some parts of whose personalities were deliberately and decisively shaped by, say, their families or religious communities. If, then, the available sociohistorical evidence indicates, as Carens claims, that "human nature

9

is so flexible that, given the proper conditions of socialization, almost any goals could be adopted on a widespread basis in a society"[3] (the essence of the "plasticity" view) and everyday experience suggests the same conclusion, radical social theorists, including Guevara, would seem to be on safe ground in accepting the proposition that at least some sort of transformation of human nature is possible.

What does the Marxist tradition say about the ways in which human nature needs to be transformed? In the works of Marx and Engels themselves, we actually find little in this regard beyond (1) some general expressions of adherence to the "plasticity" view (as in the well-known sixth thesis of Marx's "Theses on Feuerbach"[4]) and (2) a foundational commitment to a theory of history, according to which changes in a given society's mode of production inevitably effect changes in its "superstructure," which includes those constituents of human nature that I mentioned above.[5] To be sure, we also find statements to the effect that the working class will be transformed, and *must* be transformed, in the course of bringing about its own emancipation[6] and, more generally, that human beings will be very different following the abolition of capitalism.[7] On the whole, however, Marx and Engels say very little about the specific ways in which human nature will change, or need to change, and their reticence in this regard plainly derives from their aim to theorize as "scientific," rather than "utopian," socialists. As "scientific" socialists, they sought to limit themselves to identifying, and drawing conclusions on the basis of, present social tendencies and developments, instead of attempting to anticipate the future, which, they held, would be peopled by men and women who are truly free for the first time in history and therefore bound to lead their lives in ways that we, constrained and crippled as we are by capitalist society, can scarcely begin to imagine.

When we turn to later Marxist thinkers, however, we find not only agreement with Marx and Engels's views regarding the inevitability of change in human nature[8] but also far less circumspection when it comes to specifying the sorts of changes that will occur, and will need to occur, for there to exist a truly liberated society. Rosa Luxemburg, for example, not only contends that "socialism in life demands a complete spiritual transformation in the masses degraded by centuries of bourgeois class rule" but goes on to state that "one cannot realize socialism with lazy, frivolous, egoistic, thoughtless, and indifferent human beings. A socialist society needs human beings who . . . are full of passion and enthusiasm for the general well-being, full of self-sacrifice and sympathy for their fellow human beings."[9] On could also cite in this connection the "new sensibility" and "new needs"—which, to the extent that we assume them, modify our nature—defended by Herbert Marcuse,[10] the later Georg Lukács's interest in creating a new human being,[11] or, to take an example from a contemporary Marxist philosopher of an analytical orientation, Andrew Levine's insistence that "people must become more communal and more inclined to subordinate private to general interests."[12]

One could cite many more examples of statements from Marxist thinkers that postulate the kind of transformation of human nature required for a socialist or communist society. The common element in nearly all such pronouncements is the idea that the transformation in question will consist in a *moral transformation*, that in some sense human beings can, must, and will undergo such a change and that the process of creating a socialist, and ultimately communist, society will involve what we might call a *moral enhancement* of human nature.[13] This is, I take it, what Engels has in mind when he observes, "A really human morality which stands above class antagonisms and above any recollection of them becomes possible only at a stage of society which has not only overcome class antagonisms but has even forgotten them in practical life."[14] In short, many facets of the human nature—much of the individual's motivational structure—that we identify with "homo economicus" and "possessive individualism"[15] will have to disappear or, at the very least, be quite significantly attenuated if a socialist/communist society is to prove viable. But Marxists assume that they will in fact disappear, given the right institutional arrangements and provided that certain socioeconomic conditions have been satisfied.

Like other Marxists, Guevara believes that the viability of a "higher" society requires a transformation of human nature; socialist and communist societies cannot succeed without such a transformation. Yet Guevara's ideas on human transformation have attracted far more attention than those of other thinkers in the Marxist tradition, and this exceptional attention was the result of two factors in particular: the emphasis that Che himself places on the role of human transformation in the establishment of socialism (i.e., the idea's salience in his thought) and the fact that Guevara occasionally uses the striking term "new man" (*hombre nuevo*) to refer to the end product of this transformation. Unfortunately, Guevara's conception of the post-transformation human being has been widely misunderstood, when not deliberately caricatured.[16] Such a treatment of Guevara's idea of the new man makes a fair assessment of his political thought nearly impossible, and for this reason alone an accurate notion of this idea is indispensable. This is what I seek to provide in the present chapter.

THE NEW HUMAN BEING AND COMMUNISM

Before considering the specific qualities or traits with which Guevara associates the new man, it is necessary to say a bit about the use of the term—for which I shall generally be substituting the terms "new person," "new men and women," or "new human being"[17]—in Guevara's works and the role and scope of the concept in his thought. Guevara was by no means the first thinker in the Marxist tradition to stress the importance of creating a new man. Indeed, an anthology on "communist morality" published in the Soviet Union in the 1960s actually contains an index entry for the "moral makeup of the new man."[18] Still, it is probably fair to say that if the term and its variants are a familiar part of political discourse today, it is above all due to the influence of Guevara's use of "new man."

In one sense, the close association of the term "new man" with Guevara, as opposed to the characteristics belonging to this new human being, proves rather surprising for the simple reason that Guevara seldom uses it in evoking his revolutionary hopes and objectives. At the same time, this association is not at all surprising if we bear in mind that the one text in which Guevara employs the term on several occasions is in fact his best-known, and probably most widely read, political essay—namely, "Socialism and Man in Cuba." Despite its brevity (about sixteen pages in a popular English-language anthology of his writings), this essay is remarkably comprehensive, addressing topics that range from the early history of the Cuban Revolution to the status of art under capitalism and socialism, and the problems besetting attempts to promote a socialist consciousness among Cubans in the initial stages of the revolutionary process. But if there is one theme common to all of the topics discussed in the essay, it is the theme evoked in its title: the nature of the individual under socialism and communism and the measures required to bring communist men and women into being. It is precisely because the essay offers a compendium of Guevara's views on a number of essential questions pertaining to revolution and social transformation that it is generally regarded as the single most important document that Guevara produced.[19] Indeed, Cuban philosopher Fernando Martínez Heredia's characterization of the text as "Che's Communist Manifesto" hardly seems unreasonable[20]; and "Socialism and Man in Cuba" is widely considered to be a major contribution to Latin American socialist thought in general and Latin American Marxism in particular.[21] (Significantly, it is the only work by a Latin American thinker that David McLellan includes in a "chronological table" of important works in Marxist theory included in his encyclopedic *Marxism after Marx*.[22])

If, then, "Socialism and Man in Cuba" is an exceptionally important work in Guevara's oeuvre and in Latin American Marxism in general, and the term "new man" figures prominently in this text,[23] it is really no wonder that many identify Guevara with this term (especially considering that Guevara insists throughout his works on the importance of transforming human beings, albeit generally without using the term "new man"). But what does Guevara himself mean in speaking of a new man?

To begin with, we should note that the new men and women whom Guevara conjures up in "Socialism and Man in Cuba" and other texts is synonymous, for Guevara, with *communist* men and women. That is to say, in discussing the "new human beings," Guevara has in mind *human beings within a communist society*. (Note that I am following the convention, established by Lenin on the basis of his interpretation of Marx, of calling the first, immediately postcapitalist stage of communism "socialism" and the second, more advanced, stage "communism," a convention that Guevara also follows.[24]) This is often overlooked or misunderstood,[25] partly because the inconsistency in Guevara's language in "Socialism and Man in Cuba" can give rise to misinterpretations. For example, while Guevara writes at one point that "to build communism it is necessary, simultaneous with the new material foundations, to build the new man and woman,"[26] he elsewhere refers, in the very same essay and in connection with the theorization of the transition to socialism, to "the two pillars of the construction of socialism: the education of the new man and woman and the development of technology."[27] Given this ambiguity and apparent inconsistency, it is perhaps not surprising that the author of a highly praised biography of Guevara, Jon Lee Anderson, not only claims that Guevara in fact advocates the creation of a "new socialist man" but also inadvertently changes the title of Guevara's most famous essay in both Spanish and English to reflect this misinterpretation: "Socialism and Man in Cuba" becomes, in Anderson's biography, "Socialism and the New Man."[28] Yet, while Guevara's most celebrated essay deals chiefly with problems arising in the attempt to forge a socialist society and readers' confusion is therefore understandable, the new men and women to whom Guevara refers are members of a *communist* society. Guevara makes this clear when he refers to "the new society in which individuals will have different characteristics: the society of communist human beings"[29]; one of these "characteristics" is, as we shall see in the next chapter, the fact that the new human being will work in the absence of any material incentives to do so, whereas the use of some material incentives will still be necessary, according to Guevara, under socialism. We might also note in this connection the letter that Guevara wrote to Fidel Castro not long after the publication of "Socialism and Man in Cuba," in which he states that "the creation of the communist man" was one of "the two fundamental problems" faced by his new approach to economic policy, the Budgetary Finance System (discussed in chapter 5).[30] In short, the being whom Guevara evokes is neither the human being who undergoes self-transformation in the process of building socialism nor even the typical individual in a full-fledged socialist society but rather the communist human being.

Why is this consideration important? The answer is simple: it prevents us from making the mistake of assuming that Guevara believed that the transformation of human nature that he envisions, and whose advent would supposedly be hastened by the social and economic policies that he defends, could be realized in the short-term, a notion that most people would surely regard as completely implausible. Indeed, it is worth pointing out that in the very same essay Guevara declares, "What we must create is the human being of the twenty-first century"[31]; at the time in which Guevara was writing his landmark essay, the twenty-first century was still thirty-five years away—that is, at a remove of almost two generations. And he elsewhere acknowledges that his generation may have to burn itself out in the work of simply building socialism.[32] To say this is not to deny that even under socialism our human nature will already have undergone a significant modification. To the contrary, as Guevara puts it in his speech in Algeria in February of 1965 (his last major public appearance), "Socialism cannot exist without a change in consciousness resulting in a new fraternal attitude toward humanity, both at an individual level . . . and on a world scale,"[33] an attitude that, no doubt, represents a change in human nature. What is more, there may even be anticipations or glimpses of the communist person during the process of building socialism. Indeed, in an August 1964 letter to exiled Spanish poet León Felipe, Guevara relates that he had recently attended an event full of enthusiastic workers and that there was "an atmosphere of the new man in the air."[34] Still, the representative human being under socialism is a mere precursor to the new person in the classless, stateless society that is communism; in the transition from socialism to communism the moral transformation of human beings will continue, and the success of communism depends on this success of the further transformation.[35]

THE NATURE OF THE NEW HUMAN BEING

Bearing in mind that we must situate the new men and women envisioned by Guevara in a communist society, in what ways has their human nature been transformed? In other words, what are the features that make them distinctive?

Before answering this question, it is important to avoid an error found in many commentators on Guevara that consists in identifying Guevara's new human beings with various practices that Guevara advocated, such as voluntary labor, the use of moral incentives to achieve society's economic goals, or "socialist emulation."[36] These practices are, indeed, essential components of Guevara's political thought (as we shall see in the following chapter), but they serve to promote the emergence of the qualities essential to the new human beings rather than being essential hallmarks of these beings.

A careful reading of Guevara's works reveals two essential attributes or elements that distinguish the new human beings emblematic of communism and their distinctively communist ethos. The first of these is a commitment to a *radical egalitarianism*, by which I mean support for a rough equality of condition for all, coupled with an adherence to the principle of equal consideration of interests.[37] In contrast to the case of the second basic element that I shall discuss, Guevara seldom explicitly advocates or appeals to radical egalitarianism. It is, rather, a commitment that is implied, or presupposed, by many of his other positions, but that is, on the other hand, reflected in many of his own actions and practices, such as his rejection of any special privileges for himself and his insistence on strict equality of treatment among his coworkers with regard to such things as the content and size of meals. (The anecdotes attesting to Guevara's extremely egalitarian practices and policies in distributing benefits and burdens among coworkers and comrades are legion.[38]) Still, Guevara's speeches, talks, and writings do occasionally include explicit defenses of radical egalitarianism (just as they also include some statements registering his belief in the de facto equality of all[39]). At an August 1961 meeting, for example, he remarks, "It is not good . . . for there to be soap in Havana if there is no soap in the countryside: if there is no soap in the countryside, there should not be any soap in Havana. Or soap should be distributed so that there is soap everywhere. . . . Ours is a regime that wants everyone to have the same possibilities, the same treatment, and every citizen to feel that he is exactly the same as any other, another *compañero* [comrade] in the great work of building socialism."[40] During a speech in December of the same year, Guevara would underscore that socialism—an ideal he embraces—rests on "a regime in which conditions are the same for everyone."[41] Approximately three years later, Guevara would use the inauguration of a factory to declare that, while the United States represents "those who want to live off the exploitation [of others], discriminating against men because of the color of their skin, their religion, the money they have," Cuba represents "the struggle of those who seek to make all men equal, to make opportunities the same [for everyone],"[42] the viewpoint that he identifies with "Cuba" in this speech plainly being his own. In any case, this "radical egalitarianism"—a well-established concept, incidentally, in contemporary political philosophy—is, in connection with Guevara's thought, perhaps best described as a "communist egalitarianism," since it can only be fully realized in a communist (classless) society—class stratification precludes radical egalitarianism—and because Guevara identifies the bearer of this new value with the human beings who make up that society.

The second, closely related (for a reason that I will explain presently) attribute of the new human beings is a significant expansion of moral concern, in the sense of adherence to *a far more comprehensive notion of one's social duty*. In contrast to what we find in the case of the radical egalitarianism that Guevara advocates, this aspect of the new human being is reflected in countless statements throughout Guevara's works. As Guevara says in a typical expression of this idea, included in a lecture delivered in May 1964, "these individuals [who perform voluntary labor] are giving a part of their lives to society without expecting anything in return, without expecting any kind of payment, simply fulfilling a duty to society."[43] It is precisely this expansion of one's social duty that Guevara has in mind when he refers, in "Socialism and Man in Cuba," to the need to create individuals who have "much more responsibility."[44]

As I noted above, the new human being's heightened sense of social duty is closely related to the commitment to a radical egalitarianism. Indeed, it would not be incorrect to say that the former is a corollary of the latter: if we truly view others as deserving of the same consideration and treatment as ourselves, then we shall attach the same importance to the satisfaction of their needs as we do to our own, shall, in other words, grant them the same claim on our attention. Consequently, we shall strive to attend to their needs with (approximately) the same energy as we devote to meeting our own needs.[45] This commitment explains Guevara's fondness for the well-known remark by José Martí, Cuba's greatest writer and national hero, which he cites, or rather paraphrases, on innumerable occasions: "A real man should feel on his own cheek the blow inflicted on any other man's."[46]

At the same time, to describe this principle as a corollary of Guevara's radical egalitarianism may be to misrepresent it somewhat, since Guevara sometimes suggests that his notion of social duty does not entail *merely* attaching the same importance to others' needs and interests (or those of society as a whole) but that discharging one's social duty, as in fulfilling our responsibilities at work, is actually *more* important than satisfying one's own needs and those of his or her family, that "we have to be ready to sacrifice any individual benefit for the collective good."[47] In short, Guevara sometimes seems to be defending a notion of social duty that represents a rather severe degree of personal sacrifice.

Whatever the actual degree of personal sacrifice required by Guevara's notion of social duty, it will clearly diminish as communism becomes more and more fully realized in a society. There are several reasons for this, or rather several different ways in which fewer and fewer sacrifices will be required. First of all, with the increasing automation of production and the advent of abundance, society will require fewer and fewer sacrifices in terms of expenditure of labor, levels of consumption and comfort, and so on. Second, as society achieves more and more perfect equality, on the one hand, and more and more people assume the necessary sacrifices, on the other, there will be less need for sacrifice on the part of the better-off to aid those who are worse off, and the burden of sacrifice for each individual will diminish. (This is another obvious way in which a commitment to radical egalitarianism affects the scope of one's level of social duty.) Third, fewer and fewer sacrifices will be required as society evolves toward communism for the simple reason that people will cease to perceive many actions *as* sacrifices. For one thing, Guevara argues, not implausibly, that the more one accustoms oneself to sacrifice, the less burdensome the sacrifice becomes—that is, the less one thinks of it *as* a sacrifice. For another, Guevara assumes that as society evolves toward communism, the members of society will come to identify more and more fully with society as a whole, so that in working for society one is serving one's own interests and therefore much more likely to perceive sacrifices for society as directly benefitting oneself and thus barely sacrifices at all.[48] In any case, we shall have occasion to return to the question of social duty, as well as the role of sacrifice in Guevara's political thought, in subsequent chapters, as they are relevant to Guevara's views on work under socialism, internationalism, and other questions.

Once we understand what the essential—"essential" also in the sense that the proper functioning of a communist society requires them—features of the new human being are, it is easier to comprehend why this being can only exist within a communist society—that is to say, why this is the communist human being: full egalitarianism in the sense of rough equality of condition can only exist in a classless society, and people will only cease to regard social duties as a burden when abundance has ensured that all of their material needs are satisfied and automation has rendered all jobs tolerable, if not enjoyable.

A clear idea of these basic features of the new human being, or new person, also makes it easier to grasp the meaning of a term that Guevara invokes in characterizing and defending his conception of the building of socialism—namely, "consciousness."[49] References to consciousness abound in Guevara's writings, lectures, talks, and speeches. He speaks, for example, of "deepening" consciousness, "developing" consciousness, "improving" consciousness, "raising" consciousness.[50] And, while he sometimes refers to "revolutionary" consciousness or "political" consciousness,[51] as often as not Guevara uses the word without any qualification. The frequency with which Guevara uses the term attests to the importance of this concept in his political thought, as does the decision by Orlando Borrego, one of Guevara's closest collaborators during his years in Cuba, to underscore this facet of Guevara's political outlook—"his emphasis on the development of consciousness as the force driving humanity toward communism"—in his brief preface to the first multivolume edition of Guevara's works.[52]

While Guevara sometimes uses "consciousness" as shorthand for commitment to the revolutionary process, he generally also uses the word to evoke a certain moral orientation or outlook, or a set of moral commitments: indeed, this is what is distinctive about the new "consciousness." Guevara effectively says as much when he writes of the need for the "development of a consciousness in which there is a new scale of values,"[53] and, in any case, that this is what he has in mind can be readily inferred from Guevara's usage of "consciousness," mention of which is often accompanied by a reference to "duty" or "social duty."[54] The moral commitments in question, the constituents of this new consciousness, are essentially those that will lead enable Cubans to establish socialism and eventually communism, which is to say, those dispositions, attitudes, and values that help to nurture egalitarianism and a heightened sense of social duty. These are the values that need to be deepened, developed, improved, and raised, and it is because they lead to socialism that the consciousness they make up is a revolutionary consciousness. We shall return to the question of consciousness later in discussing other aspects of Guevara's political thought, and not least of all because Guevara himself says, in a little-known text (an undated report to Cuba's Council of Ministers), that he regards his approach to "the accelerated development of the worker's consciousness as a socialist producer in this stage of society" as "a shortcut for reaching socialism in less time" and, indeed, his "small contribution to the practice of Marxism-Leninism."[55]

One advantage of interpreting "consciousness" in this fashion, incidentally, is that such an interpretation sheds considerable light on Guevara's notion of *disalienation*. Guevara seldom uses the terms "alienation" or "alienated" in his works, but they do have a prominent place in "Socialism and Man in Cuba" and precisely in connection with the new men and women; indeed, "the ultimate and most important revolutionary aspiration," declares Guevara in this essay, is "to see human beings liberated from their alienation."[56] Although Guevara does not elaborate on the nature of the alienation that he mentions here, it is clear that he links disalienation with moral renewal, as is evident in a 1963 interview with journalist Jean Daniel: "Economic socialism without a communist morality does not interest me. We are fighting against misery, but we are fighting against alienation at the same time."[57] Overcoming this alienation, or producing disalienation, involves a recognition of, and practice in accordance with, social duty, the creation of an egalitarian social ethos, and the elimination of "man's exploitation of man," as Guevara will insist on countless occasions.[58] In any event, the main point is that this consciousness is the context within which those elements constitutive of the new person can begin to take shape before developing more fully under socialism and finally being completely realized under communism. And it is the practices that I mentioned above and will discuss in the following chapter—voluntary labor, the use of moral incentives, and socialist emulation—that promote this new consciousness, or moral orientation.

A STRATEGY OF DEBOURGEOISIFICATION

As noted, the consciousness that Guevara wishes to nurture is best understood as a transitional stage in the evolution from the outlook typical of a member of a capitalist society to that of the new human being who is to emerge with communism. It is worth dwelling on this point because it helps us to appreciate that the crystallization of this consciousness involves both positive and negative developments (recall the aim of "liberating" human beings "from their alienation"). Specifically, it involves freeing oneself from a certain acceptance of and attachment to capitalism, a rejection of what Peruvian philosopher Augusto Salazar Bondy once called the "capitalist conception of existence."[59] In other words, it involves a *debourgeoisification*, and it is not unreasonable, therefore, to claim that Guevara's ideas on the transformation of consciousness amount to a *strategy of debourgeoisification* (a term that, to my knowledge, he never uses).[60]

To be sure, this could be interpreted as a rather trivial claim, or as one that attributes to Guevara a rather unimpressive "strategy": after all, since the new human beings will be members of a *communist* society, they will be nonbourgeois, or postbourgeois, by definition: there can be no bourgeoisie in a classless society; hence no member of such a society can be "bourgeois" in any sense. But in my view it is not a trivial claim, although I am using "debourgeoisification" in a way that departs somewhat from standard usage. Social scientists and political commentators normally employ the term "bourgeoisification" (or *embourgeoisement*, a French term sometimes used in English-language works) to refer to the tendency of workers and other nonbourgeois social strata to assume bourgeois attitudes, values, and preferences; in a word, it normally refers to their adoption of a bourgeois lifestyle; debourgeoisification, therefore, involves the converse—namely, a rejection or repudiation of this lifestyle. As I shall be using the term, "debourgeoisification" denotes not merely a rejection of the values and attitudes characteristic of a particular social class or sociocultural stratum within capitalism but also a rejection of the values and attitudes characteristic of capitalism as such. This construal or use of "debourgeoisification" is, I submit, actually consistent with a broadly Marxist approach to social analysis, and we find warrant for it when we reconsider Marx and Engels's own use of the term "bourgeois."

Marx and Engels use the term "bourgeois" in at least three different senses. First of all, they employ the term to designate a certain economic relation: one is "bourgeois" (or *a* bourgeois) if one is a member of the bourgeoisie, the social class comprising the owners of the means production; in a word, one is (a) bourgeois if one is a capitalist.[61] This is the objective criterion employed by Marx and Engels, Marxists and a broad left-wing tradition as the basis of the concept "bourgeois" in a limited, more or less "technical," sense. Yet the term "bourgeois" is also used by Marx and Engels, as it is within the Marxist tradition generally, to refer to capitalist society as a whole when they wish to specify the mode of production that defines this society or social formation (and that corresponds to the socioeconomic nature, or designation, of its ruling class). In other words, for Marx and Engels, the term "bourgeois society" is synonymous with "capitalist society"[62]—a society whose level of capitalist development is such that capitalist relationships constitute the predominant or most decisive ones within society—so that to say "bourgeois relations of production" is equivalent to saying "capitalist relations of production." Finally, Marx and Engels and the Marxist tradition sometimes use the term "bourgeois" to refer to the economists, philosophers, political analysts, and the like who regard the capitalist mode of production as natural and inevitable, and whose work serves to justify this socioeconomic formation, even when their intellectual activity is not consciously intended to serve as such a justification.[63]

These are, then, three common, very prominent uses of the term "bourgeois" in the thought of Marx and Engels, as well as in the history of Marxist thought: the term is used to refer to a member of a certain socioeconomic category, to a specific mode of production, and to a certain attitude toward, or perspective on, prevailing economic realities. Notice that all three senses imply that to reject that which is bourgeois is, whatever else it may be, to reject capitalism, and, since one cannot reject capitalism without rejecting the values and attitudes that are (uniquely) constitutive of capitalism, we may understand debourgeoisification as a rejection of these attitudes and values. In other words, it may be used to refer not only to an opposition to the attitudes and values of some within capitalism but also the values and attitudes constitutive of capitalism as such.[64] Guevara's insistence that Cubans' consciousness must be "developed," "deepened," and so on, can be understood, I submit, as one way of speaking about, and trying to promote, just such a process of debourgeoisification. As Guevara writes, "a capitalist world . . . instills [in people] a whole series of preconceptions that remain in the subconscious and are reflected in everyone's attitudes, even when it is something unconscious,"[65] and he also observes, in a passage that echoes well-known remarks by Marx and Lenin, that "the working masses who today are beginning the task of building socialism are not pure. They are made up of human beings who carry along with them a whole series of bad habits inherited from the previous epoch. I say bad habits they have—we have—we all have those bad habits inherited from the previous epoch."[66] In short, one had to contend with the dispositions, expectations, aspirations, habits, and so on of people who had undergone a capitalist socialization whose effects were enduring and not likely to disappear overnight. Indeed, in a December 1963 meeting with his collaborators at the Ministry of Industries—that is, nearly five years after the triumph of the revolution—Guevara emphasizes that it was necessary to confront "all of the vices, all of the defects that capitalism has left us, with the same people, with all of us with our capitalist mentality, a few years ago always thinking about how much we were going to earn, how we were going to get our little house, the yacht, or in many cases food."[67] It is, in fact, precisely because of the persistence of this outlook instilled in people by capitalism that Guevara realized that Cuba would have to continue using "material" incentives and rewards—despite his own opposition to this policy—during the period of building socialism (I shall say more about this topic in chapter 2). In short, the old mindset was plainly as much of an impediment to progress as the opposition of the bourgeoisie and the machinations of imperialism, and hence the imperative of replacing this mindset, however arduous the process might be, with the values, attitudes, habits, and commitments that will help to usher in socialism and ultimately issue in the new men and women of communism.

So, the new men and women of the communist society will be, and will have to be, thoroughly debourgeosified individuals. This becomes evident when we reconsider the two features of the new human being discussed above. Consider, first, Guevara's advocacy of radical egalitarianism. Any equality that goes beyond the formal equalities typical of capitalist societies is a nonbourgeois value, for, whether or not a market economy can be designed in such a way as to achieve something approximating equality of condition, the fact is that actually existing capitalist societies have always been based on, or contained, profound social inequalities. But of course Guevara not only advocates a classless society along more or less conventionally Marxist lines[68] but also insists on nurturing an egalitarian ethos on a daily basis; that is, he emphasized the *practice*, so to speak, of equality.

Consider, next, his defense of a broad conception of social duty. The enormous expansion of moral concern that Guevara proposes represents the very antithesis, or negation, of the values fostered by capitalism, which, Guevara observes, lead to a "dog-eat-dog mentality, where each one struggles on his own, elbowing each other, kicking each other, knocking heads; each person trying to get ahead of everyone else."[69] As we shall see in chapter 2, Guevara maintains that the most effective means for producing the requisite, debourgeosified notion of social duty consists in the development of a new, debourgeosified culture of work, which will include the promotion of voluntary labor and the use of moral incentives, among other things.

In any case, Guevara acknowledges, as we have seen, that a debourgeosified consciousness cannot be produced instantaneously. All who were socialized under capitalism will need to undergo a debourgeoisification, including the Revolution's leaders, most of whom, like Guevara himself, were originally of petty-bourgeois or bourgeois extraction (but who had already evolved politically thanks to the Revolutionary War and experience of the revolution[70]). At the same time, on various occasions Guevara expresses his hope and conviction that future technicians, and administrators will come from the working classes and peasantry and that for this reason they will not only display a complete identification with the revolution but also a thoroughly egalitarian outlook[71] and presumably a greater disposition to assume an expanded view of social duty (coming as they do from a less individualistic milieu). In a word, debourgeoisification will cease to be necessary in the future.

CHALLENGES TO GUEVARA'S
CONCEPT OF A NEW HUMAN BEING

Guevara's conception of the new human being or "new man," which represents an original contribution to Marxism,[72] has been widely misunderstood. It has also met with a great deal of skepticism and criticism, even from commentators who otherwise sympathize, to one degree or another, with Guevara's broad political aims. I already noted above, and sought to dispel, one of the most common misunderstandings with regard to Guevara's notion of the new person or new human being—namely, the assumption that Guevara believes that this type of individual can be brought into being during the period of transition to socialism, or even within socialism. To the contrary, and as we have seen, the new person is the communist human being—that is, a man or woman who typifies, and can only truly exist within, a communist society. In the present section, I would like to examine some of the criticisms that Marxist and left-wing commentators either have advanced, or might be inclined to advance (given their political perspective), against Guevara's conception of the new human being.

One possible source of reservations or criticisms regarding the new human being may derive from the premise that it makes no sense to discuss the determinate attributes and qualities of this person for the simple reason that it makes no sense to speculate about the nature of a future communist society generally, including the nature of the women and men who would make up this society. The ultimate inspiration for this view derives from Marx and Engels's own rejection of attempts to specify in advance the institutions, policies, practices, and so on that would characterize a social arrangement so radically different from our own. It is a view encapsulated in Marx's well-known dismissal, in the afterword to the second German edition of *Capital*, volume 1, of the activity that consists in "writing recipes . . . for the cook-shops of the future."[73] (Some of Marx and Engels's strictures against the "utopian socialists" express the same view.) In short, it would seem that from a Marxist perspective all that one can safely say, as Trotsky once put it, is that the communist human being will have a psychology "very different from ours."[74] Yet many subsequent Marxists, including Trotsky himself, effectively disregard Marx and Engels's conviction in this regard and do indeed make attempts to anticipate some features of the emancipated human being.[75] So, it is hard to see why Guevara's decision to do so should necessarily appear objectionable from a more or less conventional Marxist standpoint. What is more, Marx and Engels may have been mistaken in contending that we should refrain from any speculation of this sort: we may indeed be able to infer, as Guevara's work implies, the kind of human qualities that a viable communist social order requires, and identification of these qualities may well facilitate the creation of such a society (e.g., by furnishing guidance in the design of certain policies).

Let us assume that the attempt to delineate the features of the new human being is a legitimate undertaking. Perhaps the problem with Guevara's notion of the new human being is that it is simply chimerical or, even if roughly attainable, undesirable. In considering the first objection, it may be well to begin by noting that Guevara's conception does not appear much less "realistic," or any more chimerical, than that of other highly respected Marxist thinkers. I have already quoted Rosa Luxemburg's vision of liberated humanity, compared with which Guevara's conception of the new human being hardly seems extravagant. On the other hand, this conception seems quite sober and positively modest as compared with Leon Trotsky's vision of "communist man." According to Trotsky, "Man will become immeasurably stronger, wiser, and subtler; his body will become more harmonized, his movements more rhythmic, his voices more musical. . . . The average human type will rise to the heights of an Aristotle, a Goethe, or a Marx."[76]

But to say that Guevara's conception seems no more extravagant than other classic Marxist thinkers' ideas is hardly the same thing as to say that it is attainable or within reach. I myself do not find Guevara's conception of the new person particularly "utopian." That is, I do not find it hard to believe that in a well-ordered society of material abundance the immense majority of human beings could embrace an ethos that combines radical egalitarianism with a far more comprehensive notion of social duty. Furthermore, even if one deems it unattainable in practice, one might still consider it a reasonable *ideal*, which human beings can closely approximate under the right conditions but never fully embody. In a word, one might regard the new human being as a normative philosophical anthropology—roughly, the human nature that people *ought* to have, or ought to aspire to have—and one that follows from a commitment to establishing a communist society. To be sure, when Guevara speaks of the new human being, it seems clear that he does not consider this being a mere ideal. Indeed, in an October 1962 speech Guevara exclaims, "If someone says we are just romantics, inveterate idealists, thinking the impossible, that the masses of people cannot be turned into almost perfect human beings, we will have to answer a thousand and one times: Yes, it can be done; we are right."[77] Moreover, according to Guevara's friend and collaborator Orlando Borrego, Guevara believed that human beings' "definitive liberation" could be attained in a not-so-distant future.[78] At the same time, we also find warrant in Guevara's works for interpreting the new human being as a normative ideal to the extent that he sometimes characterizes communism as the "perfect society."[79] If we construe "perfect" as "ideal" or "entirely without fault or defect" (two senses of the word given in *Webster's Third New International Dictionary*), then we can justifiably conceive of communism as an ideal social order and the members of this society as, accordingly, ideal human beings. In short, so construed, Guevara's new human being, *qua* communist human being, is an ideal and should be analyzed and assessed as such.

But whether or not we interpret Guevara's new human being as a human type attainable or realizable under communism, or as an ideal that human beings can approximate yet never fully embody (even if a communist society *is* attainable), one might still pose the question: Does it constitute an attractive model or vision of human life? At least one recent critic of Guevara, Samuel Farber, suggests that it does not. According to Farber, Guevara's thought leaves little room for "individual identity" and "individual self-fulfillment, expression," and his "egalitarianism left little room for individual differences or individual rights."[80] This is, in fact, hardly a new criticism: Not a few commentators appear to assume—without providing any argument—that an enlargement of one's sense of social duty, with its correlative commitment to working for the benefit of society as a whole, necessarily entails a diminution, contraction, or even nullification of one's individuality.[81] Guevara actually begins "Socialism and Man in Cuba" by acknowledging this very concern, observing, "A common argument from the mouths of capitalist spokespeople . . . is that socialism, or the period of building socialism into which we have entered, is characterized by the abolition of the individual for the sake of the state." His response in this essay consists of the claim that "the individual under socialism, despite apparent standardization, is more complete [than under capitalism]," for "the opportunities for self-expression and making oneself felt in the social organism are infinitely greater," and the individual is also free of alienation.[82] To be sure, when Guevara refers to "making oneself felt in the social organism," he has in mind mainly the fulfillment of one's social duty—that is, a type of moral self-fulfillment; and Guevara clearly subscribes to Marx and Engels's view that heightened social connections will actually enhance one's individuality, a strong integration into community life being, on their view, a precondition both for personal freedom (in the sense of free self-development) and for much of the individual's "intellectual wealth."[83] To be sure, many people today may neither embrace this particular form of self-fulfillment nor agree with Marx and Engels's view on the preconditions of freedom and individuality, and this consideration is presumably what leads Farber to conclude that Guevara's thought leaves little room for self-fulfillment as such. But if this is the case, it makes far more sense, and is much fairer to Guevara, to criticize him for insisting on a form of self-fulfillment that one finds unappealing and to show how it undermines "individuality" than to contend that his thought effectively ignores human beings' need for self-fulfillment. By the same token, it is misleading to suggest that Guevara's project involves, as another commentator puts it, "constructing a new man whose defining quality was his community-centeredness and readiness to sacrifice private interests."[84] For Guevara, the opposition between social and personal interests should and will disappear to a large degree, as was the case for Marx and Engels as well: "man's private interest," they wrote, "must be made to coincide with the interest of humanity."[85]

In any case, to say that Guevara privileges this form of self-fulfillment hardly implies that he cannot conceive of, or does not acknowledge, other sources of self-fulfillment, as is evident in the following passage from a 1963 essay: "The various branches of production will become automated, and labor productivity will rise enormously. The worker's free time will be devoted to athletic, cultural, and scientific endeavors of the highest order. Work will become a social need."[86] This passage, which recalls some well-known remarks from Marx in the *Grundrisse*,[87] is noteworthy in that it both states that in the future work will become "a social need"[88] and thereby a source of self-fulfillment *and* that men and women will dedicate their "free time" to more familiar or conventionally acknowledged sources of self-fulfillment. What is more, since Guevara, like Marx and just about every Marxist after him, assumes that socialism and communism will produce a major expansion of free time,[89] the time available for these other forms of self-fulfillment, as well as the cultivation of "individual identity" and "individual differences," will not be inconsiderable. Furthermore, since *all*, and not merely a privileged sector of society, will enjoy ample free time, far more individuals will have opportunities for self-fulfillment and self-expression, and the possibility of self-realization generally, than was ever the case in the past; in a word, the material preconditions for individual development and flourishing will be distributed far more extensively than ever before. In short, and as Marx and Engels remind us in the *Communist*

Manifesto, it is a mistake to equate "the abolition of bourgeois individuality" with the "abolition of individuality" as such.[90]

There is, however, one sense in which the charge of diminished individual differences, or standardization, not only rings true but *is* true, or so I would argue: Guevara plainly does assume that there will be a greater *moral* uniformity, or less moral differentiation, under socialism and communism. But in this regard Guevara's view is perfectly consistent with Marxist orthodoxy. For to the extent that (1) different moral outlooks derive from and correspond to different social classes,[91] (2) many moral differences represent a response to social antagonisms, which will be absent from a classless society,[92] and (3) Guevara embraces, as we have seen, Marx's view that "man's private interest must be made to coincide with the interest of humanity," we should indeed expect less moral pluralism and differentiation in a classless society. In short, the "really human morality which stands above class antagonisms" that Engels evokes in *Anti-Dühring*[93] will be a universally shared and simpler morality, and in this sense there will be fewer individual differences. That is the Marxist view, which Guevara implicitly accepts. I believe that it is one that we can endorse, too.

Finally, as for the question of whether or not Guevara's thought leaves room for "individual rights," since Guevara very seldom addresses rights and his positions and views on other issues by no means have any specific implications with regard to this topic, there are no grounds for Farber's claim—unless, of course, he simply means that Guevara does not recognize all of the standard liberal rights, which is obviously and trivially true: Marxists do of course reject liberal property rights, for example, just as liberals typically reject some of the "positive" rights defended by Marxists. (Since Farber defines himself as a Marxist, one assumes that he certainly does not equate "individual rights" with "liberal rights.")

Let me now turn to a rather different source of reservations regarding Guevara's conception of the new person or new human being, namely, that Guevara errs in placing so much emphasis on deliberate attempts to create new human beings. In other words, Guevara errs, it might be claimed, in believing that by sheer dint of willpower and revolutionary determination it will be possible to bring into being, or at least hasten the advent of, the new person when in fact this new human being can and will only emerge when objective developments in the forces of production makes this possible. In a word, Guevara's views on the creation of the new person, so it might be argued, entail a certain measure of "voluntarism" insofar as they assign a major role, and the supreme causal efficacy, to individual wills in bringing the new person into being. I will discuss the question of voluntarism at some length in the final chapter, where I also cite commentators who criticize Guevara on these grounds. For now, I will limit myself to noticing some obvious replies available to Guevara.

First of all, Guevara might well point out that critics who raise this charge effectively presuppose a rather mechanistic conception, or even a certain "automatism," regarding the change of human nature that accompanies the establishment of socialism. Yet this mechanistic view of the change, which Guevara himself disavows,[94] is difficult to maintain from a Marxist standpoint, as Ernest Mandel, for one, has pointed out. Commenting on Guevara's economic ideas, Mandel has observed that it is just as wrongheaded to insist that a major development of the forces of production must occur before there can be an expansion of socialist consciousness (the mechanistic outlook) as it is to think that education, agitation, and so on alone can immediately bring this consciousness into being. Rather, there is, according to Marxism, a constant interaction between the creation of the material conditions for the enlargement of socialist consciousness and the development of this consciousness.[95] In short, there exists a dialectical interplay, or reciprocal determination, between the material conditions and the new consciousness. One reason that pursuing a policy of deliberately promoting a socialist consciousness proves so important is that, as Hungarian Marxist philosopher Georg Lukács observed near the end of his life, "Socialism is the first economic formation in history which does not spontaneously produce the 'economic man' to fit it." According to Lukács, this is because socialism constitutes a mere transitional form, or stage, between capitalism and communism.[96] As the phase that consists in the transition from capitalism to socialism, the phase within which Guevara found himself working and whose obstacles and possibilities he sought to understand,[97] is, as it were, an *even more* transitional form than socialism and no distinctive economic formation at all, it is not surprising, assuming that Lukács's explanation is correct, that it would not spontaneously produce a corresponding economic type. As a matter of fact, Guevara sometimes comments that ideological development can be out of sync with economic development, and that the expected correspondence did not in fact exist during the transition to socialism taking place in Cuba.[98] In any case, the "economic type" needed to reach socialism will include, among other things, a commitment to substantially raising productivity as rapidly as possible, which in turn requires human beings with an expanded sense of social duty, one that motivates them to work harder and achieve the productivity gains that will benefit society as a whole. Bringing such a type into being (rapidly) may require a more direct engagement with people's mindset, even if changes in the relations of production proceed rather quickly, not least of all because one is still dealing with people thoroughly socialized by capitalism.

Finally, while not taking issue with Guevara's emphasis on fostering a new consciousness, one might argue that he conceives of this new consciousness in excessively moral terms, that is, that he reduces this new outlook or orientation to a certain moral sensibility; in a word, that Guevara places too much emphasis on the *moral* transformation of human beings in the transition to socialism.[99] In short, even granting that it is important to promote this moral transformation, it is a mistake, one might claim, to reduce the new consciousness to such a transformation, and for this reason Guevara's approach to the new person is flawed. The problem with this sort of criticism is that it is hard to imagine what else a change in "consciousness" could mean in this connection if not a new moral sensibility or perspective, a new social ethos. In other words, producing a new consciousness will always be essentially a matter of moral reform.

WAS GUEVARA THE NEW HUMAN BEING?

Referring to Guevara, Jean-Paul Sartre once said, "I believe that the man was not only an intellectual but also the most complete human being of our age."[100] Many people seem to agree with something like Sartre's view, in that they suggest that Guevara himself embodied a robust anticipation of, or approximation to, the new human being.[101] Indeed, some have gone so far as to claim that Guevara *was* an example of the new human being—that is, have not hesitated to identify Guevara with this type of person.[102]

This identification of Guevara with the new human being is both understandable and plausible. After all, Guevara embodied a radically egalitarian outlook and a keen sense of social duty—the basic hallmarks of the new person—and without question displayed the attitude to work that follows from the combination of these two commitments (and that is, as we shall see in the next chapter, its most important and visible practical consequence, or manifestation). Nonetheless, it is a mistake to identify Guevara with the new person, as opposed to viewing him as a singular harbinger of this type of human being. Guevara was not an instance of the new human being because this person can only truly appear, as was emphasized earlier, with the advent of communism. This is hardly a trivial, dogmatic assertion. The Cuba in which Guevara was living and working in the early 1960s was an underdeveloped society emerging from capitalism and undergoing a transition to socialism. In these circumstances, anyone who sought to prefigure the new person actually had to accept even more self-sacrifice, and practice even greater austerity, than would be required of the new person, who will live in a society of abundance, in which all "do their share." There is, indeed, more than a little truth in Spanish philosopher Francisco Fernández Buey's comment that Guevara "wanted to be a 'new man' in a world that was still old."[103] Yet one must add the following: precisely because he sought to be a new person in a noncommunist society Guevara actually went beyond what would be required of, or rather exhibited by, the new person in a communist society. To take but one example, achieving ethical and political "consistency" in a society that makes such consistency well-nigh impossible, or at the very least systematically discourages the values and principles (equality, social justice, etc.) to which one strives to be faithful, typically requires a superhuman effort. Consequently, avoiding compromises in such a society requires that we become not the new human beings of a communist society but human beings who would be exceptional even in that society.

It is important to underscore this idea for a fairly obvious reason. If, or to the extent that, people equate Guevara's lifestyle and practice with that of the new person, they will almost certainly find the new person—which is, let us not forget, the communist human being, or typical representative of a communist society—an unattractive ideal or goal for humanity: it simply requires too much sacrifice, is too demanding, too onerous. In this connection, it is enough to recall Guevara's grueling workdays (six days a week), which, when combined with voluntary labor on Sundays, added up to more than double a normal workweek: he was not exaggerating when, in response to a Uruguayan journalist's questions about his lifestyle and habits, he replied, "I work maybe sixteen, maybe eighteen hours a day."[104] One might also think about his self-imposed burden of constant reeducation, as he sought to master all of the relevant knowledge in assuming his responsibilities as president of the National Bank of Cuba or Minister of Industries, a commitment to reeducation that far surpasses what we expect of any official on taking up a new post.[105] More generally, while one might readily agree with Guevara when he states that "we must work for our internal improvement almost as an obsession, as a constant impulse,"[106] we should not forget that to strive for self-improvement or self-perfection in a society that is still building socialism, and hence still includes formidable institutional and attitudinal obstacles to these goals, is very different from pursuing them in a society free of such obstacles, and one that has eliminated, among other things, the exploitation of one human being by another, this being one of the ways that Guevara defines socialism,[107] and an aim that, as already noted, he underscores on countless occasions.

In light of the preceding considerations, it is probably best not to identify Guevara with the new human being but rather to think of him as a most exemplary communist in a noncommunist society, or perhaps in one of the ways that Fidel Castro characterizes Guevara in his October 8, 1987, speech commemorating the twentieth anniversary of Guevara's death: as the "model of a revolutionary man."[108] If, furthermore, revolutionaries are, as Guevara remarked in his *Bolivian Diary* a mere two months before his death, "the highest form of the human species,"[109] this is hardly an unflattering characterization, and one that would surely please Guevara.

2

The Problem of Work

Guevara refers to the topic of work, or problems relating to work, such as the need to raise productivity, time and again over the course of his speeches and writings. This comes as no surprise, considering Guevara's belief that the "new person" will view work in a way that is strikingly different from the prevailing view of work in capitalist society and that this new conception of work will be one of the hallmarks of the communist society of the future. As he writes in "Socialism and Man in Cuba," "In order to develop a new culture, work must acquire a new status," and he even goes so far as to claim that "there is . . . a need to undergo a complete spiritual rebirth in one's attitude toward one's own work, freed from the direct pressure of the social environment, though linked to it by new habits. That will be communism."[1] For Guevara, the new men and women will have, in addition to—and, as we shall see, as a result of—the features discussed in chapter 1, a fundamentally new relationship to work. It is precisely because Guevara's proposals for the transformation of work are, on the one hand, the centerpiece of his vision of social renewal and, on the other, one of his most original contributions to radical social theory that the topic of work and its place in his thought merits a chapter-length treatment.

WORK AS A PROBLEM

In order to grasp what is distinctive about Guevara's notion of work, it will be necessary to say a few words about both the topic of work as a problem for political theory generally and conventional Marxist thinking on this topic in particular. Work constitutes an important topic for political theory, whatever the theoretical tradition or school of thought, for the simple reason that work is, as Robert Dahl has written, "central to the lives of most people. For most people, it occupies more time than any

other activity. Work affects . . . their income, consumption, savings, status, friend-
ships, leisure, health, security, family life, old age, self-esteem, sense of fulfillment
and well-being, personal freedom, self-determination, self-development, and innumerable other crucial interests and values."[2] Dahl's observation is no overstatement,[3]
and it is precisely because of the decisive role of work in shaping people's lives and
in contributing to the functioning of society that the topic has always attracted the
attention of political philosophers and social theorists, not least of all those of a re-
formist bent. The fundamental question in this regard has always been the following:
How should society distribute the burdens of work? (The question is actually one
element of a much broader question for social and political thought—namely, How
are we to distribute the benefits and burdens of society?) A related problem arises
from the need to render work, or at least various aspects of many different jobs, less
onerous and more enjoyable. This is the challenge that John Stuart Mill, one of the
major figures of classical political liberalism, characterizes, in his *Principles of Political
Economy*, as "the great and fundamental problem of rendering labour attractive."[4]

If the different traditions in social and political theory have always considered
work an important problem, Marxism has certainly been no exception; indeed, it
probably attaches more importance to work than any rival theoretical tradition or
school of thought.[5] With regard to the first question that I mentioned, Marxism has
always sought to draw attention to the question of the *exploitation* of laborers while
at the same time stressing the link between control over production and the method
of allocating labor, on the one hand, and the organization of society as a whole, on
the other. Marxists have also paid a great deal of attention to the second question,
namely, the task of rendering work less onerous and more enjoyable, or what is sometimes called "the humanization of work." Indeed, their philosophical belief that labor
is the quintessential human activity and materialist assumptions concerning the role
of a worker's labor in shaping his or her psychology and personality[6] typically lead
Marxists to emphasize, and to a far greater extent than non-Marxist commentators,
the ways in which jobs as presently structured and organized severely constrain workers' prospects for self-realization. This is merely another way of saying that it severely
limits their opportunities for attaining many of the things mentioned by Dahl in the
passage cited above, such as self-esteem, a sense of fulfillment and well-being, personal freedom, self-determination, and self-development. It is precisely because work
as organized under capitalism frustrates workers' attainment of these ends and sub-
jects workers to exploitation that Marx would declare, in a speech delivered after the
fateful 1872 congress of the First International in The Hague, "One day the worker
will have to seize political supremacy to establish the new organisation of labour."[7]

When it comes to the subject of work, Guevara is in many respects a rather orthodox adherent of Marxism, in that his ideas constitute a faithful, straightforward continuation of Marx's thinking on this subject. To begin with, he shares Marx's assumptions about the centrality of labor in human experience—he calls work "the center of
human activity" in an important speech from August 1962[8]—and Marx's view that
labor, far from constituting an unavoidable "disutility," as much conventional eco-

nomic thought maintains,[9] is a vital human need. Consequently, he also shares Marx's insistence on the need to organize work in such a way as to ensure that it serves as a means of self-realization—indeed, the primary means of self-realization—rather than crippling the worker.[10] Furthermore, like Marx and other Marxist thinkers, Guevara believes that the alienation that characterizes human beings (and human relations) in capitalist societies derives in large part from the organization and experience of work under capitalism and that the essential problem with this organization lies in the commodification of labor: under capitalism "a person dies every day during the eight or more hours in which he or she functions as a commodity."[11] Accordingly, and as is again the case with Marx and other Marxist thinkers, the need to transform work from an alienating experience into a purposive activity that allows for and promotes human flourishing occupies a central place in Guevara's thought ("the ultimate and most important revolutionary aspiration" is "to see human beings liberated from their alienation"[12]), and the goal of achieving a definitive decommodification of labor informs his attempts to theorize the transformation that work must undergo in the transition to socialism and communism. Guevara also assumes, as do Marx and all Marxists, that work will have to be organized in a different way for the simple reason that the purpose of work will have changed, as the satisfaction of the needs of all and the collective welfare, rather than the maximization of profit for private individuals, will dictate society's handling of work.[13] Guevara also underscores, as does the Marxist tradition as a whole, the importance of technological progress in making liberating work possible.[14] Finally, we may note that Guevara emphasizes, like most Marxists before him, that all will bear the obligation to work in the socialist and communist societies of the future.[15]

Thus in many respects Guevara's thought on the problem of work scarcely departs from the predominant Marxist views on this topic. At the same time, Guevara's approach to work, including his views on fostering a properly socialist conception of work during the period of transition to socialism, involves a distinctive development of Marxism, as we shall see in the rest of this chapter.

RECONCEIVING WORK

Guevara takes for granted that the status of work within a socialist and (eventually) communist society will bear little resemblance to that which it has in capitalist societies. In emphasizing what is distinctive about work in an emancipated society, Guevara emphasizes one aspect of the new work experience above all: all members of society will view work as a social duty. Guevara would say this explicitly in a televised discussion in late December 1963: "In socialist society or in the construction of socialism the worker works because it is his social duty."[16] Guevara makes the same point in "On the Budgetary Finance System," an essay published shortly after this television appearance and the text that constitutes his most detailed statement of the system of economic organization he devised and implemented in the Ministry of

Industries. In this essay he writes, "We must make social duty the fundamental point of all the worker's efforts."[17] That is to say, all must come to regard work, as Guevara states elsewhere, as "the fundamental duty."[18] If, as Guevara notes in a 1961 speech to a national conference of workers, the view of work as a social duty was what distinguished the vanguard of workers in the early years of the Cuban Revolution,[19] this conviction will characterize all members of a communist society.

As Guevara repeatedly employs the term "duty" (*deber*) in evoking the distinctively socialist/communist conception of work, one might naturally assume that what he has in mind is an obligation that one assumes but may well dislike and resent. In reality, Guevara assumes that all will eventually come to embrace this duty, for he believes that all should, and eventually will, develop a *moral need* for work.[20] This is what Guevara means in saying, in a speech delivered at the University of Montevideo in 1961, that "what matters [now] is the moral satisfaction that comes from putting a bit of oneself into that collective task and seeing how, thanks to his or her work, thanks to that little individual part . . . a harmonious collective job is performed"[21]—or, as he puts it at the end of the Budgetary Finance System essay, the workplace must become "a place where their [the workers'] desire to serve society will take shape."[22]

This view of work as a social duty, but one perceived as a moral need, is, then, the essence of what Guevara calls the "new spirit of work" or "new attitude toward work."[23] It is a spirit or attitude that Guevara on one occasion likens to a "communion with work,"[24] a description he thinks justified owing to the fact that, as he would put it in an address to the Union of Young Communists, work will become "a pleasant social duty, done joyfully to the rhythm of revolutionary songs, amid the most fraternal camaraderie and human relationships that are mutually invigorating and uplifting."[25]

Before considering Guevara's ideas on how to achieve this new attitude, or relationship, to work, it is important to note two points. First of all, Guevara's conception of humans' new attitude to work is a corollary of one of the two basic features of the new person—namely, a vastly expanded notion of one's social duty. Or, rather, as Guevara often uses the phrase "social duty" in characterizing this new attitude, it may be more helpful to say that it is one practical manifestation—and to Guevara's mind, the most important one—of this new notion.

The second point to notice is that Guevara tends to maintain a thoroughly moralized conception of self-realization insofar as he identifies self-realization at (and through) work in large part with the satisfaction of a moral need—the strong desire to discharge one's social duty. In other words, to the extent that work "becomes an expression of oneself," it is because it involves "a contribution to the common life in which one is reflected, the fulfillment of one's social duty."[26] This is the sense in which people will come to identify themselves with their work: a moral identification reflected in the satisfaction of having fulfilled their obligation to a collective project that they embrace and that will lead them to willingly perform work in the absence of any material incentive. We shall return to this aspect of Guevara's view in the following sections.

How, then, is society to produce this new attitude toward work? Guevara is well aware that this new attitude will take time to materialize and that coercive policies would be required to ensure workers' fulfillment of their "social duty" in the early stages of the transition to socialism. This was in fact one way of conceiving of the "work norm" benchmarks that served as the basis for a salary scale introduced in 1964: "Nonfulfillment of a norm means nonfulfillment of a social duty . . . . The norm is more than a mere measuring stick marking a realizable or customary amount of labor; it is the expression of the workers' moral obligation, *it is his social duty.*"[27] But in addition to this measure adopted for the short term, Guevara developed two important (noncoercive) practical proposals for transforming the status of work: *voluntary labor* and *the systematic use of moral incentives.*

VOLUNTARY LABOR

Guevara's commitment to "voluntary labor" or "voluntary work"—the Spanish word *trabajo* can be translated as either "work" or "labor"—is perhaps his best-known practical proposal for building socialism, as well as being a practice that he steadfastly advocated and one to which he frequently refers. To be sure, Guevara was not the first Marxist thinker to defend and insist on the importance of voluntary labor. Four decades before the Cuban Revolution, Lenin had defended the practice of voluntary labor in a fairly well-known article.[28] However, in contrast to Lenin, Guevara developed, as Helen Yaffe rightly observes,[29] a relatively systematic conception of this practice. Moreover, Guevara was, without a doubt, a more steadfast and ardent proponent of voluntary labor than Lenin, or, for that matter, any other major Marxist theoretician.

What, exactly, is Guevara's notion of voluntary labor? As the term suggests, voluntary labor is unpaid labor that one performs in addition to the labor that constitutes one's paid occupation; it is, accordingly, labor that must be performed outside the regular workday and/or on the weekend (in a word, during one's "free time"). The labor in question must constitute useful, productive activity, and while it need not necessarily consist of *manual* labor, the most estimable form of voluntary labor is indeed manual labor of some sort.[30] In fact, the only voluntary labor that counted as such for a member of Guevara's Red Brigade within the Ministry of Industries, a group of "vanguard" workers committed to performing 240 hours of voluntary labor—the highest category—in one semester, was manual labor.[31] The rationale for this had less to do with the goal of raising productivity in certain sectors of the economy than with the value of manual labor as an example that would mobilize workers,[32] who would not only see other people performing voluntary manual labor but people who would normally be engaged in work that was a form of "mental" labor and who were, therefore, in a position to do voluntary labor that had nothing to do with manual labor.

This last point brings us to the main question: What, exactly, is the purpose of voluntary labor? According to Guevara, the true importance of voluntary labor does not lie in its contribution to production or the economic benefit that it yields, which in some cases may well be negligible, as Guevara himself acknowledges.[33] Rather, the importance of this activity derives from its "educational" value[34]—namely, its tendency to foster the development of a new "consciousness," by which he means the new attitude toward work discussed above, or "the consciousness of the social duty to produce."[35] The practice of voluntary labor produces this new attitude, Guevara maintains, by accustoming us to working for the sake of society without any concern with remuneration; this habit, which enables those who engage in voluntary labor to liberate themselves from the attitude that regards work as an instance of compulsion, eventually turns work into a need.[36] While Guevara does not explain the mechanics of this process, we may surmise that he thought that work could thereby become a need much in the way that exercise becomes a need for those who have habituated themselves to regular sessions of physical activity. In any event, to the extent that labor thus becomes a need, it constitutes nonalienated labor, and to the extent that one gives one's labor freely, it is decommodified labor.[37] In short, labor becomes, as Marx famously puts it in his "Critique of the Gotha Programme," "not only a means of life but life's prime want."[38]

This effect of voluntary labor is but one of its benefits, though the most important one. Voluntary (manual) labor also serves, for example, to familiarize administrative personnel with the array of problems faced by workers while at the same time forging bonds between these administrators and workers.[39] In addition, voluntary labor can promote solidarity and cross-class unity while furthering cooperation between town and country insofar as it brings together the working class, peasants, and intellectuals.[40] Given all of these putative benefits of voluntary labor, it is not surprising that Guevara should claim that it yields new attitudes toward "the [Cuban] Revolution, toward life, and above all toward the [working] class" or that he should have insisted that it was essential to promote and develop voluntary labor as much as possible.[41] As a matter of fact, voluntary labor is, for Guevara, one key component—or perhaps one should say "criterion"—of "socialist emulation," which also included the reduction of absenteeism, increasing savings, and improving quality.[42] Guevara conceives of "emulation" as consisting in a kind of "fraternal competition" that serves "to raise production and . . . deepen the consciousness of the masses"; it is, in other words, a "competition to see who . . . is the one who best, most rapidly builds socialism," where "socialism" is understood as referring to both a major increase in productivity and the development of the kind of "consciousness" befitting a socialist society.[43] Voluntary labor constitutes the form of emulation that most contributes to the latter, and for this very reason is also that which most decisively contributes to one's own self-transformation.

Guevara's enthusiasm for voluntary labor ultimately derives from his belief that it constitutes "the genuine expression of the communist attitude toward work in a society where the fundamental means of production belong to the society."[44] I shall return to this thesis below, after discussing Guevara's views on moral incentives. But before leaving the topic of voluntary labor, I should point out that Guevara practiced what he preached, performing an immense amount of voluntary labor himself. As noted in this book's introduction, the first day of voluntary labor was organized in November 1959, and Guevara devoted countless Sundays to voluntary labor until his departure from Cuba at the beginning of April 1965. Indeed, Ángel Arcos Bergnes, in his book of reminiscences of Guevara, lists nearly fifty plants, factories, and sugar mills where Guevara performed voluntary labor.[45] Such was Guevara's commitment to the practice that it was not uncommon for him to ask those who sought to meet with, interview, or photograph him during, or slightly before, a day of voluntary labor to join him and his colleagues in their work.[46] It is no surprise, therefore, that he should conclude his last "public" appearance in Cuba, at a meeting with members of the Ministry of Industries on March 22, 1965, by mentioning voluntary labor and telling his colleagues that they would next see one another cutting sugarcane.[47]

MORAL INCENTIVES

Guevara's second fundamental proposal for transforming the status of work consists in the generalized, systematic use of moral incentives as inducements to work. Guevara uses the concept of moral incentive (*estímulo moral*) to refer to both the worker's motivation or desire to discharge his or her duty to contribute to society (or go beyond what this obligation entails) and the social recognition of this accomplishment. Moral incentives appeal to nonmaterial needs and aspirations, including self-respect, esteem, solidarity, and the satisfaction derived from socialist emulation. A policy emphasizing such incentives rests on the assumption that one cannot generate the values constitutive of a truly socialist ethos, in which moral concerns are motivationally primary, by relying mainly on material incentives, which of course foster a very different motivational structure, while at the same time giving rise to individualistic competition for material rewards. As Guevara would say in his last published interview, "The development of the socialist consciousness is at odds with the development of direct material incentives and individual interests,"[48] and he expresses the same idea in more general terms in a well-known passage of "Socialism and Man in Cuba," observing that the notion "that socialism can be achieved with the help of the dull instruments left to us by capitalism," including "individual material interest as a lever," is a "pipe dream."[49]

Yet, while Guevara insists on the importance of moral incentives, it is by no means the case that he rejects material incentives altogether. To the contrary, he recognizes that Cuba will have to continue to rely on material incentives to at least some degree during the transition to socialism, and even during part of the period of socialism,[50] for the simple reason that people who have been socialized by capitalism will for some time tend to expect, and be most responsive to, such incentives.[51] As Guevara acknowledges in a fascinating letter written in early 1964 to a man named

José Medero Mestre, people continued to have, to some extent, urges characteristic of the old, competitive society despite Cuba's elimination of "the exploitation of man by man," and this was because "material interest" remained the "the arbiter of the well-being of the individual."[52] As this was the case, and since the objective of a society undergoing the transition to socialism must be not only to maintain the existing (i.e., prerevolutionary) level of production but to increase it—in order to meet the growing demand of those sectors of the population who emerge as "consumers" for the first time as well as to lay the foundations for a society of abundance—a revolutionary program can hardly dispense with material incentives altogether as it begins to undertake this transition.[53] Guevara accepts, then, that both moral and material incentives will be necessary during the transition to, and consolidation of, socialism.[54] At the same time, he never loses sight of the fact that any use of (individualized) material incentives reflects a regrettable necessity, a concession to capitalist socialization, or the fact that the ultimate goal is to completely eliminate the need for material incentives, a "lever" that, he contends, "is destined to die under socialism."[55]

How are we to move beyond material incentives? On the most general level, Guevara envisions a process whereby the weight and motivational efficacy of material incentives steadily declines and is superseded by moral incentives, whose weight and motivational efficacy steadily increase until they become the decisive factor in workers' disposition to work.[56] Guevara's writings and speeches contain several complementary strategies for effecting this change. One obvious strategy consists in explicitly exhorting workers to act on moral incentives by, for example, emphasizing the importance of one's social duty to work and appealing to the nonmaterial needs and aspirations mentioned above. Guevara's texts abound in such exhortations (examples of which have already been cited above), and the ceremonies in which exemplary workers, including those who had performed the most voluntary labor during a given period of time, received certificates, diplomas, medals, and so on in recognition of their accomplishments were also intended to serve this purpose. A second strategy involves investing material incentives with what Guevara calls a *qualitative* character: for example, exceptional performance might be rewarded by allowing the worker in question to attend school with no loss of salary and to acquire thereby the education and skills that would qualify him or her for a better-paying position (in accordance with the newly established pay scales).[57] The possibility of such a reward constitutes a material incentive—one improves one's material condition, receiving the same pay for less work (the equivalent of a raise)—and receives the means (the provision of educational resources) to earn more money; but the benefit serves a nonmaterial, "qualitative" end: a process of self-improvement and self-transformation that will benefit both oneself *and* society, given that the latter was in need of more highly qualified personnel. Yet another strategy for reducing the importance of material incentives consists in conferring a *collective* character on these incentives, this being one way to underscore that industrial achievements always require and rest upon a group endeavor.[58] One example of this approach would be to recognize the contributions of an outstanding worker by awarding a prize to his or her factory; this might be a new vehicle for the workers' use or the provision of certain amenities, such as a new dining hall, within the workplace. In short, the first of these latter strategies modifies the *material* aspect of individual material incentives, while the latter modifies the individualistic aspect of these incentives. Both thus contribute to undermining, in different ways, the importance of material incentives that appeal to individual self-interest.

As will be fairly obvious, Guevara's defense of moral incentives is consistent with the two features that fundamentally characterize the new human being—namely, a radical egalitarianism and a markedly heightened sense of social duty. For, to the extent that human beings come to acquire these two features, they will prove more responsive to moral incentives: a sufficiently developed sense of social duty will prompt one to work for society in the absence of any material incentive, while the assimilation of radical egalitarian values will lead one to view with disfavor any incentive scheme involving a competition for rewards that generates inequalities. (Needless to say, the more advanced the development of these features, the more effective moral incentives will be.[59]) The use of moral incentives will, at the same time, tend to reinforce this commitment to social duty and egalitarianism to the extent that it rewards—either in the form of "qualitative" benefits or collective material goods—those who act on the basis of this commitment.

One of the reasons that it is particularly important to underscore Guevara's commitment to a system of moral incentives is that Guevara himself regards the development of this system, together with the "accelerated development of the worker's consciousness as a producer" generated by it, as his "small contribution to the practice of Marxism-Leninism," as he puts it in a text cited earlier.[60] It is perhaps above all a contribution to the Marxist-Leninist theorization of the transition to socialism in that adoption of such a system will, Guevara insists, serve to accelerate development of the "subjective conditions" necessary for moving through this transition as quickly as possible.[61] But we should also note Guevara's insistence on the importance of developing a system of moral incentives because it is highly relevant to his diagnosis of the problems besetting the socialist countries in the Soviet Bloc. For example, in his notes on political economy from 1965 to 1966, first published nearly four decades after his death, Guevara emphasizes that the failure to use, or properly use, moral incentives had been one of the major sources of the deficiencies and gross inadequacies of the Soviet system.[62] Thus the very same convictions that yielded what Guevara considers his modest contribution to Marxism-Leninism also furnish the inspiration for his criticism of a political system that claimed to be the supreme embodiment of Marxism-Leninism.[63]

GUEVARA ON WORK: AN ASSESSMENT

Without question, Guevara's ideas on the status and role of work in the transition to socialism (and within socialism and communism) lend his theorization of this transition, and his development of Marxist theory generally, a very distinctive quality, for, while all Marxist theorists of any significance have, to be sure, addressed the topic of work, Guevara may be unique in terms of the relative importance that the topic assumes in his particular conception of revolutionary social transformation. (This may be due to the fact that Guevara was, as Roberto Massari has observed, one of the exceedingly few Marxist theoreticians to have spent a substantial amount of time actually working in, and touring, factories.[64]) In my view, we should commend Guevara for placing the problem of work at the center of his strategy for the transition to socialism and communism: if our aim is to build a society in which unalienated interpersonal relations prevail and a genuine sense of community exists on a collective level, we shall need to reorganize work, and this task will have to be an absolute priority. I think Guevara is also correct not only in attaching such great importance to the moral dimensions of socialist development but also in believing that giving work a new status will be both the cause and effect of moral progress (including debourgeoisification). In this connection, we can certainly subscribe to his goal of turning work into a social duty that all can embrace, an idea that constitutes a valuable contribution to radical social theory not because it is an original idea—some earlier revolutionary thinkers, including Lenin, advocated somewhat similar ideas[65]—but because Guevara's commitment to this transformation, on both a practical and theoretical level, seems unique among major radical thinkers.

But what about the two practical measures discussed in the present chapter—namely, the program of voluntary labor and the use of moral incentives? Should we endorse both of these measures as appropriate means for generating the desired transformation in the status of work, the "spiritual rebirth in one's attitude toward one's own work" to which Guevara refers? With respect to the use of incentives, I think the answer is yes. It would indeed seem to be the case, as Guevara holds, that an increasing use of moral incentives, coupled with ever less dependence on material incentives (and a modification of the character of the material incentives that *are* used), is more likely to bring into being a society in which moral incentives serve as the principal, and more or less exclusive, motivation to perform that labor that one does not seek out as a form of (nonmoral) self-realization. In short, habituation of this sort would seem to play an essential role in bringing into being the new outlook that Guevara defends. This consideration seems especially important, moreover, given that attaining true abundance—a condition in which material incentives could serve no purpose (society will be able to satisfy the needs of all) and moral incentives furnish the only rational motivation[66]—may take decades, yet it is desirable to begin reducing the role of material incentives as early as possible.

Yet, while we should endorse Guevara's views on moral incentives, careful consideration of Guevara's conception of voluntary labor reveals that it is vulnerable to a number of theoretical and practical objections. In particular, I think we should question Guevara's conception of work as a "need" as well as his claim that a commitment to—that is, participation in—voluntary labor represents the true communist attitude with regard to work.

The problems with Guevara's conception, and defense, of voluntary labor become apparent once we understand the sense in which *all* work within a communist society will be "voluntary." In a communist society, comprehensive provisions for human welfare will have eliminated the economic coercion that obliges people to work. In addition, jobs will have been restructured with a view to making them inherently satisfying, all people will share more or less equally the benefits of society's productive capacities, and the working day will have been drastically shortened. It is perfectly reasonable to assume that in such circumstances work will indeed become a genuine need (or "want" [*Lebensbedürfnis*], to use the language of Marx's "Critique of the Gotha Programme"), at least if we accept the premise—a central component of Marx's philosophical anthropology—that human beings achieve self-realization primarily through their labor (that is, through "purposive productive activity"[67]): since people will, as a rule, strive for self-realization, they will feel a strong *need* for some kind of work, even in the absence of any external compulsion or material incentives, and consequently all of their labor will be "voluntary," including that which constitutes their regular job. But notice that this is not what Guevara means by "need" when he refers to this concept in connection with voluntary labor.[68] When Guevara refers to work as a need, he has in mind a social duty, labor for the benefit of society as a whole, that an agent feels compelled to perform. That he understands "need" in this sense is clear, for example, from a passage in his 1964 speech at the "Youth and the Revolution" conference (cited at note 36 above), as well as in the one passage in "Socialism and Man in Cuba" in which he explicitly addresses this topic: "We are doing everything possible to give work this new status as a social duty and to link it . . . with voluntary work based on the Marxist appreciation that one truly reaches a full human condition when no longer compelled to produce by the physical necessity to sell oneself as a commodity."[69] Guevara's contention, then, is that work has become a need when one welcomes it as a social duty, an obligation that one eagerly assumes and discharges, without any fear of sanction for failing to perform the duty and without any expectation of material rewards for fulfilling it; by accustoming ourselves to the practice of voluntary labor, which familiarizes us with the social importance of work and severs the link between labor and remuneration, we develop this very attitude toward work. In short, Guevara thinks of the need produced by voluntary labor in exclusively moral terms, as a strong, abiding preference for acting on (i.e., discharging) a moral duty, the fulfillment of which should afford us happiness,[70] just as he believes that work in general should be viewed as "a moral necessity."[71] By contrast, when Marx observes that labor under communism will have become "not only a means of life but life's prime want," it is because he assumes that work will have become—or, rather, *also* have become—intrinsically satisfying in a nonmoral sense; that is, that we will enjoy work for itself—indeed, for what could legitimately be called self-interested reasons. I stress "also" here because the young Marx likewise refers to a need for work in the sense of a preference for benefitting others—satisfying their needs—through work.[72] Still, the main emphasis in Marx's conception of work as a need has to do with the nonmoral sense of individual self-realization just noted, whereas when Guevara refers to the need for work resulting from the practice of voluntary labor he almost invariably conceives of this need for work in a moral sense.[73]

The problem in this connection is not that Guevara's thesis involves a departure from Marx's thinking—that consideration alone would be a frivolous reason for criticizing it—but that Marx's explanation as to how and why work could become an essential need (or want) is more plausible than Guevara's. And the reason that Marx's perspective proves more plausible is that it assumes that in most cases work will not truly become a need (in the sense of "life's prime want"), no matter how much a worker identifies his or her work with a social duty, unless and until jobs are radically restructured—that is, unless and until work itself becomes inherently desirable. Indeed, Marx's declaration that labor will become "life's prime want" is immediately preceded by references to "the enslaving subordination of the individual to the division of labour" and "the antithesis between mental and physical labour."[74] It is only after transcending the conventional (capitalist) division of labor, eliminating the crippling separation of mental and manual labor, shortening the working day, and introducing job rotation that all work will be intrinsically satisfying and entirely free of the alienation that characterizes most jobs, to one degree or another, today. Once this has been accomplished, there will exist a need for work not only in the sense of a preference for benefitting others through work—which, as just noted, Marx's outlook also assumes—but also in the sense of a desire to perform labor as part of one's striving for self-realization.

To be sure, Guevara also recognizes the importance of reconfiguring the entire labor process so as to ensure that all work becomes conducive to human flourishing. This "humanization of work"—his term—will involve "putting the machine in the service of man," as he tells his colleagues at the Ministry of Industries during a March 1962 meeting; and in a speech delivered the previous year, Guevara underscores the need to "strive to make work as mild as possible, as interesting and humane as possible."[75] In a word, the future promises "the liberation" of human beings "by means of the machine."[76] However, Guevara also tends to regard these things as long-term goals, the immediate priority being to raise productivity (not an unreasonable position, given Cuba's economic situation at the time).[77] In addition, and more significantly, Guevara plainly prioritizes the resocialization of workers—that is, a policy of encouraging workers to embrace their jobs, whether or not enhanced, as their social duty—over the humanization of work ("new generations must be formed whose main interest is work"[78]). In other words, as regards the process of turning work into a need, he lays far greater emphasis on a subjective transformation of workers—the assimilation of their duty and their ability to take pleasure in discharging it—than on the objective transformation of jobs themselves.

In fairness to Guevara, there were plainly major obstacles to enacting such changes to work in Cuba in the early 1960s, given, on the one hand, the country's state of underdevelopment and limited technological options and, on the other, the US government's policy toward the island, which combined continuous efforts at political destabilization, including support for the internal counterrevolution, and economic asphyxiation.[79] Attempts to transform the labor process in such circumstances might well have resulted in temporary inefficiencies and disruptions in production and thereby curbed economic development. If Guevara pays relatively little attention to the transformation of the labor process itself, the reason may lie partly in his appreciation of these constraints and a realization that, to put it in more orthodox language, the objective conditions for liberating labor did not yet exist during the early years of the Cuban Revolution. To the extent that this was the case, Guevara's priorities reflect a political realism that belies, at least in this instance, a propensity for "voluntarism," one of the vices routinely imputed to Guevara and a question to which I shall return in the final chapter. Still, even on those occasions on which Guevara refers to the work of the future, which will be creative and enjoyable, and speaks of the pleasure that this work will afford, he typically also mentions social duty and seems to presuppose that much of the worker's pleasure will come from the satisfaction of having discharged this duty. In a speech delivered in October 1962, for example, Guevara evokes "a future in which work will be man's greatest dignity, a social duty, a pleasure given to man, the most creative activity there is."[80]

One problem with Guevara's conceptualization of unalienated work as a need, then, is that he focuses almost exclusively on, or in any case unduly prioritizes, the moral dimension of this need; and this is why the practice that he advocates as a means of effecting this transformation of work into a need—voluntary labor—appears unlikely to succeed in fully transforming work into a need—that is, a need in both a moral and nonmoral sense. In short, while voluntary labor might constitute a necessary condition for the achievement of the transformation of work into a need, it is by no means a sufficient condition: profound modifications to the content and conditions of work, changes (some of which were mentioned earlier) that would enable the activity of work itself to serve as a vehicle for self-realization, are also indispensable. One simple way to appreciate this point is to recall the several varieties of alienation that Marx identifies in his *Economic and Philosophic Manuscripts of 1844*. If Marx's account is broadly on the mark and production under capitalism typically entails, for instance, the worker's alienation, or "estrangement," from the labor process itself,[81] work will continue to generate alienation—and hence will not be perceived as a need by the workers themselves—until the labor process has been radically restructured; and this will be true even if we have successfully developed an ethos involving a commitment to work as a social duty (whether or not this arises through the practice of voluntary labor).

In reality, there would seem to be good grounds for assuming that voluntary labor in Guevara's sense may not even prove especially effective in generating the, so to speak, "moral" need for work, that is, a need in the sense of a preference for benefitting others through work. Recall that when Guevara refers to voluntary labor he means labor performed in addition to the work constituting one's normal, paying job, and also, of course, in addition to the work consisting of household labor (an important consideration when thinking about the demands that voluntary labor would impose on many women today). This is precisely what should lead us to question Guevara's assumption that the practice of voluntary labor will lead one to develop a "need" for work. First of all, the fatigue arising from regularly engaging in voluntary labor after finishing one's full-time, paid work is liable, over the long run, to diminish the appeal of work rather than enhance it. (Voluntary labor is not the same as voluntary *supplementary* labor.) Second, the notion of work as a social duty will strike most people as unattractive if discharging this duty seems overly demanding. In other words, if performing one's duty regularly requires actions that, in most people's minds, entail rather considerable sacrifice and even heroism, few will regard this "duty" as in fact constituting a duty. After all, we normally identify heroism—and Guevara actually refers to the need to "perpetuate" a "heroic attitude in daily life," such as that which prevailed during the "missile crisis" of October 1962 and Hurricane Flora the following year[82]—with deeds that go beyond the demands of duty, or what are called "supererogatory" acts in the parlance of moral philosophy. Accordingly, if voluntary labor likewise requires a "heroic attitude in daily life," it is reasonable to assume that people will not regard performance of voluntary labor as a "duty." In sum, even if voluntary labor contributes to the development of certain aspects of political consciousness and in that regard serves, as Guevara often insists and as already noted above, an "educational" purpose, there is good reason to conclude that voluntary labor may actually fail to yield what I have called the "moral" need for work.[83]

In light of the preceding considerations I think there is little justification for endorsing Guevara's proposition that voluntary labor constitutes "the genuine expression of the communist attitude toward work in a society where the fundamental means of production belong to the society."[84] Or, rather, we should only endorse, at most, a qualified version of this proposition: voluntary labor may constitute one element of a communist attitude toward work within a society still undergoing the transition to socialism, a society in which committed communists will hardly be satisfied with merely discharging the duties that are the same for everyone (Guevara emphasizes that voluntary labor is labor performed over and above the labor required by one's social duty[85]). But in such a society, a communist attitude toward work is at least as authentically expressed through an active commitment to job restructuring and enhancement, or efforts to overcome the conventional division of labor under capitalism, or rather divisions of labor: the opposition between "mental" and "manual" labor, strict occupational specializations, and divisions on the basis of gender. With regard to a communist society, on the other hand, voluntary labor as understood by Guevara will be irrelevant to the "communist attitude toward work," since, as noted earlier, all work will be voluntary in a very straightforward sense, while voluntary labor as Guevara conceives of it will be quite unnecessary. In short, the regular performance of voluntary labor in Guevara's sense proves exceedingly demanding in a society undergoing a transition to socialism and quite superfluous in a society that has already achieved socialism or communism.

SOME NEGLECTED ASPECTS OF
GUEVARA'S PHILOSOPHY OF WORK

While it is important to draw attention to the problems with Guevara's conception and defense of voluntary labor, I would like to end this chapter by emphasizing the validity of two of the general premises and considerations that inform his thinking on work in general (and that partly explain Guevara's commitment to the practice of voluntary labor), a topic that, as noted at the beginning of the chapter, represents a central problem for social theory in general and radical social theory in particular.

The first of these considerations concerns the division of labor, which Marx once said "is in a certain respect the category of categories of political economy."[86] On numerous occasions Guevara acknowledges the importance of not only overcoming the class stratification deriving from the opposition between manual and mental labor but also of eliminating the opposition itself (a basic goal for Marxists, and one reflected in the passages from Marx's "Critique of the Gotha Programme" cited in the previous section). For example, in concluding his address to the Eleventh National Workers' Congress in November 1961, Guevara emphasizes that the ultimate purpose of such things as technological development, worker education, and increased productivity was "the erasing of differences at work, the erasing of the differences between manual and intellectual labor, the erasing of class differences, [and] also the erasing of differences between the city and the country."[87] Guevara's determination to transform the division of labor is reflected, as we have seen, in his commitment to voluntary labor. But that is not the only expression of this determination. Guevara's call for greater worker participation in the management and administration of plants and factories should also be interpreted as a condemnation of the capitalist division of labor,[88] since a policy designed to heighten such worker involvement will also serve to undermine conventional forms of occupational specialization. The same is true of his "mandatory demotion" policy, introduced in 1964, which required all upper-level administrators within the Ministry of Industries to spend one month a year working at a lower position within the branch of industry under their authority, or otherwise connected to the branch that they administered. While the main aim of this policy was to familiarize administrators with aspects of production operations for which they bore ultimate responsibility, it was a measure that also challenged the traditional division of labor.[89] Finally, one could also cite Guevara's efforts to encourage his administrators to do voluntary labor in factories during at least part of their vacation periods.[90] In sum, Guevara's statements and policy proposals, as well as his own actions, plainly demonstrate his commitment to the principle enunciated by Marx in *The Civil War in France*: "With labour emancipated, every man becomes a working man, and productive labour ceases to be a class attribute."[91]

A second consideration concerns the *materialism* informing Guevara's approach to transforming the status, or meaning, of work. Simply put, Guevara assumes—in keeping with the Marxist assumption that the content of our fundamental values and attitudes derives, in the last analysis, from the material conditions of our lives—that in order to overcome what we might call the "bourgeois" conception of work people must begin working in a different way, and this is one of his motivations for so vigorously promoting the practice of voluntary labor. To be sure, Guevara engages in a great deal of moral suasion over the course of his writings, speeches, and talks, and I have already discussed his belief in the use of moral incentives. Yet he never loses sight of the need to change people's lives in order to change their ideas. In other words, Guevara's belief that new ways of working as well as exhortation were necessary to produce a new attitude toward work shows that he was neither a mechanistic (or "economistic") materialist (he does not assume that the desired change of outlook will automatically arise from the socialization of the means of production and new forms of work) nor an "idealist" (he does not hold that changing people's minds suffices to change reality). The "spiritual rebirth in one's attitude toward one's own work" would have to have both material and moral foundations.

3

Internationalism and Anti-imperialism

If there are many factors responsible for Guevara's impact on contemporary history, two major reasons for his profound and pervasive influence on radical activists and militants, in Latin America in particular, are his internationalism and anti-imperialism. These are, moreover, commitments that even people who are entirely unfamiliar with Guevara's writings, speeches, interviews, and other works but who know something about his life as a revolutionary will intuitively ascribe to him, for the simple reason that the best-known facts of his life vividly embody internationalism and anti-imperialism, often at the same time. An Argentine by birth, Guevara fought for the liberation of Cubans and the Congolese and was killed in Bolivia in the course of what he hoped would be the first stage in the liberation of the whole of Latin America; and all of these struggles at least partly involved, according to Guevara, anti-imperialist struggles.[1] (We know that Guevara was likewise prepared to fight on behalf of Guatemalans, among whom he was living when the democratically elected government of Jacobo Arbenz was overthrown in 1954.[2]) In short, Guevara's own actions attest to the sincerity of his vow, made in an exchange with representatives of other Latin American nations following his December 1964 speech at the United Nations, that he would be willing "to give [his] life for the liberation of any of the countries of Latin America, without asking anyone for anything, without demanding anything," as well as the sincerity of his conviction, expressed in his "farewell" letter to Fidel Castro, that "the most sacred of duties" is "to fight against imperialism wherever it may be."[3] But what do internationalism and anti-imperialism mean for Guevara? That is, what attitudes and actions do they entail, in Guevara's view? These are the questions I address in the present chapter.

45

THE CONTOURS OF GUEVARA'S INTERNATIONALISM

Like many important concepts in social thought, "internationalism" has multiple meanings. For example, internationalism can be understood as referring to "a policy of cooperation among nations,"[4] but the term can also mean "an attempted application of ethical considerations to international politics."[5] As we shall see, Guevara's own notion of internationalism incorporates the principles reflected in both of these definitions (along with other principles), but he also brings a very distinctive perspective to the construal of such principles. The distinctiveness of Guevara's internationalism is due in large part—as is the firmness of his commitment to this idea—to the fact that it has two different sources, or foundations, or rather arises from both moral and political convictions. (I do not mean to suggest that his political convictions do not have a moral component but only that it is possible to establish a separation of moral and political aspects for analytical purposes.) As for the moral convictions, it is clear that Guevara's internationalism follows from the two commitments that he exemplified on a personal level and that, as we have seen, would characterize the new human being: an elevated sense of social duty and the assimilation of a through-going egalitarianism. Simply stated, if we embrace a far more expansive concept of social duty and espouse a belief in universal equality of condition, then national borders as such will have little bearing on the degree of concern that we show for the well-being of other people.

At the same time, Guevara's internationalism also rests on a more narrowly political understanding of this concept that is rooted in his Marxism and involves the practice of international solidarity with all individuals and movements fighting for liberation from class oppression. In other words, Guevara's internationalism is also an expression of his commitment to the Marxist principle of "proletarian internationalism," a term that Guevara uses quite frequently. The Marxist principle of "proletarian internationalism" is encapsulated in the famous slogan "Proletarians of all countries, Unite!"—the phrase with which Marx concluded his "Inaugural Address" at the 1864 founding of the Working Men's International Association (the "First International"), as well as being the final line of the *Communist Manifesto*.[6] As these slogans suggest, "proletarian internationalism" lends "a class basis . . . to the idea of human brotherhood proclaimed by the French Revolution."[7] Lenin would subsequently spell out what this means in practice, remarking that proletarian internationalism entails "the fraternal union of the workers of all countries against the capitalists of all countries" and hence the duty of "supporting (by propaganda, sympathy, and material aid) *this struggle [i.e., the revolutionary struggle]*, this, *and only this,* line, in *every* country without exception."[8] It entails, in addition, that "a nation which is achieving victory over the bourgeoisie should be able and willing to make the greatest national sacrifices for the overthrow of international capital."[9]

It is precisely because both moral and political convictions inform Guevara's outlook that his appeals to internationalism appeal to both kinds of conviction, as when, in a 1963 preface to a book on "the Marxist-Leninist party," he characterizes "proletarian internationalism" as "feel[ing] as an affront to ourselves every aggression, every insult, every act against human dignity and against man's happiness anywhere in the world" or when, on the other hand, he suggests, in a speech from the previous year, that the Cuban Revolution would cease to be Martiano (i.e., a reflection of the principles espoused by José Martí) if it were to display indifference "when anywhere in the world the forces of repression are massacring the people."[10]

In any event, while Guevara's proletarian internationalism is indeed a genuine internationalism, it manifests itself above all as a kind of Latin Americanism: when asked during a press conference in 1961 whether he continued to consider himself Argentine, Guevara responded, "I am able to feel within myself the hunger and sufferings of basically any of America's peoples, but also [that] of any of the peoples of the world."[11] This reply echoes a view that Guevara had presented a year earlier before an assembly of tobacco workers, for whom he had evoked three levels, or one might say concentric circles, of duties: international solidarity with all countries who were suffering, solidarity with Latin American countries fighting for their freedom, and national solidarity with the men and women in Cuba worse off than themselves.[12]

There were both autobiographical and strategic, sociopolitical considerations for this special concern with Latin America. As for the former, Guevara made his personal identification with Latin America as a whole clear on countless occasions. For example, he told Argentine journalist Jorge Masetti in early 1958 (i.e., prior to the victory of the Rebel Army) that he considered all of America his "patria," and he made an almost identical remark three years later, during the press conference just cited.[13] In short, on a personal level Guevara felt a pan-American identification with Latin America *in toto*,[14] deriving in no small measure from his lengthy, youthful travels throughout South and Central America and his subsequent sojourns in Guatemala and Mexico, before eventually moving on to Cuba. These travels and experiences served to, as it were, deprovincialize and Latin Americanize Guevara, even transforming his accent and lexicon,[15] and they also help to explain why he would find it easy to identify himself as a Cuban following the revolution's triumph (shortly after which he became a Cuban citizen, thanks to a law conceived as a device for conferring citizenship on Guevara).[16] But Guevara's wanderings also acquainted him with the misery, oppression, and exploitation that defined life for a large percentage of Latin Americans, and exposure to this facet of Latin American reality, coupled with his more emotional identification with Latin America as a whole, is one of the factors that produced a certain partiality to the region in his thinking.

Yet, while this personal affinity with Latin America was undoubtedly important for Guevara's outlook, still more important in geopolitical terms were the strategic conclusions resulting from his analysis of the region's socioeconomic realities. To begin with, Guevara perceived a fundamental economic and cultural kinship among the countries of Latin America. As he observes in his "Message to the Tricontinental," a text published a mere six months before his execution, "Language, customs, religion, a common master, unite them. The degree and forms of exploitation are similar in their effects for exploiters and exploited in a good number of countries of our America"; and Guevara uses a rather similar formulation in his December 1964 address at the United Nations.[17] These common problems imply, Guevara believes, that radical transformation is necessary in all of the nations of Latin America: if these nations face the same problems, and revolution offers the solution to these problems, then revolution will be needed in all of these nations. The fact that these countries have, in addition to common socioeconomic interests, profound cultural similarities facilitates the linking of liberation movements in such a way as to make a more or less unified struggle for supranational revolution—that is, continental liberation—possible. While Guevara's conclusions regarding the need for, and value of, a supranational Latin Americanism are hardly original, the consistency with which he saw Latin America as a single community or sociopolitical entity has few parallels, as several commentators have pointed out.[18] Indeed, it may well be that case that, as Andrew Sinclair has claimed, "since Bolívar . . . there has been no man with so great an ideal of unity for that divided and unlucky continent."[19] And it was an ideal that Guevara proclaims and defends from the very start of the Cuban Revolution, as evidenced by his insistence, in one of his first public speeches after the triumph of the Revolution in January 1959, on the importance of receiving the support of the democratic peoples of Latin America.[20]

To the extent that it entailed actual participation in liberation struggles, Guevara's proletarian internationalism also prioritized Latin America. Indeed, he made it very clear upon joining Fidel Castro's group of Cuban revolutionaries in Mexico in 1955 that once they had achieved victory in Cuba, he would move on; and according to Manuel Piñeiro Losada, Cuba's intelligence mastermind and liaison to revolutionary movements throughout Latin America, "from the first moments of the victory of the Cuban Revolution," Guevara "was already thinking about carrying out what he considered his historic mission to participate in the liberation of other peoples in our continent [i.e., Latin America]."[21] As a matter of fact, Guevara had conceived the ill-fated insurgency that he launched in Bolivia in late 1966 not as a means for securing the liberation of a single country but rather as the commencement of, and initial base camp for, a revolution that would eventually spread throughout the whole of South America. These were "the continental aims of the guerrilla movement" in Bolivia, to use Guevara's phrase from his diary entry of July 10, 1967; the goal was to produce "the conditions for revoloution in the neighboring countries" or "create another Vietnam in the Americas with its center in Bolivia."[22] Within this strategy, Argentina was of central importance for Guevara.[23]

Yet, while Guevara plainly foregrounds Latin America in his global revolutionary strategy, his proletarian internationalism by no means ignores the rest of the world. As is now well known, Guevara spent some seven months fighting alongside Congolese insurgents in 1965. On a more general level, his commitment to the principle of proletarian internationalism informs his criticism of the then-socialist nations contained in what is, without question, the most controversial speech that he ever delivered—namely, his address to the Second Economic Seminar of Afro-Asian

Solidarity in Algiers, in February 1965. In this address, Guevara takes the Soviet Bloc countries to task for their "tacit complicity with the exploiting countries of the West," owing to their exploitative commercial relations with the developing nations (selling them goods at market prices, practicing "unequal exchange," and so on); "the socialist countries," Guevara argues, "must help pay for the development of countries now starting out on the road to liberation."[24] Guevara likewise upbraids the socialist countries for refusing to provide unconditional assistance—that is, armaments free of cost—to oppressed peoples engaged in armed struggle and in doing so explicitly appeals to the duties of proletarian internationalism:

> The question of liberation by armed struggle from an oppressor political power should be dealt with in accordance with the rules of proletarian internationalism. In a socialist country at war, it would be absurd to conceive of a factory manager demanding guaranteed payment before shipping to the front the tanks produced by his factory. It ought to seem no less absurd to inquire of a people fighting for liberation, or needing arms to defend its freedom, whether or not they can guarantee payment.
>
> Arms cannot be commodities in our world. They must be delivered to the peoples asking for them to use against the common enemy, with no charge and in the quantities needed and available. . . .
>
> The reply to the ominous attacks by US imperialism against Vietnam or the Congo should be to supply those sister countries with all the defense equipment they need, and to offer them our full solidarity without any conditions whatsoever.[25]

While this would prove to be Guevara's most controversial speech, given the fact that Cuba benefitted from the assistance and support of the socialist nations at the time, Guevara had in fact briefly sketched some of these ideas in a question-and-answer session following a lecture at the University of Oriente, in Santiago de Cuba, less than three months earlier.[26] And during the same exchange he mentions that he had raised these issues with representatives of the socialist nations in attendance at the United Nations Conference on Trade and Development held in Geneva about a year before the speech in Algiers. (In light of Guevara's statements in Algeria, some parts of his address at the earlier conference seem aimed at the socialist countries as much as the capitalist countries.[27])

But however critical Guevara was of some of the practices and policies of the socialist countries, the Algiers speech also leaves no doubt that the principal impediment to the establishment of a just economic system is, in Guevara's view, imperialism: "The struggle against imperialism, for liberation from colonial or neocolonial shackles . . . is not separate from the struggle against backwardness and poverty. Both are stages on the same road leading toward the creation of a new society of justice and plenty."[28] There can be, then, no development and progress toward social justice, let alone abundance and socialism, without the elimination of imperialism; and while the latter is not an end in itself—Guevara would surely agree with Peruvian thinker José Carlos Mariátegui, who had stressed a few decades earlier that anti-imperialism as such does not remove class antagonisms or conflicting class interests[29]—it is an indispensable condition for any possibility of success in achieving a definitive liberation—that is, abundance and socialism.[30] This is the conviction that inspires Guevara's passionate *anti-imperialism*, which is also the logical corollary of his internationalism: if imperialism causes the oppression of peoples in other lands and one embraces internationalism for either of the reasons inspiring Guevara's internationalism, one will favor and support anti-imperialist struggle in those lands. Considering the importance of militant anti-imperialist struggle in Guevara's thought—the historic Soviet statesman Anastas Mikoyan once said of Guevara that "he had a very specific enemy, and it is called imperialism"[31]—it is worth discussing this topic in some detail, starting with Guevara's conception of imperialism.

GUEVARA'S CONCEPTION OF IMPERIALISM

In his "Message to the Tricontinental," his fiercest and best-known denunciation of imperialism's crimes, Guevara characterizes imperialism as "a world system, the final stage of capitalism,"[32] a description that immediately evokes the title of Lenin's classic work on imperialism: *Imperialism, the Highest Stage of Capitalism*. Guevara's formulation is hardly surprising, for his speeches and writings attest to his indebtedness to Lenin's theorization of imperialism for his basic conception of, and approach to, this phenomenon.[33] (Significantly, during the question-and-answer session after his lecture at the University of Oriente, one of the books that Guevara urged students to read was precisely Lenin's *Imperialism*.[34]) For Lenin, as for Marx, imperialism in the most general sense "refers to the economic domination of one country over another as dictated by the needs of a capitalist economy," to use David McLellan's helpful characterization.[35] But Lenin identifies imperialism more narrowly with the "highest stage of capitalism," since contemporary imperialism, the most far-reaching and robust form of imperialism, is, in his opinion, a reflection or corollary of a number of fundamental economic developments that occurred in the late nineteenth and early twentieth centuries. These developments include the predominance of monopoly capitalism, as a result of the concentration of production and capital and in contrast to the competition that characterized earlier stages of capitalism; the merging of industrial capital with finance capital; the export of capital (rather than goods) to underdeveloped countries, accompanied by colonialism; the emergence of monopolistic capitalist associations that divide the world among themselves, in tandem with a division of the world among the leading powers in defense of their nations' monopolies; and intermonopolist rivalries and interimperialist competition resulting from these divisions of the world.[36] Guevara certainly subscribes to Lenin's analysis of this stage of capitalism and appropriates it for his own purposes, but we can also identify at least three factors that give Guevara's understanding of imperialism a distinctive character.

First of all, in considering the development of imperialism several decades after Lenin's landmark analysis, Guevara could study not only more advanced forms of colonialism but also neocolonialism, or, rather, "the neocolonial type of imperialism," as he calls it in his *Congo Diary*, where he also comments that this is "the most terrible" style of imperialism because, having the benefit of lengthy experience in exploitation, it is more subtle and knows how to disguise itself.[37] Furthermore, in analyzing contemporary colonialism and neocolonialism he could avail himself of the tools and insights of dependency theory, whose main theses can be roughly summarized as follows. Underdevelopment is not a phase or stage in a given country's development but rather a consequence of other countries' development; that is, the state of underdevelopment does not arise from insufficient industrialization and modernization in the underdeveloped country but from the economic needs of the wealthy, developed countries whose prosperity depends on the exploitation (of labor, natural resources, and markets) in the underdeveloped countries. The underdeveloped countries remain in a state of underdevelopment because they do not control their economic affairs but rather are subject to the domination of, and are dependent on, the wealthy, industrialized countries. We know that Guevara was well acquainted with the work of Paul Baran, whose book *The Political Economy of Growth* was a major impetus for the development of dependency theory, and references to "dependency" and the "dependent countries" abound in his writings and speeches.[38] Indeed, Guevara concludes his last major written work, *Congo Diary: Episodes of the Revolutionary War in the Congo*, a manuscript that he completed in January 1966 but that was not published until more than four decades later, with the suggestion that the "primary contradiction" of our era might be the contradiction between "the exploiting and exploited nations."[39] It is a proposition that plainly conjures up dependency theory.

Second, and in all probability as a result of his familiarity with dependency theory, Guevara seems to have a more expansive notion of the "labor aristocracy" than Lenin. According to Lenin, "the bourgeoisie of an imperialist 'Great' Power *can economically* bribe the upper strata of 'its' workers by spending on this" a small quantity of its "superprofits" deriving from its colonial exploitation, and this practice serves to "create something like an alliance . . . between the workers of the given nation and their capitalists *against* the other countries."[40] Lenin considers this development extraordinarily important in explaining the emergence of bourgeoisification (in the conventional sense) and "opportunism" within the labor movement. Guevara likewise attaches a great deal of importance to the role of a "labor aristocracy" in sustaining capitalism and imperialism, observing in his unedited and posthumously published critical remarks on the standard Soviet manual on political economy that the "labour aristocracy of imperialism" is "one of the most important phenomena at the current time."[41] Yet when he argues that first-world workers benefit from the exploitation of the underdeveloped countries, as he does in a 1965 letter to Fidel Castro in which he summarizes some of the conclusions that he had reached on the basis of his experience, study, and reflection in Cuba,[42] what he has in mind is the opportunism of the workers of the imperialist countries *as a whole* vis-à-vis the proletariat of the poor, weak, dependent countries. In other words, in the imperialist nations the concept of "labor aristocracy" applies to workers generally, who become junior partners in the exploitation of the dependent countries, as Guevara remarks in the discussion following his University of Oriente speech; or, as he puts it in later notes, having received the crumbs of colonial and neocolonial exploitation, these workers thus become accomplices of the monopolists.[43] While Guevara does not analyze this problem in any detail, his fragmentary remarks suggest that he regards the absence of contact between the workers in the exploiting and exploited nations, and the structures that create antagonisms between them, as a central element in the explanation of the labor aristocracy (as he understands this concept).[44]

The last facet of Guevara's conception of imperialism that distinguishes it somewhat from that of Lenin has to do with Guevara's own background: Guevara not only sees imperialism more directly from the vantage point of the colonized (or "neocolonized") but also brings a distinctly Latin American perspective to his understanding of the phenomenon. More specifically, this knowledge and experience of imperialist domination in Latin America lead Guevara to focus his thinking on strategies for waging an effective struggle against imperialism in situ, i.e., within those countries subject to this domination, and above all within Latin America. Of course, in order to be able to wage an effective struggle one must first of all be clear about who the principal enemy—the principal representative or agent of imperialism—is, and for Guevara the answer to this question is clear: it is the United States, which embodies the strongest, most aggressive, most brutal form of imperialism, and which Guevara does not hesitate to call, in his "Message to the Tricontinental," "the great enemy of the human race."[45] In a January 1964 speech, Guevara claims that the brutal policy that US imperialism has followed with respect to Cuba serves one purpose: to show "a destroyed Cuba, with all the leaders dead or in prison, with its people crushed by the imperialist boot in order to show what would happen to the people who dare oppose Yankee imperialism."[46] And in the same speech he warns, presciently, that US imperialism will carry out far greater aggression against the peoples of America in the future.[47] It is worth mentioning in this connection Guevara's very critical view of the United States' Alliance for Progress, which he claims in an article written in 1962, is merely imperialism's attempt to obstruct the development of revolutionary conditions in Latin America by giving some of its profits to the local exploiting classes, and thus an attempt to stop the unstoppable.[48] It is also worth noting that Guevara stresses, echoing Simón Bolívar, that "the United States intervenes in Latin America invoking the defense of free institutions,"[49] while also pointing out that when the United States is disinclined to use this pretext it will always manage to find another one, such as a betrayal of the revolution, to justify an imperialist intervention.[50]

ARMED STRUGGLE

If imperialism is "the final stage of capitalism" (or "highest stage," to use Lenin's more familiar formulation), then anti-imperialism necessarily involves a form of anticapitalist struggle. In one sense, an anti-imperialist politics represents an indirect form of anticapitalist struggle, for what both Guevara and Lenin mean with their formulations is that imperialism is the effect, or one concrete manifestation, of the latest stage of capitalism, which is the era of monopoly capitalism. (As Lenin puts it, "in its economic essence imperialism is monopoly capitalism."[51]) At the same time, anti-imperialism can indeed be construed as a direct form of anticapitalist struggle insofar as the imperialist nations' colonial and neocolonial ventures are the cause of capitalist domination in the nations subject to imperialism.

The question, at any rate, is, What to do? Or, rather, How should one fight imperialism? From Guevara's perspective, the nations oppressed by imperialist domination will, as a general rule, have to resort to armed struggle to combat and defeat imperialism. As Guevara would write in the relatively brief message that would become his "farewell" letter to his parents, "I believe in armed struggle as the only solution for those peoples who fight to free themselves, and I am consistent with my beliefs."[52] We should note that Guevara's categorical language in this letter is not entirely consistent with what he says in some other texts, in which he grants that a nation may not be obliged to adopt armed struggle to achieve its liberation. For example, in "Guerrilla Warfare: A Method," he grants the possibility of a "peaceful struggle [that] can be carried out through mass movements that compel—in special situations of crisis—governments to yield; thus, the popular forces would eventually take over and establish a dictatorship of the proletariat."[53] Likewise, in concluding a speech at the University of Montevideo on August 18, 1961, Guevara underscores the existence of freedom of expression in Uruguay and acknowledges that it may be possible to effect profound changes through the existing democratic channels.[54] Indeed, even in the "Message to the Tricontinental," a text not infrequently referred to as his "political testament,"[55] Guevara confines himself to saying that armed struggle will be necessary "in the majority of cases."[56] In light of such passages, it is somewhat misleading to attribute to Guevara a "rigid and uncompromising adherence to the method of armed struggle," as does Michael Löwy, a generally reliable and insightful guide to Guevara's thought.[57] Nonetheless, it is indeed the case that Guevara's considered view is that the world's oppressed peoples, and those of Latin America in particular, will for the most part have no choice but to take up arms if they wish to secure their liberation.

Why, exactly, does Guevara arrive at this conclusion? The most fundamental reason is that, as Guevara puts it in a speech on the eve of the 1961 Bay of Pigs Invasion, imperialism only understands the language of force, an idea that he would repeat in an interview with an American journalist three years later.[58] This is also the reason that it would be futile to appeal to international institutions,[59] which would be disinclined to restrain imperialism even if they had the power to do so: organizations such as the International Monetary Fund and the Inter-American Development Bank are, Guevara maintains, essentially in the service of US imperialism.[60] (It is worth recalling here that the Organization of American States suspended Cuba—effectively expelling it—in 1962 at the United States' urging.) And, in any event, one simply cannot trust imperialism, for "words never tally with the facts in the mouth of an imperialist ruler [*mandatario*]."[61] Moreover, Guevara assumes that, when "faced with the dilemma of choosing between the people or imperialism," Latin America's "national bourgeoisies" will inevitably side with imperialism, and this consideration also makes nonviolent national liberation virtually impossible.[62] Indeed, the alliance between local dominant classes and US imperialism will have the effect of emboldening the imperialists while at the same time shoring up the national bourgeoisie's resistance to peaceful social transformation.

With regard to the scope, scale, and ferocity of the armed struggle required to liberate the nations of Latin America (and the oppressed nations generally) and defeat imperialism, we should, Guevara insists, harbor no illusions. "We have predicted that the war will be continental," he writes in 1963. "This means that it will be a protracted war, it will have many fronts, and it will cost much blood and countless lives for a long period of time."[63] It will be necessary to fight imperialism wherever one is and with every available weapon at one's disposal.[64] As Guevara puts it in an essay published barely a week before the Bay of Pigs invasion, "Once the anti-imperialist struggle begins, we must constantly strike hard, where it hurts the most, never retreating, always marching forward, counterstriking against each aggression," and these blows must be delivered, as he stresses in a speech delivered at about the same time, without mercy.[65] One must make no concessions to imperialism, and there can be no quarter[66]; to the contrary, it will be necessary to "create two, three, many Vietnams," to use the slogan that Guevara proposes at the beginning of his "Message to the Tricontinental."[67] In the same text, Guevara writes that imperialism "must be beaten in a great worldwide confrontation"[68]—a fight to the death, as he underscores on various occasions[69]—that is to say, a war that will come to an end only with "the definitive liquidation of imperialism as an international system of exploitation of peoples."[70] It is precisely because the battle is to be of this nature that Guevara will insist (in a November 1964 speech as well as in his "Message"), somewhat notoriously, that those who join the struggle against imperialism must cultivate their hatred, which, besides making soldiers the most effective fighting forces possible, serves as a source of anti-imperialist cohesion. Hence it comes as no surprise that in his December 1964 interview with Josie Fanon, widow of anticolonial theorist Frantz Fanon, Guevara should cite "the hate which colonialism has left in the minds of the people" as one of the Africans' assets in the struggle against colonialism, neocolonialism, and imperialism in their continent.[71] Guevara's defense of hatred in these texts, incidentally, is not necessarily inconsistent with his famous assertion, in "Socialism and Man in Cuba," that "the true revolutionary is guided by great feelings of love."[72] We may legitimately feel hatred toward the agents and forces that harm or destroy that which we love, and we may only be able to help those whom we love if we develop the hatred needed to confront the forces that harm them.[73]

This battle against imperialism will require a common, united front among the anticolonial and anti-imperialist forces[74] in order to compel imperialism, among other things, to spread its forces and resources as thinly as possible, this being the most effective method of rendering imperialism maximally vulnerable while also relieving the immense pressure on Cuba, Vietnam, and other nations struggling to defend themselves against imperialist aggression.[75] (It is for reasons such as these that Michael Löwy observes that "proletarian internationalism" was, in Guevera's outlook, "above all a practical . . . necessity."[76]) This front was to include, in Guevara's day, the socialist countries: as noted earlier, proletarian internationalism entailed the duty to offer active, selfless support to national liberation movements and anti-imperial struggles, including the delivery of arms for use "against the common enemy, with no charge and in the quantities needed and available."

As for the actual mechanics of anti-imperialist struggle, Guevara is a proponent, as is well known, of guerrilla warfare, and in particular a *foco* (roughly, "center of action") version of this method of struggle, which he details in *Guerrilla Warfare*, the first of the two books that Guevara published during his lifetime (the other text being *Reminiscences of the Cuban Revolutionary War*). Guevara's conception of a foco-initiated insurgency, subsequently popularized in distorted form by French writer Régis Debray,[77] holds that an armed revolutionary vanguard, properly situated in the countryside, can spark a successful revolutionary insurrection. In his writings, Guevara provides two different sets of complementary considerations that indicate, to his mind, that guerrilla warfare is the optimal method for liberating Latin America. The first set of considerations is presented at the beginning of *Guerrilla Warfare*, where Guevara claims that the success of the insurrectionary war in Cuba contains three essential lessons for "revolutionary movements in Latin America." These three lessons are as follows: first of all, "popular forces can win a war against the army"; second, "it is not always necessary to wait until all the conditions for revolution exist; the insurrectional center can create them"; and finally, "in underdeveloped Latin America the arena for armed struggle must be basically the countryside."[78] In other words, guerrilla warfare proved its efficacy in Cuba, where a relatively small army of rebels defeated a vastly larger army of very well-equipped professional soldiers. But not only did the victory demonstrate the military efficacy of a guerrilla army, it also demonstrated the efficacy of such a force as a catalyst for the accelerated development of the sociopolitical conditions necessary for revolution. That is, the foco approach hastens the crystallization of both the "subjective" and "objective" conditions required for successfully taking power,[79] which is to say it creates both the awareness of the need, and the desire, to take power, on the one hand, and makes it possible to do so, given the chain of events that it sets in motion, on the other. Guerrilla warfare thus serves "to educate the masses in the possibility of victory,"[80] as Guevara would write in the epilogue to his *Congo Diary*, but not only the masses of the nation directly involved in the war: Guevara contends that "the beginning of a revolutionary war" also "contributes to the development of new conditions in the neighboring countries."[81] Finally, the third lesson also confirms the optimality of guerrilla warfare, albeit indirectly, in that Guevara assumes that it is the only variety of armed struggle that can succeed in the countryside, given the operational and logistical considerations that he outlines in *Guerrilla Warfare*.

In his essay "Guerrilla Warfare: A Method," Guevara mentions three additional reasons that "guerrilla warfare is the best method." First of all, as there will be resistance to revolution, it will be necessary to eliminate the oppressor army, and this can only be done by a people's army, which cannot be created overnight but rather needs to obtain its arsenal from, and develop its military skill in fighting against, the state's army. Second, the "continental" scale of the struggle for liberation will require multiple battles in many countries; these battles will inevitably take the form of armed struggle, and the only viable form of armed struggle in these circumstances is guerrilla warfare. Third, the plight of the peasantry and the intensification of its struggle against the "feudal structures" in Latin American nations generates conditions in which an insurrection in the countryside can succeed—since the peasants themselves seek emancipation and will therefore lend the insurrection their support—and, as already noted, Guevara contends that guerrilla warfare alone can succeed in the countryside.[82]

Guevara advocated guerrilla warfare, and this particular conception of it, until the end of his life. Indeed, his final communiqué in Bolivia, which he was unable to circulate, actually contains a highly compressed restatement of his vision of a guerrilla force as the agent and catalyst of national liberation.[83]

GUEVARA'S INTERNATIONALISM
AND ANTI-IMPERIALISM TODAY

Half a century after Guevara's death, it is difficult to find any grounds for challenging his uncompromising internationalism, which seems, if anything, even more sensible and attractive—not despite but because of the dramatic changes the world has undergone over the course of the past five decades—than in Guevara's day. For one thing, extraordinary technological advances, such as vastly expanded and improved forms of transportation and communication, including the Internet, have made it far easier to act in an internationalist fashion than was the case half a century ago. For another, individual countries' actions have a greater impact on other countries than was the case in Guevara's time, given the greater international economic interconnectedness and integration ("globalization") today. Finally, the forms of oppression, exploitation, and marginalization that many peoples face today may be, at least in relative terms, just as severe as they were in the 1960s. But can we say the same thing about Guevara's conception of anti-imperialism? In other words, to what extent does his particular form of uncompromising anti-imperialism, which on its own terms is certainly intellectually coherent, remain relevant to contemporary anti-imperialist struggles?

In responding to this question, let me begin by noting that I think Guevara was right to embrace Lenin's theorization of imperialism just as he was right, in my opinion, to complement this analysis of the causes and mechanics of imperialism with the insights and conceptual tools of dependency theory (which also still retains much of its explanatory power). We can also endorse, I believe, much of what Guevara says in connection with what he calls the "labor aristocracy of imperialism," even if Guevara by no means produced a systematic analysis of this phenomenon. The role that the imperialist countries' working classes play in the maintenance and success of imperialism poses an important problem, and Guevara's sketchy remarks on this issue certainly seem to point to some important truths. Moreover, we have no reason not to endorse Guevara's view that the principal agent of imperialism is the United States, whether in Latin America or in the rest of the world. Indeed, Guevara's conviction that the United States is *the* great enemy of anti-imperialist forces seems to me even less open to question than his perspective on the nature of imperialism as a socioeconomic phenomenon. To be sure, this view may not be as widely accepted as it was, say, during the era of the Vietnam War, when, for example, distinguished British philosopher Bertrand Russell, hardly a radical leftist, could write, "In every part of the world the source of war and of suffering lies at the door of US imperialism."[84] But Guevara's view is, I submit, no less valid today, within the "unipolar" world that emerged after the collapse of the socialist governments in Soviet Bloc countries from 1989 to 1991. Finally, we can also endorse Guevara's thesis to the effect that we ought to forge a common, international front against imperialism if we are to have any hope of eliminating this evil—and thereby creating the conditions for socialism and communism—once and for all. It is disheartening to realize, in this connection, that solidarity of this sort may not have increased much since Guevara's day, despite the dramatic advances in communication technologies and transportation noted above, developments that undoubtedly facilitate an international unification of movements and struggles. But here, too, Guevara's reflections may help us in understanding our challenges insofar as, for example, the existence of the "labor aristocracy of imperialism" still represents one of the major impediments to achieving the necessary solidarity and international cooperation.

In short, I think that we can still subscribe to most elements of Guevara's interpretation of the nature of imperialism, including his insistence on its barbaric character[85] and the need to combat imperialism. But this still leaves the question of *how* to combat it. That is to say, there remains the question of Guevara's ardent defense of armed struggle—by which he means guerrilla warfare—as a vehicle for national liberation and the principal route to defeating imperialism. Assuming one agrees with most of the other propositions just enumerated, how should one evaluate today Guevara's belief in, and defense of, armed struggle as the principal method for bringing about anti-imperialist revolution (which, in the case of Latin America, could be dubbed "armed Latin Americanism," to use Guevara biographer Paco Ignacio Taibo II's apt phrase[86])?

I think that it is fair to say that there is, at present, little justification for armed struggle in the form of guerrilla warfare as a method of combatting contemporary imperialism. But we should note at once that the rationale for this conclusion can in fact be found in Guevara's own defense of armed struggle. Consider Guevara's perspective on the political conditions necessary for initiating a guerrilla insurgency, as stated in the first chapter of *Guerrilla Warfare*: "Where a government has come to power through some form of popular vote, fraudulent or not, and maintains at least an appearance of constitutional legality, it is impossible to produce the guerrilla outbreak, since the possibilities of civic struggle have not yet been exhausted."[87] While imperialist domination, along with structures of oppression and exploitation, continue to characterize, to one degree or another, nearly all of the nations of Latin America today, the fact is that the nations that suffer from these ills have democratically elected governments and hence "the possibilities of civic struggle have not yet been exhausted." In other words, it is not at present the case that, as Guevara puts it in the same chapter of *Guerrilla Warfare*, "it is impossible to keep the struggle for social demands within the framework of civic dispute"[88]; to the contrary, there are channels for such struggle, and far more openings for popular participation in the political process, than in the past. Thus, while the most general political conditions that justify, in Guevara's view, recourse to guerrilla warfare or armed struggle—again, when Guevara discusses armed struggle, he means guerrilla warfare—arguably did exist in many Latin American countries in the 1960s (and even as sober an observer as K. S. Karol would remark in 1961 "that Latin American states cannot break out of their cages by peaceful means"[89]), and may reappear in the future, they do not exist in the region today. It should not surprise us, therefore, that Guevara's viewpoint enjoyed such prestige and inspired so many Latin American radicals to take up arms in the 1960s and 1970s while their contemporary counterparts are for the time being pursuing their goals "within the framework of civic dispute."

It is worth noting three other considerations, in addition to Guevara's theses on the very general political conditions that must be satisfied for guerrilla warfare to be viable, that suggest that armed struggle has little to recommend it today. First of all, there has been significant land reform throughout Latin America since Guevara's death. While the scale of this land reform has been woefully insufficient from a Marxist perspective and would undoubtedly be insufficient for Guevara, it has surely assuaged the "masses' great hunger for land," which, according to Guevara, motivates the peasants to support a guerrilla insurgency.[90] (The guerrilla fighter, Guevara writes, "is, fundamentally and above all else, an agrarian revolutionary."[91]) Second, there are considerations of feasibility: the extraordinary technological sophistication and sheer military might of contemporary imperialist powers, and preeminently the United States, significantly diminish the prospects for successful armed struggle. Finally, decades of ineffective armed struggles resulting in countless casualties, along with the increased incidence of terrorism of one sort or another, have generated a fairly widespread revulsion toward political violence among the peoples of Latin America, and no doubt even among those who would most benefit from a revolution. In light of this experience, more or less peaceful forms of radical opposition appear much more attractive and much more promising.

In short, the early 1960s seem to represent a historical juncture that was uniquely propitious for anticapitalist and anti-imperialist armed struggle, and Guevara plainly sensed as much, as Manuel Monereo has rightly emphasized. The emergence of national liberation movements in numerous places and the increasing currency of socialist ideas around the world (despite the disrepute of Soviet-style socialism), on the one hand, and the realization that US imperialism was not invincible (the defeat of US–backed mercenaries at the Bay of Pigs and the successful radicalization of the Cuban Revolution's having shown as much), on the other, gave rise to what Monereo calls a "crisis of domination." At the same time, the very real crisis of "actually existing socialism" might, were it to coincide with a recovery of US imperialism, foreclose the possibilities for change at any moment.[92] In short, "what is called the correlation of forces" was "increasingly moving toward the socialist side," as Guevara remarks in January 1962,[93] but there was also no time to lose. This perception on Guevara's part, together with his desire to return to guerrilla activity before becoming too old to do so, would explain the obvious sense of urgency or haste in Guevara that Monereo and others have noted.[94]

It is important to point out, in any event, that in rejecting Guevara's notion of armed struggle we by no means commit ourselves to a categorical rejection of violence in the fight for socialism. On the contrary, even assuming that armed struggle is unjustified in the contemporary fight against imperialism, we can still endorse Guevara's view that some violence is inevitable in the pursuit of socialism, however revolutionary forces manage to come to power, whether it be through armed struggle or by peaceful means such as elections. A government that is carrying out a revolution and embarking on the transition to socialism will, Guevara maintains, have to apply a not insignificant measure of coercion, force, and violence in responding to the opposition—much of it brutally violent (physical attacks, sabotage, bombings, etc.)—emanating from the bourgeoisie and other counterrevolutionary forces. Guevara emphasizes this very point in his 1961 essay "Cuba: Historical Exception or Vanguard in the Anticolonial Struggle?":

> If a popular movement takes over the government of a country by winning a wide popular vote and resolves as a consequence to initiate the great social transformations which make up the triumphant program, would it not immediately come into conflict with the reactionary classes of that country? Has the army not always been the repressive instrument of that class? If so, it is logical to suppose that this army will side with its class and enter the conflict against the newly constituted government. . . . What appears difficult to believe is that the armed forces would accept profound social reforms with good grace and peacefully resign themselves to their liquidation as a caste.[95]

We shall return to the question of violence, including both the measures that will provoke counterrevolutionary violence and those needed to eradicate it, in the next chapter, when we consider Guevara's conception of revolution. The important point for our present purposes is that the contrast or opposition between armed struggle and the peaceful conquest of power turns out to be largely illusory, a false dichotomy, once we realize that any regime committed to building socialism will, regardless of how it came to power, inevitably be forced to employ a considerable amount of violence against the opposition supported by imperialism, at least if it wishes to have any chance of success. As Guevara says in his May 25, 1962, remarks to Argentinean comrades, "in the last analysis, on taking power it is then necessary to take up arms," and this is presumably also what Guevara has in mind when he declares, in his February 1965 Algiers speech, that with the conquest of political power it will be necessary "to get rid of the oppressor classes" (in the original Guevara uses the word "liquidate" [*liquidar*]).[96] So, while contemporary anti-imperialist strategy should renounce armed struggle in the form of guerrilla warfare, this does not entail a total renunciation of violence. Nor does it amount to a rejection of an essential component of Guevara's political thought, notwithstanding appearances to the contrary. As I have already pointed out, Guevara expressly states that guerrilla warfare is only justified when certain conditions have been satisfied; when it is not the case that they have been satisfied, one should not pursue guerrilla warfare. It is worth noting in this connection that in his essay "Guerrilla Warfare: A Method," Guevara himself cites with approval José Marti's aphorism, "He who wages war in a country when he can avoid it is a criminal, just as he who fails to promote war which cannot be avoided is a criminal."[97] Furthermore, Guevara emphasizes, in the essay just cited, that guerrilla warfare, being "a method of struggle," is but "a means to an end"—namely, "the conquest of political power."[98] If one can achieve the same end without guerrilla warfare, or guerrilla warfare would render achievement of this end more difficult, revolutionaries have no reason to initiate a guerilla foco. It is perfectly reasonable to claim, therefore, as does Armando Hart, one of the historic leaders of the Cuban Revolution and a friend of Guevara, that "the essence of his [Guevara's] thought is increasingly valid," even if "the kinds of action chosen by Che for the realization of this ideal [of emancipation] are, obviously, very different from those that we must adopt today."[99] In sum, the method that Guevara favors as a means of promoting human emancipation was conditioned by the historical and sociopolitical circumstances of his era, and the theory of guerrilla warfare that he espoused would not justify guerrilla warfare in Latin America—his primary area of concern—today.

4

Socialism, Communism, and Revolution

Jamaican writer Andrew Salkey once observed that Ernesto Che Guevara is "the universal symbol of the modern revolution."[1] Salkey's observation certainly seems indisputable, but it seems no less indisputable that Guevara owes this status in large measure to his commitment—in both theory and practice—to guerrilla warfare. In fact, Guevara is not so much the symbol of modern revolution as, to use Francisco Fernández Buey's apt description, "the figure of the communist guerrilla par excellence."[2] But to limit Guevara's revolutionary thought to his conception and vigorous advocacy of guerrilla warfare, discussed in the preceding chapter, or to assume that this is the most significant dimension of what we might call his philosophy of revolution, is a mistake.[3] As Fernández Buey's formulation reminds us, Guevara was a communist, and he thought, spoke, and wrote a great deal about a variety of topics related to socialism and communism. The purpose of the present chapter is to elucidate Guevara's views on some of these topics, including the pace of postrevolutionary socioeconomic transformation, the dictatorship of the proletariat, and the challenges posed by the counterrevolution.

SOCIALISM AND COMMUNISM

While Guevara occasionally offers general characterizations of socialism and communism, as when he defines the former as "a social system based on equal distribution of society's wealth,"[4] he never furnishes a systematic account of these concepts, and his views on socialism and communism scarcely differ from those of Marx, Engels, and Lenin in many respects. At the same time, Guevara's writings, talks, and speeches emphasize certain aspects of these thinkers' ideas more than others, and these emphases lend a distinctive cast to his vision of socialism and communism. One example

61

of this aspect of Guevara's thought is found in his tendency to underscore, time and again, that one necessary condition for the existence of socialism is the "abolition of man's exploitation of man." Guevara uses some variation of this formulation on countless occasions in his works,[5] and while he sometimes actually defines socialism in this manner,[6] his considered view seems to be that the elimination of the exploitation of one human by another is one component of socialism. This conclusion or interpretation suggests itself for two reasons. First of all, Guevara also refers to other measures or achievements in characterizing socialism, such as the nationalization of the means of production, a very substantial increase in the production of goods required to satisfy the needs of the population, or a state that represents the working class.[7] Second, Guevara often claims that the revolution was putting an end to, or had indeed already eliminated, the "exploitation of man by man" in Cuba,[8] yet he did not believe, as we have already seen, that socialism had been established in Cuba. Rather, he assumes that his years as an active participant in the Cuban Revolution coincide with a transitional period during which Cuba has begun to undertake the task of "building socialism." In short, if Cuba had already put an end to the exploitation of one human by another but had not yet achieved socialism, then it would make little sense for Guevara to define socialism in terms of an end to humans' exploitation of one another.

Guevara's abundant references to the need to eliminate the exploitation of one human by another, quite noteworthy in themselves, also point to what is perhaps the most distinctive feature of his conception of socialism and communism, and one that I already anticipated in previous chapters: his insistence on the moral dimension of socialist/communist transformation. As noted earlier, Guevara once stated in an interview that "economic socialism without a communist morality" did not interest him, and this theme—that moral progress should have no less importance for socialism and communism than advances in productivity—is one that Guevara emphasizes repeatedly, from the time that he began publicly identifying himself as a socialist/communist until his final, unpublished theoretical manuscripts. Thus, in a televised lecture on April 30, 1961—barely two weeks after Fidel Castro had publicly declared that Cuba had undertaken a socialist revolution—Guevara stated that socialism "is the result of economic factors and factors of conscience," while in his fragmentary notes on the political economy of socialism, dating from 1965 to 1966, Guevara stresses that we should conceive of communism as consisting in a certain level of economic development, coupled with a certain level of development of consciousness, within a framework in which society has socialized the means of production.[9] As we have already seen, "consciousness" should generally be construed in moral terms, and preeminently in terms of a radical egalitarianism wedded to a quite substantially heightened sense of social duty; and it is for this reason that we should think of Guevara's conception of socialism/communism as resting on an unusually strong moral component (or, if one prefers, an unusually *explicit* moral component). Indeed, Guevara tends to conceive of the difference between socialism and communism—which Marxists have, especially since Lenin, generally envisaged as a difference between lower and higher, or immediate and more advanced, forms of a communistically oriented postcapitalist society—largely in terms of phases of moral development. For Guevara claims not only that without the "factor of consciousness" it is not possible to reach communism but also that under communism the only operative incentive to perform work or otherwise contribute to society will be one of a moral nature.[10] This will be the case not only because the development of the productive forces will make it possible to satisfy the needs of all (as a result of which material incentives will prove quite superfluous) but also because of an advanced moral development. It is precisely this conception of communism that informs Guevara's casual observation, during a 1964 meeting with colleagues from the Ministry of Industries, to the effect that society will be able to dispense with controls on people's behavior at work under communism.[11] This would, incidentally, include the desire to exploit others: To eliminate "man's exploitation of man" by rendering such exploitation structurally impossible, as occurs with the transition to socialism, is not the same thing as eliminating altogether the desire to treat others in an exploitative manner.

Let me conclude these very brief remarks on Guevara's conception of socialism and communism with a few comments on some common misunderstandings of Guevara's views on these topics. First of all, it should be noted that Guevara envisions communist society, as do all Marxists, as a classless society of abundance, whose purpose is to satisfy the needs of all. Thus, in speaking of "the central idea of entering communism" in "On the Budgetary System of Finance," his important 1964 essay outlining his theory of economic organization, Guevara refers to "a society of large-scale production and the satisfaction of man's basic needs." Furthermore, he acknowledges, in keeping with a basic premise of Marxism, that people's needs will continue to grow and that the satisfaction of these needs—which will also "become increasingly complex"[12]—will entail the production and distribution of more and more consumer goods[13]; and on numerous other occasions Guevara insists on the need to increase the supply of such goods.[14] Indeed, Guevara even endorses on occasion the most robust notion of abundance—that is, not merely *enough* for everyone but *an endless supply* for everyone[15]—as when he remarks, in a speech that also dates from 1964, that the "new society" will be one in which "all will have an infinite quantity of consumer goods at their disposal."[16] Thus, while the immediate objective during the transition to socialism is to satisfy people's most basic needs (for food, medical care, education, housing, etc.) and to prioritize the needs of the most disadvantaged sectors of the population, the long-range goal is abundance.[17] If I belabor this point, it is because at least one recent critic of Guevara has asserted that Guevara had no interest in increasing the number of consumer goods available to Cubans.[18] But the assertion is, as the passages cited attest, completely untenable.

The second misunderstanding of Guevara's thought worth mentioning here involves the claim that Guevara advocated the simultaneous building of socialism and communism.[19] This claim also proves completely untenable. While Guevara does maintain, as we shall see in the following chapter, that it is possible to compress the stages through which a society must pass in order to reach socialism and, eventually, communism, he never argues, to my knowledge, that they can be built simultaneously in Cuba or, for that matter, anywhere else. (One should also bear in mind in this connection that Guevara's thought focuses above all, as we have already seen, on the political economy of the *transition to socialism*, which he does not identify with the political economy of *socialism*.) Moreover, it is precisely because Guevara does *not* believe that socialism and communism can be built simultaneously that he accepts Marx's familiar distinction between the distributional principles appropriate for the former and the latter: whereas under socialism, the "lower" phase of communist society, an individual's contribution to the social product will necessarily determine his or her share of social benefits, under communism, the "higher phase of communist society," the operative principle of distribution will become "From each according to his abilities, to each according to his needs!"[20] As Guevara invokes and endorses Marx's distinction on numerous occasions,[21] the claim that he does not accept that "the principle of 'from each according to his ability and to each according to his work' was the one appropriate to 'socialism,'" a claim recently advanced by Samuel Farber,[22] makes little sense.

GUEVARA'S CONCEPTION OF REVOLUTION

"Remember that the revolution is what is important."[23] These words, from a letter that Guevara wrote to his children in the last year of his life, offer a concise statement of the importance of the Cuban Revolution, and revolution generally, for Guevara's worldview. Yet, the depth of his commitment to revolutionary social transformation notwithstanding, Guevara never attempted to produce a systematic treatment of his conception of revolution. To be sure, Guevara occasionally offers a general characterization of revolutions, as when he defines them as "accelerated radical social changes," or explains that they consist in "cries of desperation from the people, who take up arms and solve the immediate problem of an oligarchy, or a government, that is oppressing them."[24] But his comments on the nature of revolution are for the most part of an incidental character. Nevertheless, a number of these comments on the nature of revolution are of some interest, as are his more developed thoughts on the measures that socialist revolutionaries will have to enact if their revolution is to succeed. (I am not referring here to Guevara's more specific ideas and policies for building socialism, which we shall examine in the following chapter.) Consideration of these comments and thoughts reveals, if nothing else, that it is hardly the case that, as one author has argued, Guevara tends "to reduce revolution to armed struggle, the armed struggle to rural guerrilla warfare, and guerrilla warfare to the core group of the foco."[25]

Let us note, to begin with, that Guevara often emphasizes—in keeping with Marx's well-known thesis that "the working class cannot simply lay hold of the ready-made State machinery, and wield it for its own purposes"[26]—the need to utterly transform the prerevolutionary state institutions. While Guevara would not exempt any of the state's central institutions from this transformation, he tends to attach paramount importance to the destruction of the existing army—that is, to the dismantling of the army inherited from capitalist society and its subsequent replacement by a "people's army." (This is not the same thing as the need to defeat the oppressor's army, a topic touched on in the preceding chapter.) As he says in an essay titled "The Cuban Revolution's Influence in Latin America," written in 1962, "One of the premises of the Cuban Revolution is that it is absolutely necessary to immediately destroy the army in order to take power seriously."[27] Yet this is not, for Guevara, merely a premise of the Cuban Revolution; to the contrary, "the defeat and subsequent annihilation of the army by the popular forces" is "*an absolutely necessary condition for every genuine revolution.*"[28] Indeed, this is not only "an absolutely necessary condition" but is also the very first task that must be undertaken after a successful revolution.[29] The reason for prioritizing the elimination of the old professional army is that it constitutes one of the principal impediments to the enactment of popular demands, "the enemy of the people par excellence."[30] In rehearsing this same argument in June 1961, shortly after the Bay of Pigs Invasion, Guevara invokes Spain and Guatemala (allusions to the pre–civil war Second Republic and the early 1950s government of Jacobo Arbenz, respectively) as examples of popular movements that failed because they did not establish their own people's army to defend the social gains achieved.[31]

Besides the need to dismantle the oppressor army, the newly victorious Cuban Revolution had to deal with—as will all successful anti-imperialist or socialist revolutions, thinks Guevara—the problem posed by those who not only served in the previous regime's forces of repression but also were individually guilty of torture, murder, and so on. Guevara approved of executions in such cases. It is worth mentioning in this regard that on arriving in Havana in January 1959, Guevara was put in charge of the city's La Cabaña fortress, and while there his responsibilities included the supervision of the revolutionary tribunals that tried and sentenced hundreds of people accused of crimes, often of a quite abhorrent nature, in service to the dictator Batista. Some of these people were executed,[32] and while Guevara did not participate in the trials, he did have the last word on every sanction. Guevara defended the tribunals, a form of "revolutionary justice," arguing that the revolutionary government only executed war criminals and those guilty of crimes against humanity. He suggested, moreover, that part of the negative reaction that these executions, which enjoyed nearly universal support within Cuba, provoked abroad arose from the fact that the foreign press, and preeminently the US news services, had failed to convey the true extent of the killings and torture under Batista, and in Latin America more generally.[33] In any event, Guevara plainly believed that some executions were necessary and unavoidable, a view he reiterated in his response to criticisms from Latin American delegates following his address at the United Nations in 1964: "Yes, we shoot people, we have shot people, and we shall continue to shoot people as long as it is necessary. . . . But I must say this: we do not commit assassinations."[34]

Another noteworthy aspect of Guevara's notion of revolution concerns his understanding of the dynamic of radicalization within a revolutionary process, and his views on the experience of radicalization within the Cuban Revolution in particular. Regarding the general topic of radicalization, Guevara holds that "a revolution that does not constantly expand is a revolution that regresses."[35] That the word "expand" here means something like "become more radical" or "intensify" (the original Spanish is *que no se profundice*—"is not deepened") is obvious from other passages in which Guevara states or implies the same idea.[36] A constant deepening and heightening of revolutionary measures reduces the possibility of a reversion to the prerevolutionary condition; that is, this procedure tends to make the revolution irreversible or, if one prefers, to forestall and neutralize counterrevolutionary tendencies. To be sure, Guevara sometimes characterizes the actual process of radicalization of the Cuban Revolution—namely, its evolution from the defeat of Fulgencio Batista's army to the consolidation of policies and measures aimed at establishing socialism in Cuba—as a historically specific response to both external and internal pressures. The external pressure consisted of the resistance of the United States in the form of punitive measures taken against Cuba (such as the annulment of the annual sugar quota in July 1960), while the internal pressures included both antirevolutionary resistance emanating from the Cuban bourgeoisie and others who sided with American imperialism *and* popular support for the revolution, with its demands to push the revolution forward.[37] Yet there can be no doubt that the radicalization of the revolution was, in Guevara's view, not merely an appropriate response to contingent pressures. Rather, just as the elimination of the prerevolutionary army is, for Guevara, "*an absolutely necessary condition for every genuine revolution,*" so, too, is the constant expansion of revolutionary measures. Guevara's thesis is, in any case, hardly original; it is, rather, a familiar Marxist idea, and Guevara actually invokes and paraphrases Marx himself in the sentence preceding the remark that I cited at the beginning of this paragraph.[38]

Guevara occasionally claims, in keeping with his (sometime) contention that contingent historical factors and circumstances dictated the radicalization of the Cuban Revolution, that it was the revolution's tendency to follow a more and more radical course that led the revolution's leaders to embrace Marxist and communist ideas. In other words, it was not merely true, as Guevara remarked to Jorge Masetti in 1958, that it was only in the course of making a revolution that the guerrillas themselves became revolutionaries,[39] or that, as he maintains in *Guerrilla Warfare*, the interaction between the guerrillas and the people caused "a progressive radicalization" of the revolutionary struggle (as the former demonstrated the value of armed struggle and the lives of the latter revealed the true extent of oppression in Cuba).[40] It was also the case that this process of relentless radicalization had eventually turned the revolution's leaders into Marxists and communists.

This is a questionable thesis but not because anyone would challenge the proposition that the Cuban Revolution underwent a very profound radicalization in a very brief span of time. Indeed, most observers would not only grant this proposition but also agree with Guevara's interpretation of the revolution's early development.

For example, in an article published on the very day that the Rebel Army attained its victory, January 1, 1959, Guevara refers to the revolution as a cross-class movement, and twelve months later he would characterize the initial stages of the Cuban Revolution in more or less populist terms, describing it as antifeudal and opposed to the big landowners (*antilatifundista*).[41] Not long after this, Guevara would note, in a parenthetical periodization included in a document for the Council of Ministers, that the "bourgeois-democratic" phase of the revolution lasted no more than twenty months (i.e., until September 1960),[42] a claim that likewise appears quite plausible. The problem arises when Guevara goes on to suggest, as he does on some occasions, that he and the other leaders of the July 26 Movement (named after the date of Fidel Castro's unsuccessful attack on the Moncada army barracks in Santiago de Cuba in 1953) discovered, and subsequently came to embrace, Marxism and socialism/communism as a result of their experience during the revolution. For example, in his July 1960 speech to the First Latin American Youth Congress, Guevara tells his audience that, "if today we are putting into practice what is known as Marxism, it is because we discovered it here."[43] Likewise, in a question-and-answer session with American students in August 1963, Guevara, referring to the July 26 Movement, says, "We were not communists. It was necessary to fight for the people's well-being and to change the existing reality. We saw, as the struggle developed, how Marxism had foreseen answers to the problem and how the behavior of American imperialism forced us to choose. . . . The study of the development of this struggle showed us the truth of Marxism."[44]

While this account is certainly consistent with a Marxist approach to social analysis, with its emphasis on the social determination of our ideas, and may well offer an accurate description of the ideological evolution of much of the leadership of the Cuban Revolution, it hardly applies to the development of Guevara's own political outlook, for the fact is that Guevara already adhered to a Marxism of some sort and espoused communist ideas prior to the triumph of the Cuban Revolution in January 1959.[45] These commitments are reflected, for example, in a December 1957 letter to an important figure in the July 26 Movement, René Ramos Latour; in this letter, Guevara declares that on account of his "ideological preparation" he belonged "to those who believe that the solution to the world's problems lies behind the so-called iron curtain."[46] Similarly revealing is an April 1963 speech in which Guevara remarks that he was thinking about a "socialist revolution" during the revolutionary war—and hence well before the Rebels' victory—and in an interview published in *Look* magazine the very same month, Guevara admitted to his interviewer, Laura Bergquist, that he had a "Marxist-oriented revolution in mind" (the phrase is Bergquist's) when he was "fighting in the Sierra Maestra mountains."[47] Approximately a year later, Guevara would state, in an interview with another American journalist, that he had had an intuitive sense that the revolution would follow the radical path that it took without foreseeing the "Marxist-Leninist formulation" of the revolution. When journalist Lisa Howard subsequently posed a question regarding Fidel Castro's denial, while fighting in the Sierra Maestra, that he was a communist,

Guevara, contradicting to a large degree his previous statement, replied, "I knew he was not a Communist, but I believe that I also knew that he would become a Communist. Just as I knew at that time that I was not a Communist but I also knew that I would become one within a short time and that the natural development of the revolution would lead all of us to Marxism-Leninism. I cannot say that it was a clear or conscious knowledge, but it was an intuition . . . the result of an examination, of careful assessment of the development of the attitude of the United States."[48] We might also note, finally, the significance of a famous joke relating to Guevara's appointment as president of the National Bank of Cuba in November 1959. At a meeting of the revolution's leadership, the story goes, Fidel Castro asked if anyone in the room was an economist. Guevara, half dozing in the back of the room, immediately and energetically raised his hand. When a nonplussed Castro later told Guevara that he never knew that he was an economist, Guevara replied that he thought Castro had asked if anyone present was a *communist*.[49] It is seldom noticed that the joke's comic effect requires the presupposition that Guevara already considered himself a communist prior to his appointment as director of the National Bank—were this not plausible, the joke would make no sense and would hardly be amusing—in late 1959. And if he did indeed identify himself as a communist less than a year into the revolution, long before it had implemented its truly radical early measures (e.g., the nationalizations of US companies) and during a time in which the revolution was still passing through its "bourgeois-democratic" phase, the idea that Guevara became a Marxist and communist as a result of the social changes in Cuba appears utterly implausible.

So, when Guevara denies his own prerevolutionary adherence to Marxist and communist views, as in his exchange with the American students, his remarks are highly misleading, at the very least: while the evolution of the revolution no doubt radicalized him in many ways, Guevara plainly espoused a Marxist, communist political outlook at the revolution's inception, however ill-defined this outlook may have been. No less misleading, therefore, is his assertion that he "discovered" the Marxist perspective through the Cuban Revolution. It is significant, in this regard, that just three months after his speech to the First Latin American Youth Congress (cited above) Guevara would remark, in "Notes for the Study of the Ideology of the Cuban Revolution," that "there are truths so evident, so much a part of the people's knowledge, that it is now useless to debate them. One should be a 'Marxist' with the same naturalness with which one is a 'Newtonian' in physics or a 'Pasteurian.'"[50] The latter remark, from October 1960, appears more than a little inconsistent with the uncertainly that Guevara expresses in July 1960 regarding the possibly Marxist character of the Cuban Revolution and, more generally, with the notion that he, along with the rest of the Cuban Revolution's major leaders, gradually discovered Marxism through the revolution. Likewise, when Guevara denied being a "communist," as he did in a mid-1959 letter to the editor of Cuba's most important weekly magazine, it was plainly a matter of political expediency, a tactical untruth, as it were.[51] As Guevara told Cuban journalist José Vázquez, while the revolutionary press should never lie, there are some truths that should be kept secret so as to avoid giving weapons to the enemy,[52] a precept that seems especially reasonable when one faces an enemy as powerful as Cuba's.

ACCELERATING DEVELOPMENT

Another noteworthy aspect of Guevara's general conception of revolution is his insistence on the possibility of accelerating the tempo and pace of the revolutionary transformation of Cuba well beyond what Marxist theory, as well as mainstream economics and political science, would judge feasible. Before turning to Guevara's remarks on this question, it is important to underscore that, contrary to what one might assume given Guevara's largely undeserved reputation for "voluntarism," Guevara never disputes the Marxist premise that a revolution will not succeed in the absence of the requisite "objective conditions," such as a given level of economic development, certain structural problems or "contradictions" that prove irresolvable within the existing sociojuridical framework, one of various kinds of political crises, oppressive or exploitative social conditions, and so on. Indeed, if Guevara believed that outbreaks of revolutionary struggle were imminent and inevitable throughout Latin America,[53] it was because, in his opinion, these objective conditions already exist. It is likewise owing to his recognition of the indispensability of these objective conditions that Guevara insists that revolutions cannot be "exported" while at the same time acknowledging that revolutions do "expand ideologically," influencing other countries besides those in which they occur; insofar as this has been the case with the Cuban Revolution, one could say that the revolutionaries "exported" their example.[54] But this is very different from exporting the objective conditions that give rise to, and are necessary for the occurrence of, a revolution, which is simply not possible.

Thus, as revolutions cannot be exported, Cuba could not export them, even if it wished to do so. While this may appear to be a trivial point, a mere truism, Guevara found it necessary to underscore this idea on a number of occasions, since other countries often accused Cuba of "exporting revolution." For example, representatives of other Latin American countries leveled this accusation against Cuba following Guevara's address to the United Nations General Assembly on December 11, 1964, and two days later Guevara confronted the same charge from a journalist on the American television program *Face the Nation*.[55] Of course, Guevara also supported armed struggle in nations striving to attain their liberation and believed that Cuba, and other liberated nations, should support these liberation struggles. Was he inconsistent? In fact, there was no inconsistency in Guevara's position, for, as Guevara himself observes in his reply to other representatives' comments during the same UN session, exporting revolution is not the same thing as offering "assistance," which "can be given or not given to liberation movements; above all they can be supported morally."[56] Yet one might still maintain that Guevara is inconsistent to the extent that he also claims, both before and after he began to explicitly acknowledge his Marxist convictions, to eschew interference in the internal affairs of other nations in general. For example, at the Inter-American Economic and Social Council conference held in Uruguay in August 1961, Guevara said, "We guarantee that not one rifle will be moved from Cuba, that not one weapon will be moved from Cuba for fighting in any other country in Latin America."[57] Indeed, Guevara even refused invitations from students and professors to take part in a march starting at the University of Montevideo, where he gave a speech not long after delivering the address from which I have quoted, on the grounds that joining the march could be construed as interference in Uruguay's internal affairs.[58] Yet there is no inconsistency in this regard either, assuming that Guevara subscribes to the position of the Cuban Revolution's leadership—namely, that this principle did not apply in the case of those Latin American countries openly hostile to the revolution—that is, those countries that had broken off relations with Cuba.[59] This was the case with Bolivia, for example, which had severed relations with Cuba in 1964, two years before Guevara arrived in the country with the intention of establishing a guerrilla insurgency there. (As for the Congo, an insurrection was already underway when Guevara's contingent of Cuban forces arrived in April 1965.)

So, Guevara accepts many standard Marxist assumptions about the importance of "objective conditions" for revolution and does not depart from Marxist theory at all in his views on the kinds of conditions required for the establishment of a socialist society. In Cuba, however, a revolution had taken place even though the objective socioeconomic conditions required for socialism did not yet exist, on account of Cuba's underdevelopment. For Guevara, the absence of these objective conditions need not—and did not—constitute an insurmountable obstacle to the creation of socialism in the near future, for he holds that it is possible, and eminently desirable, to dramatically accelerate the development of these conditions. In other words, he holds that it is possible, in certain circumstances, for a country to make rapid progress in its development, advancing by *quemando etapas*—that is, by leaps and bounds, which is just another way of saying "to go as quickly as possible in the building of socialism."[60] In practical terms, this would require, among other things, expediting the modernization of agriculture, an acceleration of job training (especially in technical fields), optimal use of new technology, and a major commitment to intensive industrial development. Since proceeding "by leaps and bounds" entails a contraction of the process of economic development, and this contraction is achieved in part by omitting some steps constituent of traditional patterns of economic growth and evolution, Guevara's notion is largely synonymous with the more familiar notion of "skipping stages" of development. In any case, while it is certainly no wonder that Guevara should think it desirable to hasten the advent of socialism (since it is an extremely desirable goal), we might well wonder why he should think it was possible to do so, why it was the case, as he remarks at the beginning of 1962, that Cuba had "all of the conditions to advance at an extraordinary speed."[61] The answer lies in Guevara's belief that individuals' enthusiasm and determination could play a critical role in enabling Cuba to dramatically reduce the amount of time required to push development forward.[62] In other words, a certain level of commitment and ardor will generate the disposition to sacrifice and interest in problem-solving needed to shorten the amount of time that economic development, and in particular the kind of development required to lay the foundations for socialism, normally requires. The idea of compressing and skipping stages was, as Manuel Monereo has rightly observed, something of an obsession for Guevara.[63] If he was optimistic about the possibility of harnessing revolutionary enthusiasm and fervor to this end, it was no doubt in part because of the favorable international context briefly noted in the preceding chapter: Guevara seems to have assumed, and not unreasonably, that this particular historical context, marked by the appearance of national liberation movements, the recent setbacks for US imperialism, and so on, might heighten, or at the very least help to sustain for some time, ordinary Cubans' prodigious enthusiasm for, and commitment to, the revolution during the first several years of its existence. These were some of the "exceptional historical circumstances" that led Guevara to believe that it would be possible, at least to the extent that Cuba adopted his system of economic and industrial management (briefly discussed in the following chapter), to hasten the development of "consciousness" and thereby the development of the forces of production.[64] There were, in short, "objective" factors informing Guevara's belief that the "subjective" conditions for "skipping stages" in building socialism in Cuba were especially favorable. But even where the conditions were less favorable, revolutionary struggle could still make it possible to skip stages. In reflecting on his experience in the Congo in 1965, for example, Guevara insists that the Congolese will pass "through the different stages of history at breakneck speed," proceeding from a state that was "in some cases . . . close to primitive communism . . . to feudalism . . . to the most advanced concepts."[65]

THE DICTATORSHIP OF THE PROLETARIAT

One familiar Marxist concept that Guevara often invokes in his reflections on the revolutionary process is "the dictatorship of the proletariat," which is surely one of the most widely misunderstood and distorted of Marxist concepts. As Hal Draper has convincingly shown, "For Marx and Engels . . . 'dictatorship of the proletariat' meant nothing more and nothing less than 'rule of the proletariat'—the 'conquest of political power' by the working class, the establishment of a workers' state in the immediate post-revolutionary period."[66] That is, it refers, to borrow Harold Laski's definition, to "an organisation of society in which the state-power was in the hand of the working class, and used with all the force necessary to prevent it being seized from them by the class which formerly exercised its authority."[67] Guevara uses the term in this broad, original Marxist sense and, accordingly, regards the dictatorship of the proletariat as a form of "democracy,"[68] a form of majority rule or rule by the people. In Guevara's view, the Cuban Revolution had established such a "dictatorship," at least once it had adopted an unmistakably socialist orientation.[69] Guevara's identification of this period of the revolution with the dictatorship of the proletariat is significant in that it reflects his belief that this form of rule, this "dictatorship," can be established "in the countries that are beginning the building of socialism"[70] and not only after the creation of socialism, the "lower stage" of communism. This belief represents a departure from what Marx himself appears to maintain in his "Critique of the Gotha Programme," as Guevara himself acknowledges,[71] but one that seems justified and reasonable given the nature of the transitional period whose basic features Guevara sought to understand and theorize.

Aside from this particular modification of Marx's notion of the dictatorship of the proletariat, two other aspects of Guevara's construal of this concept are worth mentioning briefly. First, Guevara claims, in "Socialism and Man in Cuba," that the dictatorship of the proletariat involves a dictatorship not only over "the defeated class" but also over "individuals of the victorious class."[72] Guevara's point in this passage is that the new state, which he elsewhere calls a "proletarian state,"[73] will find it necessary to heighten the political consciousness of the many workers whose revolutionary commitment lags well behind that of the "vanguard group," which is "ideologically more advanced"; this consciousness-raising consists in fostering an understanding of the workers' new responsibilities, which on one occasion, a televised speech from June 1960, Guevara identifies with the duties to produce, save (i.e., avoid waste at work), and become organized so as to be able to give more (*rendir más*) to the revolution.[74] This new class consciousness is to be achieved by "incentives and pressures of a certain intensity."[75] The kinds of measures to which Guevara alludes here—the "pressures" that he has in mind are doubtless mainly exhortation, moral suasion, the promotion of socialist emulation, and so on—are hardly comparable to the measures constitutive of the dictatorship over the "defeated class," some of which I discuss below, but the passage has proven controversial nevertheless.[76] Significantly, nearly half a century before Guevara spoke of the proletariat exercising its dictatorship over itself, the extremely influential Marxist philosopher Georg Lukács presented a similar idea in almost identical terms. Lukács observed that it may be the case that, after having overthrown the bourgeoisie, some members of the proletariat fail to realize that "the strengthening of labour discipline and thereby raising productivity" is in their own interest. Should this occur, it will be necessary, writes Lukács, for the proletariat to create "a legal order by means of which the proletariat compels its individual members . . . to act in accordance with their class interests," in which case "the proletariat . . . exercises dictatorship even against itself."[77] There is no indication that Guevara also had the creation of "a legal order" in mind when referring to "pressures of a certain intensity," but even if that were the case the proletariat's dictatorship over itself would still have little in common with that which the proletariat exercises over the "defeated class."

The second aspect of Guevara's notion of the dictatorship of the proletariat worth underscoring is his insistence on the compatibility of this form of rule with broad freedom of discussion and debate. To be sure, Guevara never claims that there is complete freedom of discussion in Revolutionary Cuba. In his view, and as he would put it in his lengthy press conference in Punta del Este, Uruguay, in August 1961, full freedom of expression existed neither in Cuba nor in the capitalist nations, but in Cuba the masses who had been oppressed until recently—all of the peasants and workers—could now express themselves, and this increased their options in life.[78] Regarding his reasons for saying that full freedom of expression does not exist in Cuba, Guevara explains on more than one occasion that the revolution will not tolerate the expression of certain views. As he tells students and professors of architecture in a speech delivered in September 1963, "the only thing we do not permit is blackmail through ideas, or sabotage of the Revolution"; in other words, "the only thing we demand is that the general lines of the state in this stage of socialist construction be respected."[79] This is why the revolution does not allow, for example, public criticism from those who do not feel any ties to the revolution and denies a hearing to those who claim to be dissenters but do nothing more than speak for the United States.[80] Yet, while "we do not permit the dictatorship of the proletariat to be attacked, . . . within it there exists a wide margin of discussion and expression of ideas."[81] The position that Guevara articulates, however sketchily, in this passage (which likewise comes from the architecture conference and is preceded by a reference to debates with artists who remained in Cuba but did not sympathize with socialism) bears a great resemblance to Fidel Castro's well-known encapsulation of the revolution's cultural policy presented at the National Library barely two months after the Bay of Pigs Invasion, on June 30, 1961: "Within the Revolution, everything; against the Revolution, nothing" (*dentro de la Revolución, todo; contra la Revolución, nada*).[82] In any event, there is no reason to question the sincerity of Guevara's support for "a wide margin of discussion," since we know that he encouraged vigorous policy debates with his collaborators and colleagues, not least of all when it came to his own ideas on economic management.[83] Guevara himself would emphasize, during a meeting with collaborators in August 1963, that he always allowed his colleagues to say whatever they wanted, even about him, the only condition being that they also do their work.[84] In addition, and perhaps more significantly in this regard, as Minister of Industries Guevara went so far as to issue a circular, applicable to all workplaces within his ministry, that prohibited managers from conducting any interrogations of workers with respect to their ideology. We could also note here Guevara's decisive intervention, in 1964, in defense of Trotskyists facing imprisonment or his condemnation of the vandalization of a Trotskyist publisher that prevented it from bringing out a Cuban edition of Trotsky's *Permanent Revolution*.[85]

CONTAINING THE COUNTERREVOLUTION

The main function of the dictatorship of the proletariat is, of course, to ensure a revolution's success by eliminating any resistance from the counterrevolution—that is, from those who wish to undo the revolution and overthrow the government that defends it. But how does one identify the counterrevolution—many people who do not embrace a given revolutionary project will not actively oppose it, let alone constitute a threat to its existence—and what measures are justified in attempting to thwart its designs?

Before considering Guevara's views on counterrevolutionaries and the appropriate methods for dealing with them, it is important to point out that the counterrevolution, supported from the outset by the US government, was a very real threat in Cuba following the January 1959 victory of the Rebel Army. There were many bombings, frequent acts of sabotage, countless attempts at economic destabilization in one form or another, an insurgency in Cuba's Escambray Mountains, and on and on. (It is perhaps not widely known that the most famous, most frequently reprinted photograph of Guevara, taken by Alberto Korda on March 5, 1960, is an image captured at the funeral for several dozen victims of an act of sabotage that had occurred the previous day. This funeral was also, incidentally, the first time that Fidel Castro uttered the slogan *Patria o muerte* ["Fatherland or death"].[86]) Moreover, though internal counterrevolutionary resistance would sharply decline after the early years of the Cuban Revolution, as many who would support or join the counterrevolution went into exile and the Cuban state efficiently suppressed the activities of those counterrevolutionaries who remained on the island, actions undertaken by counterrevolutionary groups abroad, and most notably those who operated out of South Florida, would continue for decades.[87] And this threat to the survival and consolidation of the Cuban Revolution was compounded by the devastating economic embargo imposed by the United States in late 1960.[88]

The fighting, therefore, did not stop on the first day of the revolution, as Guevara reminds his audience in his speech at the University of Montevideo in August 1961.[89] Indeed, Guevara contends, effectively confirming one of Lenin's theses, the class struggle actually intensified after the Revolution; and it is for this reason that revolutionary leaders must exercise repression, "the hardest and gloomiest side" of a revolution.[90] Early on, in the crucial, initial stages of the revolution, these leaders had come to realize that every relaxation of this repression was inevitably followed by a corresponding increase in the activities of "the forces of reaction."[91] As Guevara puts it in a speech delivered to militia members in January 1961 and that draws together some of these themes, "Now comes the phase of fighting against all those who are trying to undermine our Revolution internally; against all those who belong to the exploiting social classes, who have been defeated in Cuba once and for all, but do not know it. And, not knowing this, they fight day after day, and that also is a lot of work for Cubans—to crush attempts at counterrevolution every time."[92]As Guevara says in this speech, the counterrevolution must be crushed. (Notice, incidentally, the reference to the "exploiting social classes" in a speech that antedates by a few months Fidel Castro's declaration that the Cuban Revolution was a socialist revolution; it represents an anticipation of Guevara's explicit use of Marxist categories, concepts, and terminology.) Guevara reiterates this idea on a variety of occasions, including in his interview with American socialist historian Leo Huberman: "Our intention," he told Huberman, "is to eliminate the counterrevolutionaries."[93] Just as the immediate viability of a revolution requires the destruction of the prerevolutionary army, so, too, its long-range survival requires the eradication of the counterrevolution.

Guevara's views on the inevitability of counterrevolutionary opposition, and the imperative of thoroughly eradicating it, differ little from the views of the other major figures in the Marxist tradition.[94] But these views no doubt owed more to Guevara's firsthand experience of the 1954 coup that overthrew Jacobo Arbenz's progressive, democratically elected government in Guatemala than to his theoretical preparation—or, for that matter, to his experience of counterrevolutionary activity in Cuba from the very start of the revolution. In fact, Guevara often cites the lessons of Guatemala in analyzing challenges and developments in postrevolutionary Cuba, and his reflections on the problem of the counterrevolution are no exception in this regard.[95] And it was those reflections that would lead him to adopt an uncompromising attitude with respect to those who sought to overthrow the revolution: "We have no mercy for those who take weapons [sic] against us; it does not matter if they are weapons of destruction or ideological weapons."[96]

But if Guevara counsels severity in dealing with counterrevolutionaries, he also insists on the importance of respect for those who, while not supportive of the revolution, do not engage in counterrevolutionary activities and should therefore not be deemed counterrevolutionaries. Indeed, how one treats members of groups that may not instinctively sympathize with the revolution (in its transition to socialism), such as the petite bourgeoisie, may determine whether or not they eventually come to embrace it.[97] But revolutionaries should respect the attitude of even those who have no sympathy for the revolution at all and likely never will, provided these people do their jobs and do not combat the revolution.[98] These people are less of a problem than "anyone who uses his influence for his personal benefit or for that of his friends," for such conduct also makes one a counterrevolutionary, just like "anyone who fights against the revolution." "Those who violate revolutionary morality while speaking of revolution," Guevara adds, "are not only potential traitors to the revolution but are also the worst detractors of the revolution."[99]

THE SIGNIFICANCE OF GUEVARA'S VIEWS ON SOCIALISM, COMMUNISM, AND REVOLUTION

There is, to my mind, little to challenge in Guevara's views on the aspects of socialism, communism, and revolution discussed in the present chapter (the need for a new revolutionary regime to systematically dismantle oppressor armies, the function of the dictatorship of the proletariat, the problems posed by counterrevolutionaries, and so on). Moreover, what is most noteworthy about Guevara's views on these topics is surely their overall similarity, despite the novel modifications of some details, to standard Marxist views on these same topics. Yet one of Guevara's views, his conviction that it is possible to "skip stages" in building socialism, also offers striking parallels to a theory that, while put forward by a major Marxist theorist, was anathema to many twentieth-century communists—namely, those of a Stalinist persuasion. This theory is, as many familiar with the Marxist tradition will doubtless have already guessed, Leon Trotsky's theory, or doctrine, of "permanent revolution." These parallels, which are by no means the only similarities between the two thinkers, have admittedly not gone unnoticed in commentary on Guevara's thought[100]; what I wish to do here is merely summarize them in a very brief form.

It may be helpful to begin by summarizing Trotsky's theory of permanent revolution, whose main elements can be briefly stated as follows. First, Trotsky's theory holds that "for backward [e.g., "colonial and semi-colonial"] countries the road to democracy passed through the dictatorship of the proletariat. Thus democracy is not a régime that remains self-sufficient for decades, but is only a direct prelude to the socialist revolution." That is, contrary to much conventional socialist thinking, it is not the case that a lengthy period of democracy must precede the dictatorship of the proletariat; rather, the dictatorship of the proletariat ushers in democracy and national liberation. Second, "the dictatorship of the proletariat which has risen to power as the leader of the democratic revolution is inevitably and very quickly confronted with tasks, the fulfillment of which is bound up with deep inroads into the rights of bourgeois property. The democratic revolution grows over directly into the socialist revolution and thereby becomes a *permanent* revolution." In other words, social emancipation requires the enactment of policies and the establishment of practices that transcend and undermine the (bourgeois-) democratic framework. As a result, "for an indefinitely long time and in constant internal struggle, all social relations undergo transformation. Society keeps on changing its skin. Each stage of transformation stems directly from the preceding. . . . Revolutions in economy, technique, science, the family, morals, and everyday life develop in complex reciprocal action and do not allow society to achieve equilibrium." There is a blending of successive stages of economic development, such as precapitalist and advanced-capitalist methods and relations of production, and this is made possible by the presence of advanced industry and technology alongside primitive productive processes ("combined and uneven development"); this blending corresponds to different phases of political evolution, together with a shortening of the duration of these stages. Finally, the theory holds that the socialist revolution must of necessity assume an "international character" so that "the completion of the socialist revolution within national limits is unthinkable." While "the socialist revolution begins on national foundations . . . it cannot be completed within these foundations. . . . In an isolated proletarian dictatorship, the internal and external contradictions grow inevitably along with the successes achieved. . . . The way out for it lies only in the victory of the proletariat of the advanced countries. Viewed from this standpoint, a national revolution is not a self-contained whole; it is only a link in the international chain." This vital need for support from other nations means that "socialist construction is conceivable only on the foundation of the class struggle, on a national and international scale."[101]

As these are the theses that constitute the essence of the theory of permanent revolution, it is no wonder that many have found a kinship between some of Guevara's views and Trotsky's theory. While Guevara would likely agree with the first postulate mentioned in the preceding paragraph,[102] the most striking parallels between his thought and Trotsky's theory of permanent revolution have to do with the second and third postulates mentioned here. First, Guevara's notions of "skipping stages" and the "radicalization" of the revolution plainly invite comparison with Trotsky's notion of a democratic revolution that "grows over directly into the socialist revolution" and is thus characterized by "revolutions" within different domains of social life that "do not allow society to achieve equilibrium." To be sure, when Guevara speaks of the possibility and desirability of skipping stages (*quemar etapas*), he is typically referring to distinct phases of economic development, whereas the emphasis in the passage from Trotsky cited above refers to phases of political development. But we should bear in mind that for Marxists a correspondence obtains between the economic organization of a society and its political institutions (an idea contained in Marx's famous "base-superstructure" metaphor[103]). And just as Trotsky elsewhere focuses on the skipping of stages of economic development, Guevara also alludes to the process of skipping stages with respect to the institutional arrangements of politics, a process that he likely thought had been facilitated by the rapid and profound changes in the mentality of most Cubans that he had witnessed during the first few years of the Cuban Revolution.[104] As for parallels with Trotsky's insistence on the unavoidability of effecting "deep inroads into the rights of bourgeois property," it is enough to recall Guevara's support for a thoroughgoing nationalization of industry and, more generally, his commitment to a ceaseless "radicalization" of the revolution.[105]

As for the third postulate of the theory of permanent revolution, Guevara never ceases to argue that the triumph of socialism requires internationalization and the international coordination of revolutionary struggles. Most emphatically expressed in his "Message to the Tricontinental," including its exhortation to "create two, three, many Vietnams," Guevara's belief in the necessity of internationalizing national and socialist liberation struggles, and of internationalizing the support for these struggles, is, as we have already seen, an important motif in many of his speeches and writings. His essay "Guerrilla Warfare: A Method" offers something of a summation of his perspective in this regard, for in this piece he remarks that "it is difficult to achieve and consolidate victory in an isolated country," and he insists on "the continental nature of the struggle," which will be a war with "many fronts."[106] It is significant that Guevara returned to the theme of a continental struggle, and the need for international unity and coordination of this struggle, in his last "public" appearance in Cuba, a talk given before his collaborators at the Ministry of Industries in March 1965[107]; barely a week later he would depart Cuba to join rebel forces in the Congo. It is likewise significant that in one of his final texts, an unfinished proclamation or communiqué drafted in Bolivia, Guevara claims that obtaining Bolivia's "independence" will require the assistance of friendly nations, which will enable those who are fighting for the country's liberation to break through the imperialist encirclement.[108]

The resemblance between Guevara's theses and Trotsky's theory of permanent revolution is, then, undeniable. It also has quite significant implications: as Tamara Deutscher has rightly observed, "The cornerstone of Trotskyism has been and remains the theory of permanent revolution."[109] This is one reason that it should not surprise us that Soviet authorities would come to suspect Guevara of being a "Trotskyist"—though one must bear in mind, of course, that after the rise of Stalinism the Soviets used the term, always meant as a slur, quite loosely—or that students in Moscow would level the same accusation during a meeting with Guevara in November 1964.[110] What *is* surprising is that Guevara arrived at his theoretical conclusions despite a near total unfamiliarity with Trotsky's works.[111] Likewise surprising, in light of the kinship between Guevara's and Trotsky's views (but not in light of Guevara's ignorance of Trotsky's views), is Guevara's rather dismissive attitude toward Trotsky throughout most of his political "career": only in the last three years or so of his life did Guevara begin to believe that one might need to take Trotsky's ideas seriously. For example, Guevara remarks during his December 1964 lecture at the University of Oriente that Trotsky had represented an "ultra-left" current, or one of "left-wing opportunism," at the time of Lenin's death, and at a meeting in the Ministry of Industries just a few days later he would state that some of the fundamental bases for Trotsky's ideas were mistaken, as were his actions (Guevara seemed to be referring to Trotsky's actions after being forced into exile). Yet in the very same meeting Guevara would tell his collaborators that "it is clear that we can take a series of things from Trotsky's thought," while a year later he would include Trotsky's works in a proposal for an ambitious publishing project sent to Armando Hart, an important figure in the Cuban Revolution's leadership (the Bolshevik leader's works were to be included in a section covering "Heterodox" Marxist thinkers).[112] Furthermore, Guevara read Trotsky's *History of the Russian Revolution* during his guerrilla campaign in Bolivia and in fact praised it in his brief notes on his reading.[113]

Guevara's attitude toward *Trotskyism* and *Trotskyists*, on the other hand, was, if anything, even less favorable and may not have changed much in the last years of his life. During his major press conference at the Inter-American Economic Conference in Uruguay in August 1961, Guevara condemned the Cuban Trotskyists' "ultra-leftism" and criticized them for fomenting "subversion," insinuating that they might even be working on behalf of the United States.[114] (It so happened that Cuban Trotskyism was particularly strong in Guantánamo, a city located just a few minutes away from the US naval base in Cuba.) Two years later Guevara would complain, during a meeting with American students, that the Trotskyists "are more revolutionary than anyone, but they do nothing and they criticize everything," while during the December 1964 meeting just cited he would claim, in a similar vein, that "the Trotskyists have not contributed anything to the revolutionary movement anywhere."[115] Finally, in a brief note on C. Wright Mills's *The Marxists* dating from the days of Guevara's guerrilla struggle in Bolivia—that is, the last year of his life—Guevara observes that Mills's opinions are "tinged with a Trotskyist type of senile anti-Stalinism."[116] On the other hand, Guevara accepted an invitation to meet with a group of Uruguayan

Trotskyists, representing "Trotskyists the world over and those of Latin America in particular," only a few days after the press conference in which he had denounced their Cuban counterparts' "ultra-leftism," and Guevara's close collaborator Orlando Borrego has pointed out that it was widely known that there were Trotskyists working in the heart of Guevara's Ministry of Industries, including one who held the position of "director," and that this never represented a problem.[117] Guevara's more or less uninformed dismissal of Trotskyism was compatible, therefore, with his support for broad freedom of debate "within the Revolution," a commitment that would involve him, as we have seen, in defense of Trotskyists on more than one occasion.

5

Consolidating the Revolution and the Building of Socialism

In the previous chapter I discussed Guevara's views on certain general aspects of revolution, socialism, and communism. The present chapter represents a continuation of chapter 4 to a certain extent but, as the title suggests, focuses somewhat more narrowly on the policies and practices that should, in Guevara's view, govern the consolidation of a revolution and the building of socialism. Accordingly, I will consider some additional, general principles espoused by Guevara, but I will also discuss the concrete system of economic management devised by Guevara, a form of administration that he believed would enable Cuba to effect the transition to socialism more quickly and more efficiently. As we shall see, contrary to what many seem inclined to believe, perhaps because they are only familiar with his military exploits or uncompromising anti-imperialism, Guevara took the task of "building socialism" very seriously, bringing the same zeal and dedication to the mundane bureaucratic and managerial tasks of administration that he brought to the theorization and practice of guerrilla warfare.[1] In fact, besides his writings and speeches on political and military questions, Guevara produced numerous reports on his visits to production centers and on the progress of different sectors and activities within his ministry. Moreover, many of his speeches, talks, presentations, interviews, and other communications contain extensive discussion of practical problems relating to production and industrialization, including abundant data and highly detailed observations on all manner of economic questions.[2] Furthermore, and as already mentioned earlier, Guevara typically worked at least sixteen-hour days, often staying at the Ministry of Industries until 3 a.m. or later. Guevara was indeed a "man of action," but, as we shall see, it was not merely in the more romantic sense that his name evokes for many.

THE CUBAN TRANSITION TO SOCIALISM IN CONTEXT

Before discussing Guevara's ideas on the consolidation of the revolution and the construction of socialism, it will be useful to consider the context in which Guevara developed and defended these ideas. In political terms, this was a context characterized, first of all, by unrelenting hostility on the part of the United States and, to a lesser degree, those nations that embraced the United States' position toward Cuba and, second, by the violent opposition of counterrevolutionaries (typically with US support). In economic terms, the principal problem was the relatively "underdeveloped" state of the Cuban economy at the beginning of the Cuban Revolution.

Guevara often refers to both sets of factors, the political and the economic, in discussing the obstacles to social transformation in Cuba. As for the former, Guevara would remark, as early as mid-1961, in an interview with Polish-French journalist K. S. Karol, "In very quick succession, we have been taught the meaning of economic blockade, subversion, sabotage, and psychological warfare."[3] Two years later, during a seminar on planning held in Algiers in July 1963, Guevara sketches what this means in more concrete terms: "But the struggle continued. The imperialist blockade was at its apex, and we saw ourselves forced to fight day after day just to give our people enough to eat, to maintain our industry, develop our fields, our commerce, to defend ourselves against sabotage from outlaw groups, from direct foreign aggression, their aerial bombardments, their daily violation of our sovereignty, and in addition, we had to smash reactionary opposition at home, expose traitors, and expel them from government. Sometimes they fled into exile, sometimes they were jailed, sometimes they were shot."[4] And Guevara would also make use of his address to the United Nations in December 1964 to draw attention to the frequency and scale of the "provocations" against Cuba, claiming that they numbered 1,323 in 1964 (up to the date of his speech, that is), or "approximately four per day," and citing one lethal incident from the previous summer.[5]

But while this unrelenting political hostility inevitably constrained the process of social transformation, the structure of the Cuban economy in 1959 also represented a major obstacle to development. In economic terms, Cuba was, in Guevara's view, both semicolonial and underdeveloped—in his draft preface for a planned study of Marxist political economy and socialism Guevara declares that the book will be "a cry let out from underdevelopment"[6]—and one had to reckon with such circumstances in theorizing and preparing the path to socialism.[7] These adverse circumstances included the fact that semi-illiteracy characterized the peasantry in its entirety and nearly all of the working class at the start of the revolution, or so Guevara claims in an August 1964 speech.[8] The challenges posed by this state of affairs were merely exacerbated by the effects of US policy toward Cuba: prior to the revolution, 80 percent of Cuba's trade was with the United States, and it imported all of its spare parts from the United States.[9] Before the revolution, Cuba could import needed goods (food, spare parts, consumer products, etc.) within hours, or at most a couple of days; after the United States imposed its economic embargo of Cuba, it could take weeks to obtain comparable goods from the socialist countries, and up to two months in the case of goods imported from China.[10] Guevara summarizes the resulting scenario well in his 1963 essay "Against Bureaucratism": "We have begun the gigantic task of transforming society from top to bottom in the midst of imperialist aggression, of an increasingly tighter blockade, of a complete change in our technology, of drastic shortages of raw materials and foodstuffs, and of a massive exodus of the few qualified technicians we have."[11]

These were the circumstances, then, in which Cuba would initiate the transition to socialism. They offered, in effect, a textbook illustration of the three major difficulties that, as C. B. Macpherson once pointed out, the twentieth-century's socialist states had to confront. Nearly all of these states, Macpherson argued, (1) were established in underdeveloped societies, with a large peasant population among which illiteracy was widespread, (2) faced the Western powers' hostility, including support for counterrevolution and "encirclement," and (3) were born in revolution or civil war, with the inevitable result that deviations from the leadership's line would tend to be viewed as treasonous.[12]

In any event, just as he would often draw attention to the obstacles and difficulties noted in the first three paragraphs of this section, Guevara often underscores the importance of bearing in mind that the process on which the Cuban revolutionaries had embarked was the *transition* to socialism rather than socialism as such.[13] The revolutionaries therefore faced problems arising from an instance of what Georg Lukács refers to as "the nonclassical genesis of socialism in an underdeveloped country."[14] Lukács speaks of a "nonclassical genesis" because the standard Marxist model of historical evolution assumes that socialism will emerge from a highly advanced and fully developed capitalist society. The model does not posit any transitional phase between capitalism and socialism, the latter being the social arrangement that follows a successful proletarian revolution in a capitalist society; it is the "lower" stage of communism (and in this sense is itself a "transitional" phase). If Guevara often stresses the fact that the Cuban Revolution had embarked upon the transition to socialism rather than establishing socialism, it is because this transition poses problems that are very different from those that would arise in a socialist society that develops in accordance with the "classical" genesis of socialism. "How," Guevara asks in "The Meaning of Socialist Planning," "in a country colonized by imperialism, its basic industries underdeveloped, a monoproducer dependent on a single market, can the transition to socialism be made?"[15] The central problem is to overcome underdevelopment and establish the economic foundations for socialism—and to accomplish this feat without much theoretical guidance. Marx and Engels, whose works focused on the operation of capitalism, had said very little about the structure and institutional mechanics of a socialist society; as noted in chapter 1, Marx declined to offer "recipes . . . for the cook-shops of the future," an "unscientific" and futile enterprise in his view (How could we possibly foresee how truly free human beings in a radically different social and institutional environment would organize their society?). He and Engels said even less about a stage involving a transition to socialism, a stage in which, as Guevara himself points out in the essay just cited, the relations of production need not correspond to the forces of production, despite what one might expect from a superficial interpretation of Marxist theory.[16] On the other hand, what the Soviet Union and China offered in terms of lessons regarding this transitional phase was of limited value, both because Cuba's economic and political history had little in common with that of either of these nations and because the concrete aspects of this phase, whose main task consists of overcoming economic underdevelopment, had not been adequately analyzed and theorized by either the Soviets or the Chinese.

Guevara was acutely aware of this dearth of reflection on the transition to socialism in underdeveloped or semicolonial countries. Significantly, Guevara's planned study of Marxist political economy and socialism was to include, according to the tentative outline for the book, not only a section that dealt with "the transition period" but also one that would underscore the fact that even though both Marx and Lenin theorized two stages of communism (in the "Critique of the Gotha Programme" and *The State and Revolution*, respectively) Lenin in reality posited the existence of *three* stages; the explanation for this additional stage was to be found in underdevelopment.[17] This outline reflects an idea that Guevara stresses in one of his last public lectures in Cuba, the late 1964 appearance at the University of Oriente in Santiago cited earlier, during which he also notes his great level of interest in the political economy of the transition period.[18] Guevara's interest in the nature of, and problems characterizing, this phenomenon is readily comprehensible: besides the fact that the transitional period, or building of socialism in underdeveloped and neocolonial countries, had not received the theoretical consideration that it deserved, the practical problems attending this phase of radical social transformation were the ones that Guevara had to confront on a daily basis during his years in Cuba. This dual motivation to make sense of the transition period explains both Guevara's degree of concern with this aspect of socialism and communism and the enduring value of his analysis of it.

THE VALUE OF UNITY

In chapter 3 I briefly discussed Guevara's insistence on the importance of international unity in the anti-imperialist struggle. But this is not the only form of unity that Guevara espouses; the success of the transition to socialism, Guevara argues, also requires maximum unity, albeit of an internal sort, within the country undergoing this transition, or even a nation merely carrying through the more limited type of revolution represented by the Cuban Revolution during its initial phase. In fact, Guevara was literally declaring the paramount importance of unity from the first day of the Cuban Revolution—in an article written at the end of 1958 and published on January 1, 1959, the date of the Rebel Army's triumph.[19] Less than a month later he would conclude his first major speech after the Rebels' victory by warning that "we must be aware of all efforts to divide us and struggle against those who try to sow the seeds of discord among us."[20]

The value and importance of unity would be a recurrent theme in Guevara's speeches, talks, and writings throughout his years in Cuba, but the unity he advocates and appeals to is generally not the international or transnational unity required for the broad anti-imperialist struggle but rather either internal (national) unity or class unity. Internal or national unity, the kind of unity that Guevara envisions in both of the passages just mentioned, is crucial for both the defense of Cuba vis-à-vis external enemies and for the possibility of implementing a revolutionary program, especially when it takes a socialist turn, which necessitates greater social cohesion and solidarity, as well as uniformity of purpose. So, for example, in his 1959 May Day speech delivered in Santiago de Cuba, Guevara declares, "There must be nothing other than unity of all the people if we wish to win the great battle that is approaching." He then goes on to explain that there is both a "great battle" that is peaceful—whose object is "the building of a prosperous, industrial country"—and "the great defensive battle against those who want to drown our Revolution in blood."[21] Significantly, Guevara also emphasizes the value of internal unity in his address to the United Nations in December 1964—he actually uses the word "cohesion" (*cohesión*), but two standard English versions of the address translate it, reasonably enough, as "unity"—although on this occasion he seems to have in mind primarily, if not exclusively, unity as a condition of national defense and survival.[22] (It is also significant that Guevara refers to the general question of unity near the end of his final public appearance in Cuba in March 1965, but the context is a discussion of unity and disunity within national liberation movements.[23])

While not as frequent as his calls for national unity, Guevara likewise upholds working-class unity from the early stages of the revolution on—that is, even during the period preceding Fidel Castro's declaration of the Cuban Revolution's socialist character in April 1961. So, for example, in an October 1959 speech Guevara would emphasize the fundamental importance of worker unity as a weapon through the ages, and uniting and unity therefore constituted a duty for workers, given that the "oppressive" capitalists always seek to foment division, on the basis of race, sex, and other kinds of differences. Similarly, in a televised lecture from June of the following year, Guevara stresses how "colonialist powers" and "large international enterprises" promote divisions within the working class and thus undermine solidarity among the workers.[24]

It is important to point out, in discussing Guevara's defense of workers' unity, that with the increasingly socialistic orientation of the Cuban Revolution Guevara's conception of such unity would undergo a significant modification. After all, the elimination of capitalism meant the elimination of capitalists and hence the disappearance of the old antagonism between the owners and their representatives, on the one hand, and the workers, on the other. In a word, the traditional class antagonism no longer existed: "When the domination of one class over another disappears, when the means of production belong to everyone, contradictions do not exist."[25] This means that workers' "unity" takes on a new meaning in a society building socialism, for the simple reason that in a society that is not character-ized by class domination it no longer makes sense to speak of unity *against* the adversary of one's class. This idea decisively shapes Guevara's perspective on trade unions and unionism. As he explains in the same December 1964 meeting with his collaborators at the Ministry of Industries from which the preceding quotation is taken, "The union is the association of workers to be against the employer." Since this employer has ceased to exist and the workers who assume administrative roles can hardly be regarded as enemies of the working class, unions lose their principal reason for being and, indeed, are no longer needed.[26] Guevara holds, then, that the union as an institution will eventually disappear because the progress toward socialism will gradually render them superfluous, much in the way that the state will eventually fade away, and he points out that Lenin, too, had prophesied that unions would not exist in the future.[27] In the short term (i.e., so long as it contin-ues to exist as an institution), the union's function should be, according to Gue-vara, to promote a new conception of work among the masses and raise production levels, defending the other interests of the workers only until such bodies as the Workplace Justice Councils (Consejos de Justicial Laboral), established in 1963, had completely taken over that role.[28]

So, revolutionary unity—which is nothing other than a certain form of political unity—is plainly a fundamental concern for Guevara and should be understood as a composite of the unity achieved among the workers, internal or national unity, and international anti-imperialist unity. The latter would include unity not only among the peoples of colonial and neocolonial nations but also within the international Communist movement: it was in the name of unity, in fact, that Guevara criticized the Sino-Soviet split.[29]

In considering Guevara's insistence on unity, it is important to realize how this view is related to two other aspects of Guevara's thought. First of all, notice that "unity" and "social duty" are complementary notions. If members of a given society act in accordance with a notion of social duty, some sense of social unity will inevi-tably emerge from their efforts, as their actions will create bonds with others and greater social cohesion. On the other hand, to the extent that people feel that all of the members of their society constitute a unified whole, they are more likely to embrace a strong notion of social duty, for in attending to the needs of others they will be benefitting the whole of which they themselves form one part, effectively serving their own interests. Second, maintaining unity inevitably entails sacrifice among those who are united: the acceptance of policies and practices whether or not one agrees with them, forgoing certain benefits or renunciation of some ambitions, limitations on one's scope of action (including, in some cases, expression of criticism or dissent), and so on. But for Guevara, sacrifice for the sake of unity is but one of the multiple varieties of sacrifice assumed by a revolutionary as one of his or her du-ties, a topic that merits a separate discussion.

THE DUTIES OF REVOLUTIONARIES

Guevara never precisely defines what he means by "revolutionary," although it is clear that the "revolution" in question is one whose goal is human emancipation as understood from a communist perspective. However, Guevara's writings, speeches, and talks do contain plenty of references to the dispositions, qualities, and ethos that define true revolutionaries during the process of building socialism. (While it is true that he also discussed revolutionaries' duties before the leaders of the Cuban Revolution stated that their aim was socialism, Guevara's comments on the revolutionaries' duties from that period are consistent with his comments during the openly socialist phase of the revolution.) I have already discussed the two most important components of the revolutionary's ethos in chapter 1—namely, one's embrace of a radical egalitarianism and a far more comprehensive notion of one's social duty. To be sure, these attributes are, as noted in that chapter, actually the two most important attributes of the new, communist human being. But the true revolutionary is the person who in important respects anticipates or prefigures the new person envisioned by Guevara. "Important" respects does not mean *most* or *all* respects, which would be false: the members of a communist society will lead lives very different from those of the members of a society that is building socialism, as the former will have undergone a very different socialization process, live within very different institutional arrangements, enjoy the benefits of abundance, and so on. In any case, these two values or qualities are doubtless the true revolutionary's two most important *substantive* commitments. The elements of the revolutionary's ethos that I wish to discuss in the present section, by contrast, are the more general qualities and dispositions that, according to Guevara, characterize a revolutionary during the phase of building socialism, and presumably also during the initial phase of socialism itself.

In considering the qualities that distinguish the revolutionary, one might well begin with Guevara's "farewell" letter to his children. In this letter, dating from 1965, Guevara writes, "Above all, always be capable of feeling deeply any injustice committed against anyone, anywhere in the world. This is the most beautiful quality in a revolutionary."[30] Yet this quality would seem to be, in essence, little more than a corollary of the enlarged sense of social duty just mentioned. Furthermore, the "most beautiful" quality in a revolutionary need not be one of the most *important* ones, at least during the period of building socialism. For these reasons, we need not consider this quality at any length.

In one sense, the most distinctive and important quality of revolutionaries is an unqualified devotion to the revolution itself. In his essay "Socialism and Man in Cuba," Guevara cites occasions in which many Cubans displayed a "total dedication to the revolutionary cause," and it is obvious, from his remarks in this essay and elsewhere that Guevara identifies such an attitude with that of the true revolutionary. Or, rather, he identifies the revolutionary with the *routinization* of this attitude, which is why Guevara goes on to add that "to perpetuate this heroic attitude in daily life is . . . one of our fundamental tasks."[31] It is, in any event, a view more or less implicit in another sentence from the letter to his children cited in the preceding paragraph—"Remember that the revolution is what is important, and each one of us, alone, is worth nothing"—as well as in the comment that Guevara once made to his close collaborator Ángel Arcos Bergnes: "The principles of the Revolution come before personal principles."[32] Guevara's own life, needless to say, exemplified "total dedication to the revolutionary cause" more than anyone else's.[33] In any event, this thoroughgoing dedication to, and identification with, the revolution is what inspires and sustains two other salient qualities of the revolutionary: a disposition to endure major personal sacrifices and a commitment to exemplary conduct.

The value—and inevitability—of sacrifice is an important theme in Guevara's conception of the revolutionary. The sacrifices that a revolutionary must endure can take many forms: material goods forgone, leisure time lost due to work of one kind or another for the benefit of the revolution, and renunciation of certain personal aspirations (as regards, for example, professional ambitions or the choice of where to live). Such sacrifices prove necessary and unavoidable not only because revolutionaries have undertaken to build socialism at an accelerated pace in an underdeveloped country but also because they must do so in the midst of what Guevara calls "capitalist reaction."[34] What is more, this "capitalist reaction" includes not merely the lack of support from capitalist nations but also the belligerent enmity of the United States, a country only ninety miles away.[35]

Significantly, Guevara never made any attempt to mislead Cubans regarding the magnitude of the sacrifice that the transition to socialism in Cuba would require. To the contrary. For example, in a January 1962 appearance on televsion, the public forum par excellence, Guevara informed viewers that "the time ahead is a time of hard work and a time of sacrifice, in which many things will have to be scarce, in which it will take us a lot of effort to develop our industry, our agriculture."[36] But he was no less forthright when it came to acknowledging that not everyone in Cuba fully grasped the need for such sacrifice.[37]

In any event, while Guevara insists that all will have to accept sacrifices in the building of socialism in an underdeveloped country, it is the most committed revolutionaries who, because of their special responsibilities, will have to endure the greatest sacrifices. This is true, for example, in the case of the "vanguard" youth who become Young Communists (i.e., members of the Union of Young Communists), who must be "the first to be ready to make the sacrifices demanded by the revolution," but in fact all cadres must possess a "capacity for sacrifice."[38] As a specific example of sacrifice, one might cite Guevara's description of the optimal revolutionary administrator of a factory or enterprise who, whatever his or her relation to the party, is capable of forgetting all personal interests and of placing adherence to revolutionary laws and the performance of revolutionary duties before personal friendship.[39]

The true revolutionary must not only be indefatigable but also always seek more work and more sacrifices with which to discharge his or her duties; or, as Guevara says in a meeting in February 1964, for those in the vanguard, making sacrifices must be so habitual that sacrifice itself becomes their way of life.[40] Most self-sacrificing of all is the revolutionary who becomes a leader at the highest levels[41]; and, as a matter of fact, on several occasions, including in "Socialism and Man in Cuba," Guevara notes that the Cuban Revolution's supreme leaders had to sacrifice much of their family life, besides enduring the other sacrifices that define the life of a revolutionary.[42] Guevara claims, incidentally, that this understanding of the revolutionary leader's sacrifices derives from José Martí, who "taught us that a revolutionary and a ruler can have neither a private life nor pleasures. He must give everything to the people that choose him, and this places him in a position of responsibility and combat."[43] In any case, as a man who often worked *at his office* until 3 a.m. and who worked on the weekends as well (part of this work consisting of voluntary labor),[44] Guevara exemplified this spirit of self-sacrifice like no one else; and he specifically mentions the extent of this self-sacrifice in a highly revealing comment during his press conference at the 1961 Inter-American Economic and Social Council Conference: "I am convinced that I have a mission to fulfill in the world, and that for the sake of this mission I have to sacrifice my home, I have to sacrifice all of an individual's pleasures of daily life, I have to sacrifice my personal security, and perhaps I'll have to sacrifice my life."[45]

The second quality that defines the true revolutionary is, as noted, a commitment to exemplary conduct. Revolutionaries should, according to Guevara, set an example, and the greater the responsibilities of a revolutionary (the higher the position of authority occupied by the revolutionary), the greater the importance of his or her exemplariness, for one's duty to make sacrifices is commensurate with one's responsibilities. As Guevara puts it in his 1962 essay "The Cadre: Backbone of the Revolution," revolutionaries should always be "demonstrating through personal example the truths and watchwords of the revolution."[46] In short, they should, as he stresses in a speech from January of the same year, preach by example, and he specifically mentions "sacrifice" and "work" as two areas in which the revolutionary must prove exemplary.[47]

For Guevara, an important corollary of this idea is that no one ought to recommend or call for actions that one does not, or will not, perform oneself. Indeed, in a report prepared for the Council of Ministers and that covers 1961 to 1962, Guevara notes that this principle had been, in effect, the official policy applied to those who held leadership positions in his Ministry of Industries.[48] (There is no question that Guevara was unrivaled in his adherence to this principle, as those who knew him and worked with him are quick to emphasize.[49]) This readiness on the part of revolutionaries, and especially those who hold positions of authority, to perform difficult work or endure major sacrifices would create what Guevara, borrowing a term from Fidel Castro, calls "moral compulsion," which refers to an example's effect in motivating or inspiring similar actions in others.[50] At the same time, Guevara does not hesitate to claim that a revolutionary who has invariably displayed exemplary conduct may have the right to demand similar conduct from others when this is indispensable. As he would remark in a January 1964 speech during a ceremony in which "communist labor" certificates were awarded, "The one who can show with his example day after day, without expecting from society anything but recognition of his merits as a builder of the new society, has the right to demand sacrifice of others when the time comes."[51]

In sum, we can identify the duties of revolutionaries with five basic qualities: a profoundly egalitarian outlook, a very strong sense of social duty, an exceptional devotion to the revolution, a disposition to endure major personal sacrifices, and a commitment to exemplary conduct. As noted earlier, the first two qualities also characterize the new human being, but the latter three properly characterize revolutionaries during the period of transition from capitalism to socialism. Guevara's identification of the revolutionary with these qualities, and in particular with great, even extraordinary, personal sacrifice, helps to illuminate the striking remark from his *Bolivian Diary*, cited earlier, to the effect that the revolutionary is "the highest form of the human species." If revolutionaries represent this level of achievement, it is not only because of the difficulty of their struggle and the value of their objective but also on account of the sheer range and magnitude of the sacrifices that they must endure, which far exceed anything that the new human being will face. After all, the new human being will inhabit a society in which a communist institutional framework will already exist, as will abundance; in which a very robust sense of social duty will, thanks to a different process of socialization, be the norm, and thus inevitable social burdens will be shouldered by a far larger number of people; and in which, as a result of the technical revolution, work will be far less onerous than it is at present and all will be able to dedicate themselves to the kind of work they most wish to pursue.[52] If we grasp the extent to which the optimal revolutionary is in some sense even more estimable than the new human being, it will not be difficult to understand why Guevara holds revolutionaries in such high regard. But to grasp as much is also to understand the error in assuming that the revolutionary accurately "prefigures" the new human being, or that a revolutionary's lifestyle should be construed as an instance of "prefiguration," a term now regularly used to designate the practices of individuals, movements, or organizations that attempt to reflect or embody—in their relationships, forms of organization, tactics and methods, and so on—the society that they seek to create, the goal that they aspire to attain.[53] To be sure, some of the revolutionary's specific practices are prefigurative. One example is the manual labor performed by senior managers and technical personnel, which, as Marta Harnecker has pointed out, prefigures the communist society—this was its purpose—in which the opposition between manual and mental labor has ceased to exist.[54] As a whole, however, the revolutionaries' actions amount to something that we might more accurately call "superprefiguration," as they must endure far more sacrifice than the new human being, have to be "exemplary" (and overcome formidable obstacles in the process), and should exhibit a level of devotion to social transformation—that is, the revolution—that will prove quite unnecessary in a communist society.

Before concluding this discussion of Guevara's conception of revolutionaries, it may be useful to say something about one facet of a revolutionary's sacrifice, understood as the practice of making sacrifices, that I have not mentioned previously— namely, the acceptance of *discipline*. Of course, one might just as well assert that sacrifice is one aspect of discipline, rather than the other way around. In reality, sacrifice and discipline seem to reciprocally condition each other: discipline makes sacrifice possible (it ensures that we make obligatory sacrifices), but it is also a consequence of sacrifice (we achieve discipline through sacrifice—by resisting certain promptings, renouncing certain pursuits, and so on). But whatever the relationship between sacrifice and discipline, the fact is that Guevara attaches a great deal of importance to the question of discipline—it is, for example, one of the attributes of a cadre mentioned in "The Cadre: Backbone of the Revolution"[55]—and, accordingly, contends that significant breaches of discipline must not be tolerated. So, for example, he would declare in the epilogue to *Guerrilla Warfare*, "It can never be permitted . . . that a revolutionary of any category should be excused for grave offenses against decorum or morality simply because he is a revolutionary."[56]

Mention of this topic is important if only because one of Guevara's most controversial policies at the Ministry of Industries was precisely a policy for handling certain breaches of discipline. The policy in question consisted of sending administrators guilty of certain serious violations of basic norms to the Guanahacabibes rehabilitation center on the western tip of Cuba. Those whose sanctions consisted in confinement at Guanahacabibes were sent to the center for periods ranging from one month to a year, and at the center they spent their days performing physical labor of various sorts, labor that was, according to Tirso Sáenz (another of Guevara's close collaborators in the Ministry of Industries), no worse than that of a forest worker.[57] After they had completed their "sentence," the sanctioned administrators could return to the Ministry of Industries, and, since they had discharged their debt to society, no one was to criticize them for the error that had warranted the sanction.[58]

As Guevara underscores in the January 1962 Ministry meeting in which he discusses Guanahacabibes at some length, the center was for people (i.e., management personnel) whose error—which might be a disciplinary problem, an act of nepotism, or a violation of ethical guidelines[59]—constituted a breach of "revolutionary morality"; those who were guilty of criminal misconduct should be sent to jail—that is, they were to be handled by the normal criminal justice system.[60] For this reason, he regarded the corresponding sanction as a "moral" sanction, as he would say in another meeting two and a half years later.[61]

In any assessment of Guanahacabibes, one must bear in mind two factors. First, confinement in the rehabilitation center was the most severe sanction meted out. Second, and more important, the punishment was hardly tantamount to a standard penal sanction: the ministry administrator could in fact reject the sanction, but if he did so he would have to abandon the Ministry. Indeed, the administrator sent to Guanahacabibes was even responsible for getting to the center himself.[62] Together with the fact that it was a "moral" sanction and one intended to improve the administrator's revolutionary caliber, the relatively "voluntary" nature of the punishment (by contrast, one cannot "reject" a state's sanctions for breaches of the law) helps to account for Guevara's claim that a spell at Guanahacabibes represented a "revolutionary sanction."[63] It is also worth pointing out that Guevara visited Guanahacabibes on many occasions and that during his visits he would perform physical labor alongside the other men "sentenced" to the rehabilitation center and give a talk at the end of the workday.[64]

While some of Guevara's closest collaborators, including Orlando Borrego and Ángel Arcos Bergnes, defend the legitimacy of the rehabilitation center at Guanaha-cabibes, a place that they themselves saw firsthand,[65] one could certainly challenge the value and wisdom of this approach to rehabilitation and reeducation. Unfor-tunately, the currency of distorted accounts of the nature of Guanahacabibes have made a serious evaluation of the center, and the rationale behind it, very difficult. Jorge G. Castañeda, one of Guevara's biographers, deserves some of the blame for this state of affairs. In his widely praised biography, Castañeda devotes two para-graphs to the rehabilitation center, one of which consists of some of Guevara's own remarks from the meeting cited above. Castañeda implausibly links Guanahacabibes to a broader "crackdown" in Cuba and also contends that the center established a precedent for, among other things, the later "confinement of dissidents,"[66] no mat-ter that no one was sent there for being a dissident and that the punishment was in a certain sense voluntary. Unfortunately, some subsequent commentators have acritically accepted Castañeda's ill-informed and highly misleading characterization of Guanahacabibes, and their own studies of Guevara have suffered accordingly. For example, Mike González, basing his account on Castañeda's biography, leads readers to believe that anyone who violated "revolutionary morals" could be sent to the cen-ter,[67] as though it were not the case that Guevara only sent administrative personnel from his own ministry to Guanahacabibes, the "morals" that had been violated were important norms and regulations, and one could refuse to accept the punishment. Like González, Samuel Farber also cites Castañeda and basically extends his line of thought, writing that "Guevara played a key role in inaugurating a tradition of administrative, nonjudicial detention subject to no written rules or laws."[68] (To be sure, Farber also cites Helen Yaffe's account of the rehabilitation center—far more comprehensive and scholarly than Castañeda's two-paragraph treatment of Guana-hacabibes, but unavailable when González's book was published—yet altogether ignores her analysis and that of the Cubans whom she cites.) In sum, and as is the case with so many other ideas and practices associated with Guevara, it is necessary to dispel a number of widespread misconceptions before one can even begin to un-dertake a dispassionate assessment of the rehabilitation center at Guanahacabibes.

WORKER EMPOWERMENT AND WORKERS' RULE

For Guevara, the Cuban Revolution was a "proletarian revolution" in the sense that it transferred ownership of the means of production to the working class, gave this class power, made possible worker control of both the means of production and the entire production process, and looked to the working class to guide the building of socialism.[69] (It was not necessarily a "proletarian revolution" in the sense that the working class had "made" or led the revolution.) As Minister of Industries, Guevara emphasized that dimension of workers' rule most relevant to his own area of responsibility: participation in, and control of, decision making within factories, workshops, and other industrial operations. Guevara emphasizes the importance of attaining this goal on numerous occasions.[70] Besides affording workers effective control over production in the workplace, the aim was, as Guevara writes in an early 1962 essay, "Our Industrial Tasks," to "create a socialist conscience by enlisting the workers in all of the practical tasks of the building of socialism; in participation in the management of the factories and enterprises and in the centers of technical study."[71] Guevara realized that much remained to be done in order to attain this goal and, in keeping with his commitment to workers' rule, would criticize the lack of worker involvement in the management of factories in a meeting in the same month in which he published the "Our Industrial Tasks" article.[72]

One of the chief obstacles to establishing complete worker management in factories was the general level of education and training among Cuban workers at the beginning of the Revolution. While Guevara insists that the administrators, managers, and technicians—most of whose well-trained predecessors had abandoned the country—will have to come from the working class,[73] he also stresses the need for "the working class to begin attaining the technical level required to take completely in its hands the administration of factories and the entire state."[74] Guevara's desire to produce the worker-managers who would be able to oversee every aspect of production—that is, to generate a system of wholly worker-operated factories (in which the workers would take charge of not only decision making but also *every* aspect of the factory)—accounts for two of the motifs that appear time and again in Guevara's speeches and writings: the importance of education and training and the need to promote a culture of collective discussion and consultation. In his address to the Eleventh National Labor Congress in November 1961, for example, Guevara remarks that "we have to develop the working class so that it can take charge, technically, of the workplaces."[75] Guevara actually links learning and education—which for many Cuban workers meant, in the short term, attaining the equivalent of a sixth-grade education (a fundamental goal in the first years of the Cuban Revolution)—to his notion of social duty, and it is precisely through the concept of work that he does so: as he says in another speech from the same month, the aim should be to "link study with work and work with duty."[76] Interestingly, in discussing the importance of study and continuous learning, Guevara suggests that what one at first experiences as external compulsion will gradually become a vital need,[77] which is of course also the process of psychological development that he describes in connection with voluntary labor. At any rate, while acquisition of the rudiments of a basic education was the short-term goal, the most important task in the long term was occupational and professional training at all levels.[78]

For Guevara, collective discussion and consultation complement study and training as preparation—and one could just as well say (additional) "education"—for worker control of production and for socialism more generally. In referring to discussion and

consultation, Guevara has in mind both the handing of all manner of problems arising at the workplace and worker involvement in the process of production planning.
As for the former, Guevara advocates "discussion of all problems without fear, openly
discussing them"—or, as he puts it in a July 1961 article, "criticism and self-criticism
will be [in the new society] the foundation of daily work but carried to their utmost in
the Production Assembly . . . where the work of the Administrator will be subject to
questioning and criticism on the part of the workers he manages."[79] Guevara's commitment to worker participation in economic planning, which of course includes decisions
bearing on production, is no less robust. Collective planning is as feasible and essential
in an economy in the process of building socialism as in a socialist economy itself, since
collective ownership of the major means of production already exists and the purpose
of production is already the satisfaction of the needs of all; and on numerous occasions
Guevara underscores the importance of involving workers, or rather the "masses" as a
whole, in this planning. Thus, in a very brief speech delivered in February 1961, Guevara stresses the need for "the participation of the masses in all of the work of planning
the nation's economy," and it is a theme that he likewise highlights in the "Our Industrial Tasks" article cited above.[80] In a word, Guevara espouses democratic planning—he
himself uses this terminology[81]—and his commitment to this principle was such that
it actually appears in one of Guevara's final texts, an unfinished communiqué drafted
in Bolivia in early 1967, which demands, among other things, the "participation of
workers and peasants in the tasks of planning the new economy."[82] (Incidentally, Guevara also defended the democratic self-organization of peasant associations in Cuba,
explicitly urging that they be formed from the bottom up.[83])

Among the many reflections of Guevara's commitment to collective discussion
and consultation are the bimonthly meetings with senior administrative staff from
the Ministry of Industries (including provincial delegates), which were held from
January 1962 to December 1964. Volume 6 of *El Che en la Revolución cubana*, the
first comprehensive edition of Guevara's works, includes the transcripts of many of
these meetings (taken from recordings of the sessions). With their frequent shifts between theoretical discussions and considerations and detailed analyses of very specific
practical problems and challenges confronting administrators within the Ministry
of Industries, the meetings demonstrate the depth of Guevara's commitment to a
view that he articulates in a speech before newly trained administrators in December 1961: "Theory is indispensable for the development of the revolution and for
acquiring a superior consciousness, but it must always be combined with practice."[84]
Besides reflecting Guevara's belief in the unity of theory and practice, the meetings
exemplify his commitment to collective discussion and consultation; and while these
sessions involved administrators and senior management personnel, Guevara sought
to institutionalize the practice of discussion and consultation in every workplace
within his ministry and to enable all workers to participate in these collective de-
liberations. (It was a practice that he followed with his guerrilla comrades-in-arms,
too.[85]) If, as Orlando Borrego reports, Guevara found this volume of his "collected
works"—which he saw, along with the rest of the collection, shortly before leaving

Cuba for the last time—particularly "interesting,"[86] this was surely due in part to the value of the discussions it contains, a value that they would lack had the meetings not included such extended exercises in collective deliberation.

One of the reasons that it is worth discussing this aspect of Guevara's thought at some length is the fact that two commentators already mentioned have faulted Guevara for in effect ignoring the working class. According to Samuel Farber, giving "economic and political power" to "the working class and its allies" was not "a defining element" of Guevara's Marxism, and Farber likewise maintains that Guevara "would not even consider anything resembling workers' control of production."[87] In a similar vein, Mike González asserts that Guevara "did not see the organised working class as a central actor in his vision of revolution" and that "it is the revolutionaries, and not the working class, who are the key actors in his conception of revolution."[88] As should be obvious from the summary of Guevara's ideas in the present section, Farber's claims prove wholly untenable. With regard to González, the notion that the working class was not a key actor in Guevara's conception of revolution—a claim also made by Farber—is minimally plausible only if one reduces "revolution" to actions leading to and culminating in the overthrow of a capitalist social order and one is concerned only with Guevara's position on "the central question of the role of the working class as the agent of revolution" (to use Farber's words[89]). While Guevara does stress, in an interview just a few months after the triumph of the Revolution, that "working class participation in the struggle to achieve freedom was absolutely essential,"[90] it is true that he ascribes a preeminent role to the peasantry and armed revolutionary vanguard in his theory of guerrilla warfare and holds that this form of struggle is the most effective and reliable method for overthrowing capitalist regimes. One could, therefore, plausibly maintain that the working class was not a key actor in Guevara's conception of revolution *if that is all that is meant by "revolution."* For Guevara, however, the overthrow of an oppressive regime constitutes but one aspect or phase of the revolution; that is to say, Guevara's "ideology of revolutionary warfare" does not exhaust his conception of "the revolutionary process" (I take both phrases from González[91]). This should go without saying in light of the section on Guevara's conception of revolution in chapter 4 above, is implicit in the idea of "socialist revolution"—one does not find a functioning socialist society on the morrow of the capitalists' capitulation—defended by Guevara,[92] and can be inferred from any number of passages in his works.[93] Adherence to such an outlook hardly makes Guevara an unorthodox Marxist: Marx and Lenin likewise identify "revolution" not only with the conquest of political power but also with the ensuing period of social transformation.[94] Indeed, both González and Farber themselves plainly regard the events that occurred after January 1959 as forming part of the revolution that occurred in Cuba, as does virtually everyone who addresses the topic of the Cuban Revolution. Consequently, it is difficult to understand why they should come to the conclusion that Guevara's notion of revolution marginalizes or ignores the working class. Similarly, one wonders why they should both maintain that Guevara departs from Marxism on the issue of worker's self-emancipation.[95] Guevara plainly believes that much of the process of worker self-emancipation takes place *after* the overthrow of capitalist rule, as did Marx,[96] whether or not the working class was the principal agent of this overthrow. Indeed, many of the practices and policies that Guevara advocates, such as education and training or voluntary labor, are intended precisely to facilitate the self-emancipation of workers in the postrevolutionary period—that is, in the period following the overthrow of capitalist rule and during which society begins the work of building socialism. Naturally, one might dispute the value of these practices and policies in attaining the desired end or even question Guevara's conception of "proletarian self-emancipation"[97] but not Guevara's commitment to the principle itself. "The seizure of power by the working class is a historical necessity," said Guevara in April 1962,[98] and he did not hesitate to embrace all of the corollaries and implications, including proletarian self-emancipation and worker control of production, of this view.

GUEVARA'S ECONOMIC PHILOSOPHY

While an extended treatment of Guevara's ideas on economics, economic theory, and economic policy lies beyond the scope of this work, it is important to mention at least some aspects of these ideas in a study of Guevara's political thought, if only on account of the numerous connections between the political and economic dimensions of this thinking.

It should be emphasized at the outset that, contrary to what one might assume, given the fairly common perception of Guevara as a "romantic" or "utopian" whose political project exemplified a "voluntarism" blind, or indifferent, to economic realities, Guevara developed his economic outlook in light of a comprehensive yet detailed understanding of the Cuban economy. That Guevara was extraordinarily well informed as regards the characteristics of the economy, and its industrial sector in particular, will be apparent at once to anyone who reads his speeches, lectures, and articles bearing on this topic, which, as noted at the beginning of this chapter, abound in statistical data and lots of other information on production and the operation of the Cuban economy in general. Some typical examples of such texts include Guevara's March 1961 lecture on foreign aid and Cuba's development, with its highly detailed discussion of factories, or the December 1963 televised lecture in which Guevara explains new salary scales and production norms.[99] Guevara also possessed an impressive knowledge of both the economic and technical dimensions of that sector of production that has historically dominated the Cuban economy— namely, the sugar industry—as is evident in both his January 1962 television appearance to discuss the second "People's Sugarcane Harvest" and his speech a few months later at a national conference on sugar.[100] In addition to speeches and talks such as these, one could also cite various essays that demonstrate Guevara's command of data on production and the Cuban economy generally, not to mention the countless reports—on visits to factories, on the state of the "consolidated enterprises," on his ministry's goals—contained in volume 6 of *El Che en la Revolución cubana*, which also illustrate just how seriously Guevara took his managerial and bureaucratic responsibilities.[101]

Guevara was, then, hardly a starry-eyed radical bent on imposing his blueprint for a new social order on a socioeconomic situation about which he understood little. In fact, it was precisely this respect for economic realities that would eventually lead Guevara to concede, as he does in a speech delivered in Algeria in July 1963, that his early hopes and projections for Cuba's growth rate had been grossly unrealistic.[102] Similarly, Guevara did not hesitate to admit, in a meeting with Latin American visitors the following month, that his initial strategy for industrialization had been misguided (for instance, the raw materials for certain goods that were going to be produced cost nearly as much as what it would cost Cuba to purchase the finished goods themselves) or that it had been a mistake to neglect the sugar industry in the drive for agricultural diversification, a topic that he returns to in his 1964 article "The Cuban Economy: Its Past and Its Present Importance."[103] Incidentally, Guevara's public acknowledgment of these errors testifies not only to his determination to fashion policy in accordance with actual socioeconomic conditions and possibilities but also to his sense of obligation to tell the truth, which, as he tells us in a note that prefaces his account of his guerrilla campaign in the Congo, was a rule—tell the truth—that he had always followed.[104] And, indeed, according to Alfredo Muñoz-Unsain, an Argentine journalist who spent most of his working life in Cuba, it was this quality—he was "the sort who took the microphone and spoke the truth"[105]— that endeared Guevara to the Cuban people.

Another aspect of Guevara's economic outlook worth mentioning—since it, too, diverges from the image of Guevara as a revolutionary dreamer—is his insistence on *efficiency.* This concern with efficiency is evident, for example, in Guevara's remarks in the August 1963 bimonthly meeting with administrators from the Ministry of Industries, during which he discusses the need for financial discipline, reliable statistics, employee qualifications, management control mechanisms, and staffing strategies, among other things.[106] Besides these topics, Guevara also discusses such questions as salaries, individual productivity norms, the indispensability of good accounting, and the importance of sound investment practices on the numerous occasions in which he stresses the need to strive for maximum economic efficiency.[107] Of course, Guevara's concern with efficiency was not merely the response of a dedicated Minister of Industries to some of the obvious economic problems in Cuba's plants and factories. It was also the result of his desire to accelerate economic development to the greatest possible extent so as to shorten the transition to socialism; improved efficiency would contribute to this accelerated development by helping to dramatically raise productivity. The latter objective was, as Manuel Monereo has observed, something of an obsession for Guevara.[108] "The slogan of the moment," declares Guevara at a ceremony recognizing outstanding workers in the Ministry of Industries, "must be produce and produce and produce, every day and with more enthusiasm!"[109] While Guevara normally favors less dramatic forms of expression in underscoring the urgent need to substantially increase productivity, the idea that raising productivity (including the creation of surpluses for export) is an absolute priority is a recurrent theme in his speeches and writings.[110] In fact, even in his speech of April 15, 1961, to militia members, delivered after the bombing raids preceding the Bay of Pigs Invasion that would begin less than two days later, Guevara insists that "the people's task is more and more important, in the sense of holding the rifle in one hand and to be working beside their machine, or with their pick or machete, producing every day, disciplining themselves to produce more, disciplining themselves to produce better."[111] Guevara links this idea to his other "obsession"—namely, the deepening of consciousness—these being the two paths that must be followed in order to hasten the transition to socialism.[112]

If Guevara's commitment to economic efficiency would come as a revelation to many, his concern with *quality* would likely also prove quite surprising, if only because Guevara's personal austerity and indifference to material possessions might lead one to assume that he would take no interest in whether products were well made. The fact is, however, that Guevara took the quality of goods being produced in Cuba very seriously and urged workers and administrators to improve their quality —"our workers and administrators" should "offer the finest quality of goods possible to the people"[113]—starting with those goods that were "for popular consumption."[114] Indeed, Guevara claims that a commitment to quality is a—or rather forms part of one's—social duty, and he attributed the decline in quality of many goods produced in Cuba in the early years after the revolution to a lack of "revolutionary consciousness."[115] For Guevara, in short, quality should be a socialist value, and it was therefore a mistake to regard it as a capitalist vice and identify it with the counterrevolution, as did some *compañeros*.[116] As he would put it in August 1962, "by no means is quality at odds with this stage in the construction of socialism"; or, as he says a year earlier and in a less prosaic register, "Beauty is not something that is incompatible with the Revolution."[117]

AN ALTERNATIVE APPROACH TO SOCIALIST ECONOMIC MANAGEMENT

During 1963 and 1964, Guevara took part in a series of lively theoretical exchanges, whose participants included other Cuban officials with expertise in industry or the economy as well as two foreign Marxist economists.[118] Now commonly referred to as "the Great Debate," a name first used by Ernest Mandel (one of the two foreign economists),[119] the exchanges ranged over a variety of questions bearing, on the one hand, on Marxist economic theory and, on the other, on the correct system for the management and administration of industry, and the economy as a whole, as Cuba initiated the transition to socialism. Perhaps the most salient theoretical question concerned the status of the so-called "law of value" during the transition to socialism. Though often used rather loosely, the law of value refers primarily to the thesis, posited by Marx, that the socially necessary labor time required to produce a commodity determines its exchange value and thereby regulates the way in which producers exchange the products of their labor in capitalist societies.[120] One of the central questions addressed by the participants in the Great Debate concerned the persistence of the law of value in a society already undergoing the transition to socialism. Helen Yaffe provides a lucid summary of this aspect of the debate: "All the participants in the Great Debate agreed that the law of value continued to operate because commodity production and exchange through a market mechanism continued to exist after the Revolution. The social product continued to be distributed on the basis of socially necessary labour time. However, they disagreed about the conditions explaining the law's survival, its sphere of operation, the extent to which it regulated production, how it related to the 'plan' and, finally, whether the law of value should be utilised or undermined, and if so, how."[121]

What was at stake here? If—or rather to the extent that—the law of value still operated in Cuba, the capitalist market continued to function within the Cuban economy. As Guevara writes in his essay "On Production Costs and the Budgetary System," "It is, in fact, impossible to consider the law of value outside the context of the market. By the same token, one could say that the expression of the law of value is, in fact, the capitalist market itself."[122] The basic problem, from Guevara's perspective, was that the continued use of market mechanisms in enterprises that were not only state-owned but striving to lay the foundations for a socialist society represented a self-contradictory policy, as did, more generally, the continued existence of market transactions in accordance with exchange values. (Recall the passage from "Socialism and Man in Cuba" in which Guevara declares that it is a "pipe dream" to think that "socialism can be achieved with the help of the dull instruments left to us by capitalism.") Indeed, as Guevara would put it in his last published interview, "[T]he definition of capitalism is: to give free rein to the law of value. Every time that we give more latitude to the law of value, we move closer to capitalism again."[123] Guevara's reasoning would seem to be as follows: Where the law of value obtains and economic life consists in market transactions in terms of exchange values, one's motivation to produce derives from the promise of receiving greater material rewards, and one strives to create more value only so as to be able to obtain more value through exchange. This motivation issues in competition to produce more than others so as to be able to obtain as much as possible from a finite supply of goods. The most appropriate incentive for production where the law of value obtains—that is, the incentive most consistent with producers' aspirations—will be a material incentive, use of which will in turn reinforce this motivational disposition that responds to material incentives.

As the quotation from Yaffe indicates, Guevara readily acknowledged that the law of value continued to operate in revolutionary Cuba, yet he also held that economic policy should be fashioned in such a way as to ensure that "the law of value will be reflected less and less in the plan."[124] The provision of some essential goods at very low prices, through the use of mechanisms like subsidies and price controls, would be one example of curtailing the operation or presence of the law of value.[125] Forms of regulation such as these, which serve to undermine the relation between value and price, constitute a very direct interference with the law of value. Hence Guevara's statement, in 1964, that "we do not deny the existence of the law of value" but "the possibility that price really represents value under the current conditions of socialism."[126]

As far as Guevara's political and economic thought is concerned, the importance of the Great Debate lies not in the rather arcane analyses of the law of value and the other general theoretical issues addressed by the participants but rather in the fact that Guevara would, in the course of the exchanges, expound his own, distinctive ideas on economic management in a more or less systematic fashion. These ideas were the components of a novel form of economic management and organization devised by Guevara and generally known in English as the "budgetary finance system."

Guevara's system of management starts from the assumption that once the state has assumed ownership of all industrial operations (factories, plants, etc.)—Guevara advocates nationalization of all industry, all the means of production[127]—it is both possible and desirable to view all of the different enterprises in an economy as constituent parts of a single production operation, of "one big factory."[128] Once production units have been organized in accordance with this conception, "there is no need for commodity relations between enterprises," and "the transfer of a product from one enterprise to another, whether within one ministry or between ministries, should be construed as merely a part of the production process in which values are added to the product."[129] Within Guevara's system, therefore, the product only becomes a commodity—understood as "that product which changes ownership through an act of exchange"[130]—when it leaves the state-owned industrial sector and is appropriated by some individual or group.[131] Guevara's system of management also includes centralized control of the operations and activities of individual enterprises, which is made possible by the unitary ownership already mentioned, and by using the most advanced methods and techniques of accounting and administration. A third distinctive feature of Guevara's system is the fact that enterprises do not have their own funds. Rather, "at the bank there are separate accounts for withdrawals and for deposits. The enterprise may withdraw funds in accordance with the plan from the general expense account and the special wage account. But its deposits automatically pass into the hands of the state."[132] Banks thus become little more than allocation mechanisms, and money "functions only as money of account, as a reflection, in prices, of an enterprise's performance that can be analyzed by the central bodies in order to control its functioning."[133] Finally, and not least important, Guevara's system prioritizes moral incentives (of the sort discussed in chapter 2) as a means of maintaining and increasing productivity, including the lowering of costs.[134] By relying primarily but not exclusively on moral incentives, the budgetary finance system begets a "deepening" and development of consciousness, as Guevara underscores in a March 1964 speech,[135] and it is for this reason that Guevara deems the use of moral incentives an absolutely crucial element of his system, and the system as a whole "part of a general conception of the development of the building of socialism"[136] (moral transformation being, as we have seen, central to Guevara's own conception of this development).

Guevara implemented this system of economic management in the Ministry of Industries at the same time as another system—whose name has been variously translated as the financial self-management system, economic calculus, the system of self-finance, the auto-financing system, or the economic accounting system—was being used in the agricultural sector and in foreign trade. This other system embodied, in crucial respects, the very antithesis of Guevara's position. Under the financial self-management system, each enterprise has its own juridical identity and, as terms like "self-management" or "self-finance" suggest, is responsible for managing its own finances; the enterprise's performance is measured by its profitability. Under this more decentralized system, "the production unit's relations with the bank are similar to those a private producer maintains with capitalist banks" (control over accounts, use of credit, interest on loans, etc.),[137] and market (commodity) relations regulate trade between different enterprises. Finally, and not least important, the financial self-management system uses material incentives to reward worker performance and enhance productivity.[138]

Interestingly, and perhaps surprisingly in light of the foregoing summary, Guevara remarks on a number of occasions that his system of management, the budgetary finance system, actually involves procedures and techniques borrowed from capitalism, or, rather, from monopoly capitalism, and during his December 1964 lecture at the University of Oriente he even goes so far as to say that this system is "a form of capitalist administration with a revolutionary Marxist content."[139] What Guevara means, quite simply, is that the budgetary finance system incorporated the most advanced administrative and accounting techniques of monopolistic and quasimonopolistic enterprises within contemporary capitalism.[140] One way in which Guevara's system plainly differs from a capitalist system of economic management, however, is in its emphasis on moral incentives, and this is likewise one of the salient differences between the budgetary finance system and the financial self-management system. In fact, what most troubled Guevara about the alternative to his system of economic management was precisely its reliance on material incentives. For Guevara, a system that rests on such incentives does not serve to foster a truly socialist/communist outlook, and for this reason he views the budgetary finance system as "a more efficient way of reaching communism."[141] While Guevara insists that his rejection of the financial self-management system by no means represents a dogmatic dismissal of this approach and that he does not regard that system as inherently "antisocialist,"[142] its unqualified acceptance of material incentives was, in his view, a major, decisive drawback, given that use of such incentives does not promote the outlook that ought to characterize, and probably constitutes a necessary condition of the success of, socialist and communist societies. Guevara's view of the pernicious effects of material incentives was in fact the central element in his explanation, both during his last years in Cuba and after he left the island in 1965, for the Soviet Union's failure to realize the promise of socialism. For Guevara, the New Economic Policy (NEP), adopted under Lenin in 1921, was the climacteric in this regard, for this policy, which was intended to revive and stimulate an economy devastated by civil war and social unrest, introduced market mechanisms, and hence material incentives, in some sectors of Soviet economic life. Accordingly, Guevara would claim in the introduction to the book on political economy and socialism that he began to prepare in 1965 and 1966 that the NEP fundamentally shaped the subsequent, extremely disappointing, evolution of Soviet society.[143] The NEP was responsible for introducing nothing less than "the great Trojan Horse of socialism, direct material interest as an economic lever."[144] Guevara acknowledged Lenin's responsibility in establishing the NEP—he was the "culprit"—and in failing to adequately explain that it represented a tactical retreat,[145] but he was also certain that Lenin would have rectified this decision and radically modifed the NEP had he lived longer.[146]

Guevara's attitude toward Lenin in this connection was, then, complex. John Gerassi, a journalist and academic who had some conversations with Guevara in the summer of 1964, later recalled, "In our discussion of Lenin, Che made me feel that he looked upon that great revolutionary as almost tragic, as a man who knew that a society built on material incentives was doomed to fail morally, and yet the man who instituted the New Economic Policy. That policy, as successful as it was, brought back material incentives at the expense of moral incentives."[147] But whatever the extent of Lenin's responsibility for the economic path taken by the Soviet Union, Guevara was openly declaring as early as 1963 that the Soviet model required a major, urgent overhaul and that one of the principal problems besetting that model arose from its use of material incentives.[148] Indeed, Guevara not only drew attention to this problem with the model but also was already claiming in 1965 and 1966 that the Soviet Union and socialist nations in general were returning to capitalism.[149] While we cannot know to what extent Guevara's explanation for the developments that eventually led the socialist countries back to capitalism was correct, his conclusion proved, as we now know, remarkably prescient.[150]

GUEVARA'S IDEAS ON BUILDING SOCIALISM

In his writings and speeches, Guevara frequently emphasizes the importance of Cuba—that is, the Cuban Revolution—as an example for the peoples of the colonial and neocolonial nations, and for Latin Americans in particular. Cuba is, to use the metaphor favored by Guevara, a "beacon" (*faro*) for these nations,[151] and Cuba enjoys this status because it represents, as he writes in the epilogue to *Guerrilla Warfare*, an example of "national and international dignity" (which is the very reason that it constitutes a *bad* example from the point of view of the North American monopolists).[152] Cuba provides "the hope of redemption of all of the nations of America" and, indeed, "all countries that fight for their liberation."[153] But this status also entails, Guevara emphasizes, responsibility—namely, "the obligation to show the nations of America what can be done with a just social regime."[154] This is one reason that so much hinges on our assessment of the correctness of Guevara's ideas, principles, and policies for building socialism.

I began this chapter with a brief overview of the formidable obstacles and difficulties that Cuba faced in undertaking the transition to socialism in the early 1960s. One reason for drawing attention to these problems is that some familiarity with the context in which Guevara was attempting to "build socialism" is essential for understanding his insistence on, say, the value of unity or the importance of (and some initial impediments to) worker control. And, indeed, if we bear in mind this context, Guevara's views on these issues hardly prove unreasonable. This is even true, in my view, of Guevara's notion of the duties of revolutionaries, including his emphasis on sacrifice. Guevara had no illusions regarding the magnitude of the privations that Cuba would be forced to undergo during the transitional period. If even socialism might involve, as Engels would write in 1891, "a short transitional period involving some privation,"[155] presumably owing to the effects of initial redistributive measures and the inefficiencies attending radical economic restructuring, it was hardly unreasonable for Guevara to assume that the transition to socialism in an underdeveloped country under siege would involve fairly severe privations and would therefore require a correspondingly greater disposition to endure sacrifices—the "heroic attitude in daily life" that Guevara evokes in "Socialism and Man in Cuba"—among those most committed to bringing socialism into being. In maintaining that revolutionaries would benefit both from the experience of privation and the development of a "heroic attitude" in response to it, Guevara articulates a view that, contrary to what some might assume, is consistent with Marxist orthodoxy: in the passage from his introduction to Marx's *Wage Labour and Capital* just cited, Engels notes that the short transitional period (one "perhaps . . . involving some privation") that he mentions would be "at any rate of great value morally."[156]

As for more narrowly economic questions, one could hardly take issue with Guevara's views on the need for efficiency and high standards of quality in the presocialist and socialist economy. Guevara's concern with efficiency and quality in production—two objectives that, needless to say, should be priorities in any economy—is especially noteworthy in light of the fact that inefficiency and poor quality in manufactured goods were problems that plagued the centrally planned economies of the Soviet Bloc countries throughout their history.

Finally, how should we assess Guevara's system of economic management? I have provided little more than a skeletal outline of this system in the present chapter, and for this reason alone I will not attempt to provide a detailed evaluation of this system here. Instead, I will offer two very general observations. First, at a time in which an alternative to capitalism is needed as urgently as ever yet many on the left despair of the possibility of developing an economically viable socialism, Guevara's budgetary finance system offers, at the very least, some useful elements for the development of a practicable, noncapitalist form of economic management. One of the reasons that the general framework of Guevara's system remains quite promising is that he consciously attempted to incorporate, as we have seen, the best administrative and management techniques from contemporary monopoly capitalism. Second, while giving due weight to bureaucratic and administrative efficiency, Guevara's budgetary finance system also serves the "educational" end of moral transformation discussed in chapters 1 and 2. In short, Guevara's arrangement combines operational efficiency and moral appeal, two essential elements of any minimally acceptable model of economic organization and management for socialism (and the transition to socialism). Of course, what makes the budgetary finance system most distinctive as an approach to managing a centrally planned economy is its emphasis on moral transformation, but this emphasis on moral transformation is also what is perhaps most distinctive of Guevara's Marxism as a whole. This is one of the topics that I discuss in the next chapter.

6

The Guevarist Legacy

The previous chapters of this book have examined and assessed what are, in my view, the most important facets of Guevara's political thought. In this final chapter, I will present some general considerations on Guevara's legacy as a political thinker. Specifically, I will be focusing on the difficulties attending commentators' attempts to situate Guevara, or classify him, within the history of Marxist political thought, difficulties that arise in large part from the eclectic, nondogmatic quality of his interpretation of Marxist doctrine. I will also discuss two of the more salient features of Guevara's Marxism—namely, its humanism and its strongly moral cast, as well as Guevara's putative "voluntarism," this being one of the most frequent criticisms of Guevara from commentators on the left. In the penultimate section of this chapter I restate some of the reasons for holding that *Guevarism* remains relevant to the contemporary left while also briefly discussing a few of the questions that the left will not find addressed in Guevara's works. I conclude with some very brief reflections on the familiar slogan in Revolutionary Cuba, "Be like Che."

AN ECLECTIC MARXISM

The term "Guevarism" is often associated primarily with Guevara's theory of guerilla warfare,[1] yet, as I have sought to show in the previous chapters of this book, Guevarism is, as a theoretical orientation and concrete political project, first and foremost a variety of, or current within, Marxism. While most informed commentators would doubtless agree with this characterization, there is considerable disagreement as to where, exactly, to situate Guevara within Marxism, as his main ideological affinities seem to defy any simple classification. This uncertainty as regards Guevara's basic theoretical and political affinities is surely due, at least in part, to the lack of dogmatism in Guevara's thought. Indeed, countless commentators have drawn attention to the nondogmatic, or rather antidogmatic, quality of Guevara's thought,[2] and it is hardly insignificant in this connection that Guevara himself mentions the danger of dogmatism in his most emblematic essay, "Socialism and Man in Cuba."[3] In fact Guevara's works contain many examples of his aversion to dogmatism, the most notable being his highly critical notes on the Soviet manual of political economy from 1965 to 1966. But Guevara's antidogmatic attitude is also evident in his acceptance of the use of the two rival systems of economic management discussed in the last chapter, the budgetary finance system and the financial self-management system, until one or the other had proven its superiority.[4] One might also mention here Guevara's interest in reading Trotsky when, around 1960, a Peruvian revolutionary named Ricardo Napurí expressed surprise at Guevara's refusal to accept the collaboration of a distinguished intellectual because the man was supposedly a Trotskyist. After subsequently acknowledging that he had not read any Trotskyist literature, Guevara asked Napurí to bring him a book by Trotsky, which he did (*The Permanent Revolution*) and which Guevara subsequently read and discussed with Napurí.[5] Considering that Cuba was at this time just beginning to consolidate its relationship with the Soviet Union, for which everything smacking of "Trotskyism" was anathema, Guevara's response to Napurí amounts, in effect, to a rejection of dogmatism. This very same antidogmatic, somewhat heretical outlook can also be seen, and likewise in regard to the question of Trotsky and Trotskyism, in Guevara's proposal, mentioned in chapter 4, that Trotsky's works be included in a publication program for the popularization of Marxist thought in Cuba. In 1965 the Marxism studied and promoted in Cuba was the official Soviet version, which vilified Trotsky and viewed all things connected with Trotskyism with extreme disdain, and thus this gesture likewise attests to Guevara's eschewal of dogmatism. What is more, Guevara displayed the same support for those who wished to familiarize themselves with Chinese Communist literature at a time when Cuban Communists, who sided with the Soviets in the Sino-Soviet dispute, condemned the reading of political literature from China.[6] This freedom from dogmatism is, in any case, surely one source of Guevara's appeal to many Marxists.

Partly as a result of this absence of dogmatism in Guevara's thought, Guevara's Marxism has been interpreted, and either embraced or dismissed, under the most disparate and contradictory labels. For example, Guevara has been thought to be something of a Maoist by some and a Trotskyist of sorts by others, while the Soviets actually believed that Guevara was *both* things at one and the same time.[7] Others have suggested that he was to a large degree a Stalinist or a kind of libertarian Marxist or even an anarchist.[8] Still others include Guevara's thought under the rubric "Castroism."[9]

There is, without question, a bit of truth in all of these characterizations, and others that have been or could be made. (One might even make the case, for example, that Guevara had syndicalist leanings, given his statement that "one could think of the work center as the basis of the future society's political nucleus."[10]) Let us briefly consider a couple of the more interesting—either because of their plausibility or implications—classifications of Guevara's thought, starting with the label "Trotskyist." It is undoubtedly true, as Donald C. Hodges has written, that "politically, Che came to recognize some of the same revolutionary priorities as Trotsky," including the "objective of internationalizing the revolution," just as it is true that "like Trotsky, Che deemed it necessary to combine revolutionary stages through a simultaneous struggle for national liberation and socialism" (as we saw in chapter 4), or that "Che had more in common with Latin American Trotskyism than with the established Communist parties. In fact few Trotskyists have spoken as persistently and as articulately for continuing revolution as Che Guevara."[11] These affinities help to explain the sympathy for Guevara's political thought found among some figures and organizations rooted in the tradition of classical Trotskyism, including Ernest Mandel, Michael Löwy, and the US Socialist Workers Party. At the same time, Hodges rightly notes that insofar as Guevara's foco theory dispenses with the need for a "vanguard party," or implies that the guerrilla force can in some sense assume the same role, his thought "marks a decisive break with classical Bolshevism" and thus Trotskyism.[12]

What about Maoism? Significantly, in the very same December 1964 meeting in which he criticizes Trotsky and the Trotskyists, Guevara observes that many of his "opinions" are close to those of the Chinese, and he specifically mentions four questions: guerrilla warfare, "people's war," voluntary labor, and opposition to the use of material incentives.[13] Guevara was certainly correct in finding many fundamental similarities between his positions and Maoist doctrine—the Chinese positions that he mentions are Maoist positions—and I touched on some of these similarities earlier, most notably Guevara's emphasis on the centrality of the peasantry in revolutionary struggle—that is, his thesis that "the peasant class of Latin America . . . will provide the great liberating army of the future" and that in the "dependent countries" in general the peasants are, in a word, "the revolutionary force."[14] Moreover, whereas Guevara seems never to have had a positive attitude toward Trotsky himself,[15] he was already an admirer of Mao prior to the start of the Cuban Revolutionary War—after the birth of his daughter in Mexico, Guevara wrote to his mother, "My communist soul expands plethorically: she has come out exactly like Mao Tse-tung"[16]—and in April 1959, not long after the triumph of the revolution and two years before Fidel Castro officially declared it "socialist," Guevara told Chinese interviewers, "We have always looked up to Comrade Mao Tse-tung."[17] If, as Jon Lee Anderson writes in his biography of Guevara, the Soviets suspected that Guevara's ideological sympathies lay more with Beijing than with Moscow,[18] one can hardly ascribe this perception to the Soviets' lack of sound information. At the same time, Anderson cites a Soviet official to whom Guevara explained, in the course of a protracted conversation, "'why' he wasn't a Maoist."[19] It would be fascinating to know the reasons that Guevara cited on that occasion, in early 1964, for rejecting the Maoist label (the official did not recount Guevara's reasons, unless Anderson chose to omit them from his narrative), but there are, in any case, plainly important differences between Guevara's political thought and Maoist doctrine. To begin with, one might cite Guevara's views on economic development: Mao's Great Leap Forward, for example, involved a practice and degree of decentralization wholly at odds with Guevara's thinking on planning under socialism. Guevara would also surely reject Maoism's approach to ideological struggles, the problem of bureaucracy, and the evil of inequality, at least to the extent that the principles and practices of the Great Proletarian Cultural Revolution exemplify this approach.

Let me say, finally, something about Guevara's relationship to Stalin and Stalinism, if only because some commentators fault Guevara for failing to fully grasp the evil of Stalinism or even accuse him of strongly sympathizing with Stalin and Stalinism. In considering Guevara's relationship to Stalin and Stalinism, it is important to begin by acknowledging that Stalin's writings did in fact shape Guevara's early interpretation and assimilation of Marxism, socialism, and communism. Indeed, in his December 1964 lecture at the University of Oriente, Guevara himself states that he "got involved in" communism through Stalin.[20] But it is equally important to point out that it was by no means unusual in the early and mid-1950s for a young person of a leftist, anti-imperialist political orientation to hold a highly favorable opinion of both the Soviet Union and Stalin.[21] However, while Guevara initially held the figure of Stalin in very high regard, and even in his last years continued to maintain that Stalin's writings should form a part of the education of Marxists and others,[22] it hardly follows that we are justified in speaking, as does one of Guevara's critics, of an enduring "identification with Stalin."[23] Admittedly, Guevara's works contain little direct criticism of Stalin himself. The most notable exception is to be found in Guevara's posthumously published notes on the Soviet manual of political economy, where he writes that Stalin's "tremendous historical crime" was "to have scorned communist education and instituted the unrestricted cult of authority."[24] Yet there are two fairly obvious explanations for the absence of any significant critical assessment of Stalin, and Stalin's crimes, in Guevara's works. First of all, Guevara believed, as odd as it may seem, that the Soviet Union's most fundamental problems ultimately derived from the adoption of the NEP, which occurred under Lenin. Second, Guevara also held the belief, likewise expressed during his appearance at the University of Oriente, that one must judge Stalin within the historical context in which he lived and acted[25]—a belief probably strengthened by the knowledge that the Cuban revolutionaries' failings were not being properly contextualized by their critics—and providing the necessary contextualization was no simple undertaking.

But even if it is false to say that Guevara was a Stalinist, might it not still be correct to claim, as do some writers sympathetic to Guevara, that he had an extremely inadequate grasp of Stalinism as a political phenomenon? One encounters this criticism in texts by, for example, Manuel Monereo and by Oliver Besancenot and Michael Löwy.[26] Unfortunately, these authors neglect to provide clear explanations as to what it was that, in their view, Guevara failed to understand about Stalinism. This is not to say that these authors are necessarily wrong, and it is true, without question, that Guevara's essays, articles, speeches, and other communications contain virtually no real analysis of Stalinism, just as they contain almost no criticisms of Stalin. On the other hand, on the couple of occasions on which Guevara does refer to "Stalinism," he tends to identify it with *repression in defense of the revolution*. As he told K. S. Karol, "Every revolution, like it or not, inevitably has its share of Stalinism, simply because every revolution faces capitalist encirclement. . . . We have had to defend ourselves against the imperialist threat, and the [Bay of Pigs] Invasion of April 17 reminded us that no measure, no sacrifice, is too great as far as this is concerned."[27] Guevara used an almost identical formulation in a conversation with John Gerassi: when Gerassi asked Guevara about, among other things, executions in Cuba, Guevara replied, "Every social revolution has to have its Stalinist phase."[28] Needless to say, if this is more or less all that "Stalinism" means, then not only is Stalinism inevitable in the course of a real social revolution, but those who favor such revolutions can hardly have grounds for condemning it. In short, it may be fair to say that Guevara's understanding of the phenomenon of Stalinism was indeed inadequate, but it seems somewhat unfair to criticize Guevara for not failing to make more of an effort to analyze Stalinism: as we have seen, Guevara's diverse activities and responsibilities barely left him time for intellectual pursuits, and, on the other hand, the unremitting counterrevolutionary violence that Cuba endured in the early years of the revolution (including an insurgency in the Escambray Mountains) no doubt reinforced his acceptance of *his own* understanding of Stalinism, and this would hardly prompt him to devote more thought to the nature of this problem.

In any event, my main point is that it is incorrect to describe Guevara as a Trotskyist or Maoist (or Stalinist). Guevara borrowed from many different currents within the Marxist tradition and sometimes arrived independently at ideas that bore a strong resemblance to views developed by other Marxist theorists. His fundamentally antidogmatic, nonsectarian orientation enabled him to use ideas deriving from different currents within Marxism, along with contributions from other intellectual traditions (such as dependency theory and anticolonial thought), to forge a distinctive political project.

GUEVARA'S MARXIST HUMANISM

While commentators may disagree about the nature and extent of the affinities between Guevara's thought and other currents and tendencies in the Marxist tradition, there is widespread agreement among those who have studied Guevara that his political outlook plainly constitutes (whatever else it may or may not involve) a distinctive variety of Marxist humanism.[29] To be sure, some writers prefer to use the term "revolutionary humanism" or "socialist humanism" in this connection,[30] but it is clear that, whichever label is used, the point is that Guevara's thought involves, in Juan Valdés Paz's words, a "recovery of the humanist tradition of Marxism."[31] The origins of this tradition can be found in Marx's early writings, in which Marx actually identifies communism with humanism, with the latter consisting, as T. B. Bottomore writes, in "the ideal of a community of men who are able to develop freely, and in harmony with each other, all their personal qualities."[32] While Marx develops his defense of this ideal in rather general terms, he does emphasize that the ideal entails an end to all forms of alienation and dehumanization (whether due to oppressive work conditions or competitive social relations), fostering the all-around development of individuals and individual autonomy, the defense of human well-being and the satisfaction of human needs, and the opportunity for true self-expression. In a word, it entails, as Marx puts it in a well-known phrase from a text published in 1844, "the *categorical imperative to overthrow all relations* in which man is a debased, enslaved, forsaken, despicable being."[33]

Commentators are right to describe Guevara's thought as a variety of Marxist humanism, for many of the objectives and themes from Marx's works just noted, and more generally the concepts and terminology properly associated with Marxist humanism, also abound in Guevara's writings, speeches, lectures, and talks. Indeed, when Guevara proclaims during an August 1961 speech that "the fundamental goals of our Revolution . . . are the dignification of man, to secure for the citizen all of the advantages of culture, social assistance of every sort, and all of the material goods necessary for a happy life,"[34] he is in effect declaring his adherence to the tradition of Marxist humanism. In this same speech, Guevara declares, with a phrase that likewise evokes Marxist humanism, that the aim of "socialist development" is none other than "the happiness of man."[35] In another speech, Guevara refers to the goal of producing a country in which "the people will really become the creator and leader of their history," and, in his essay "Notes for the Study of the Ideology of the Cuban Revolution," he approvingly cites Marx's "revolutionary concept" that the world must be transformed so that "man ceases to be the slave and instrument of his environment and becomes an architect of his own destiny."[36] We may also note that at his very last bimonthly meeting of administrative personnel in the Ministry of Industries, Guevara says that Cuba's new "Marxist, socialist system" is one in which "man is placed at the center, one speaks of the individual, one speaks of man and the importance that he has as an essential factor in the Revolution" (and Guevara had earlier lamented the fact that this was sometimes forgotten during the transition to socialism).[37] Quite apart from such passages as these, many of the themes discussed earlier are of course also quite relevant to Marxist humanism, starting with Guevara's frequent references to the need to end the exploitation of one human being by another, his concern with alienation, and, of course, the creation of a new human being. In short, as in the case of the young Marx, Guevara tends to identify, albeit less explicitly, communism with humanism. Yet, just as Marx insists that we must "overthrow all relations" preventing human beings from living dignified lives and achieving self-realization, Guevara takes it for granted that "it is necessary to eliminate [*liquidar*] the layer of exploiters the world over"[38] in order to establish a true humanism. It is an idea that Guevara in effect restates in his "Message to the Tricontinental," where he maintains that in Africa "the impoverished masses of a country" will have "to conquer their right to a decent life."[39]

Like the young Marx's humanism, Guevara's humanism does not by any means consist of a systematically articulated theory, and, accordingly, it does not lend itself to extensive analysis. Still, it is undeniable that Guevara—whose conception of humanism may have been shaped in part by Aníbal Ponce's concept of "proletarian humanism"[40]—furnishes some elements for developing such a theory. It is worth noting, moreover, that Guevara was fashioning a variety of Marxist humanism just as a number of prominent philosophers and social theorists were beginning to analyze the topic of socialist humanism in general, and Marxist humanism in particular. For example, Erich Fromm's landmark collection of essays on the subject of "socialist humanism"—which does not contain any contribution by Guevara—would appear in 1967.[41] In any event, and as Michael Löwy has observed, Guevara's commitment to a form of socialist humanism is surely part of what makes him one of the revolutionary figures from the Third World who has best stood the test of time.[42] In elaborating on this claim, Löwy seems to include Guevara's emphasis on moral questions within his "humanism."[43] While I think it important to separate at least some of Guevara's moral concerns from his humanism, Löwy is certainly right to underscore the importance of moral concerns to Guevara's Marxism. Indeed, I think they are perhaps even more important than Löwy believes, and it is both because I think we should separate Guevara's moral concerns from his humanism and because I think they are central to his thought that I will deal with them in a separate section.

MARXISM AS A MORAL OUTLOOK

Just as there is widespread agreement among commentators as regards Guevara's nondogmatic outlook and his humanism, so, too, a great many who have studied Guevara's works agree on the importance of moral considerations and moral transformation in Guevara's political thought. For example, in his October 18, 1967, speech in memory of Guevara, Fidel Castro would note that "moral resources" were, for Guevara, "the fundamental lever in the construction of communism in human society," while just two years later philosopher Alasdair MacIntyre would astutely point out, in a review of books on and by Guevara, that "the word 'moral' recurs throughout Che's writings."[44] Since these early observations regarding the importance of morality and moral considerations in Guevara's thought, numerous other commentators have also emphasized this aspect of Guevarism.[45]

We have already seen, of course, many of the ways in which moral considerations are of the utmost importance to Guevara's political outlook and that a central component of his particular political project consists in the creation of a genuinely communist ethos. The "consciousness" that Guevara frequently invokes in some sense corresponds to the preparation of this ethos, and that is why, as noted earlier, when Guevara uses the term "consciousness" he normally has in mind a cluster of moral attitudes or a set of moral commitments, including those that define the new human being. Guevara considers moral transformation essential to the transition to socialism—as well as the eventual

transition from socialism to communism—and, accordingly, he prioritizes moral transformation in his everyday praxis, which aims at, among other things, individual self-
transformation. (We should also recall that Guevara embraces a largely moral notion of
self-realization.) To a certain degree, Guevara's comment in an interview cited earlier,
"Economic socialism without a communist morality does not interest me," encapsulates
this viewpoint. In short, socialist and communist societies are, for Guevara, radically
different, morally speaking, from capitalist societies, and the requisite moral transformation must begin during the transition to socialism.

Guevara's concern with moral transformation is noteworthy for a number of
reasons. To begin with, we should note that Guevara's emphasis on the moral dimensions of socialism and communism, and the ways in which the political culture
of these social arrangements essentially consists in a new moral culture, results in
a moral radicalization of the Marxist project. Indeed, among Marxist thinkers and
theorists, Guevara plainly ranks among those who attach the most importance to
these dimensions: while the young Lukács, for example, may have underscored the
Marxist thesis that "the power of morality cannot become effective . . . as long as
there are still classes in society,"[46] Guevara not only describes the contours of the
postclass morality but also actually devotes many of his efforts to nurturing this
morality and, as we have seen, has few reservations about explicitly invoking moral
considerations, or even appealing to the conventional language of morality, in order
to do so.[47] Particularly revealing in this regard are Guevara's remarks at the end of a
talk at the University of Havana in May 1959, remarks in which he asks his audience to consider whether "there is not something beautiful about lending all of their
efforts to a government that represents the majority of the people; if it is not better
to have a bit less money, but to know that a great mass of peasants is benefitting
[from this], and to know that they cannot liberate themselves until these measures
are taken."[48] Also revealing in this regard is a comment that Guevara made to Tirso
Sáenz, a senior administrator within the Ministry of Industries, after Sáenz's 1963
trip to Poland. Upon hearing Saénz describe his political disappointment (the Polish
officials with whom he had interacted were interested in doing business rather than
solidarity and mutual aid), Guevara replied, "They're screwed. A country in which
moral principles do not prevail . . . cannot be called a socialist country."[49] Yet not
only does Guevara emphasize moral considerations more insistently and explicitly
than other major Marxist theorists, he also displays a degree of personal consistency
in practicing what he preaches—as regards moral issues—that is surely unsurpassed
among Marxist thinkers; and this commitment can also fairly be described as a moral
radicalization of Marxism to the extent that it requires near perfect consonance between one's political and personal morality, near perfect integration of the personal
and the political. As Juan Valdés Paz has observed, both in his theory and practice
Guevara "propounds an uncompromising fusion of ethics and politics," and this was
reflected on a personal level in "an absolute need for consistency."[50]

Guevara's theorization and foregrounding of the moral dimension of the transition to socialism and communism, his "moralization" of Marxism, is also notewor-

thy because, apart from the fact that few other Marxists attached such importance to moral considerations at the time,[51] it anticipates to a certain extent the "ethical turn" in later twentieth-century Marxist theory. Indeed, a moralization of socialism in general, and Marxism in particular, remains one of the principal legacies of the body of thought known as "analytical Marxism," a theoretical movement developed by numerous, mainly Anglo-American philosophers and social scientists in the 1970s and 1980s. Many of the thinkers associated with this "school" devoted at least part of their efforts to an analysis—and frequently defense—of the normative moral dimensions of Marxist doctrine even as they criticized and rejected many of Marx's basic claims and theses. A good reflection of this position can be found in Jon Elster's conclusion to *Making Sense of Marx*: "It is not possible today, morally or intellectually, to be a Marxist in the traditional sense. . . . But . . . I believe it is still possible to be a Marxist in a rather different sense of the term. I find that most of the views that *I* hold to be true and important, I can trace back to Marx. This includes methodology, substantive theories, and, above all, values. The critique of exploitation and alienation remains central."[52]

In any case, whatever the similarities and differences between Guevara's views and the conclusions reached by the analytical Marxists, we may note that in emphasizing the moral dimensions of Marxism, and in presenting socialism and communism as resting centrally on a set of moral commitments, Guevara's thinking represents an important departure from the mainstream of the Marxist tradition. Largely inspired by Marx's own example, most Marxists have stressed the "scientific" character of Marxism's denunciation and rejection of capitalism (i.e., the view that it is no longer defensible in light of certain laws of social development) and/or argued that appeals to morality are unnecessary and misguided, since the material interests of the oppressed will suffice to generate the motivation to undertake a revolutionary transformation of society. As a result, explicit appeals to moral principles or considerations were anathema to most Marxist thinkers, who typically viewed such appeals with disdain. Guevara's robust, unapologetic appeals to morality in the early 1960s represented, therefore, a significant departure from mainstream Marxist theory; it would be a long time before Marxist thinkers would acknowledge without hesitation that the Marxist condemnation of capitalism rests on moral considerations (among other things).

In the end, Guevara's emphasis on moral considerations suggests that he conceives of the commitment to building socialism as a kind of *moral vanguardism*: the political vanguard is, in the last analysis, a moral vanguard. If many who do not subscribe to Guevara's specific political objectives nonetheless find him an attractive, even irresistible, figure, the explanation may well lie in Guevara's concern with moral renewal.

THE QUESTION OF "VOLUNTARISM"

Just as a large number of commentators emphasize Guevara's humanism and underscore the essentially moral orientation of his Marxism, so, too, many who have

studied Guevara's thought contend that it exemplifies a species of "voluntarism."
Thus it is that Francisco Fernández Buey, for example, refers, in the introduction to
his short anthology of Guevara's texts, to Guevara's "voluntarist" proposals as head
of the Ministry of Industries, while Rolando E. Bonachea and Nelson P. Valdés
write, in the introduction of *their* anthology of Guevara's works, that "the essential
element in *Guevarism*" is "the great emphasis on voluntarism."[53] Samuel Farber, for
his part, goes so far as to accuse Guevara of "extreme" voluntarism and even "hy-
pervoluntarism."[54] And various other commentators likewise identify Guevara with
voluntarism, or something very much resembling it, whether or not they use the
term "voluntarism."[55] However, whereas people generally find Guevara's humanism
and espousal of a morally oriented Marxism praiseworthy,[56] practically no one who
concludes that Guevara's Marxism amounts to a form of voluntarism defends it on
these grounds—that is to say, defends it as voluntarist. This is as one would expect:
"voluntarism" is a pejorative term within the Marxist theoretical tradition. But does
Guevara's approach to revolutionary social transformation really represent a form of
what has conventionally been called voluntarism? Or, rather, is this a fair criticism
of Guevara's Marxism?

Needless to say, in order to answer this question, we must first understand what
is meant by the label "voluntarism." In general, voluntarism refers to the tendency
to emphasize human intentions, rather than material conditions or objective laws of
social evolution, in explaining historical development. That is, it involves the claim
that the human will, either that of an individual or the collective will of a group, is
the decisive factor in sociohistorical development; it, and not objective conditions
and processes, is the force that dictates the course of history. Accordingly, to characterize a position as "voluntarist" is to assert that the position in question assumes that
human willpower suffices to overcome seemingly insurmountable objective, or "material," impediments to achieving a given goal. In the more specific context of radical
social theory, and Marxism in particular, voluntarism is often characterized as a tendency to give undue weight to "subjective" conditions—political commitment and
motivation—at the expense of "objective" conditions, or as the belief that the former
are of much greater import when it comes to effecting radical social change, so that
people who are sufficiently motivated and properly guided can succeed in achieving
their aims even in the face of highly adverse or "unripe" material conditions. This
emphasis on the decisive importance of "subjective conditions" is precisely what
Bonachea and Valdés have in mind in referring to Guevarism's "great emphasis on
voluntarism," and this is likewise what Mike González has in mind in attributing to
Guevara the thesis that "the will of the revolutionary can overcome objective conditions and substitute the individual for the movement of an entire class."[57]

So, does Guevara's political thought amount to a voluntarist conception of Marxism? Careful analysis of Guevara's works shows, I believe, that the accusation of
voluntarism is far less justified than is widely believed, at least with respect to his
approach to the building of socialism. (Whether or not we can justifiably speak of
voluntarism in connection with Guevara's approach to the theory of guerrilla war-

fare, or his actual military strategy in the Congo or Bolivia, is a separate question and one that I will not address.) In order to understand my grounds for saying this, it is important to realize that two different aspects of Guevara's thought on the transition to socialism are targets of the charge of voluntarism. The first is Guevara's thesis that, given sufficient motivation and resolve, revolutionaries can effect a very rapid acceleration in the development of the forces of production (i.e., far beyond their "normal" pace of development) and thus create the single most important condition for the establishment of socialism. The second is Guevara's assumption that it is possible to make great progress in producing an ethos appropriate for socialism and communism—consisting mainly in the embrace of egalitarianism and new conception of social duty, as argued earlier—before the establishment of the material conditions of abundance and new relations of production, which, according to standard Marxist theory, would naturally yield this new ethos, and more or less spontaneously.

Let us begin with the first thesis. As a matter of fact, Guevara does assume that a "deepening of consciousness" can serve as a "method" for "developing production"[58] and explicitly links the two phenomena on many occasions.[59] We have already seen a specific reflection of this in Guevara's contention that it was possible to "skip stages" (*quemar etapas*) of economic development thanks to an enhancement of workers' political consciousness and, consequently, heightened psychic investment in the revolutionary process. Guevara's most detailed and explicit statements of this thesis appear in his contributions to the Great Debate on economic policy in Cuba. In "The Meaning of Socialist Planning," perhaps the essay in which Guevara states this idea most emphatically, Guevara writes that the aim of the budgetary finance system is "a more accelerated growth of consciousness and, through consciousness, of the productive forces."[60] Indeed, Guevara goes so far as to claim, in the article that details the mechanics of this system, that "in a relatively short time . . . the development of consciousness does more for the development of production than material incentives do."[61] While in this passage Guevara is clearly referring to the growth of "consciousness"—which in this context seems to mean roughly "revolutionary commitment"—among all members of society, in "The Meaning of Socialist Planning" he focuses on the role of "the vanguard of the revolutionary movement," which, "increasingly influenced by Marxist-Leninist ideology, is capable of consciously anticipating the steps to be taken in order to force the pace of events, but forcing it within what is objectively possible."[62]

For many people of a conventional Marxist cast of mind (and others), these passages furnish proof of Guevara's fundamental "voluntarism" to the exent that they assert that sheer willpower suffices to bring about a certain form of economic development in the absence of the objective conditions supposedly required for such development. Guevara's use of the expression "force the pace of events" proves especially significant, or rather damning, from this point of view, as does his contention, also found in "The Meaning of Socialist Planning," that the "consciousness" of those who make up the vanguard "can perceive the proper paths by which to lead a socialist revolution to victory in that country, even though, at their level, the contradictions

between the development of the productive forces and the relationships [i.e., "relations"] of production that would make a revolution imperative or possible . . . might
not exist objectively."[63] However, if we bear in mind other considerations and qualifications stated by Guevara in these essays and elsewhere, Guevara's claims cease to
appear voluntarist, or, if one prefers, "unduly" voluntarist.

To begin with, Guevara does not make a sweeping claim to the effect that "consciousness" always enjoys the efficacy that he attributes to it in these and other texts.
Rather, Guevara's claim is that consciousness—in the general sense of commitment,
motivation, and resolve—can play this role during the period in which he was writing. As we have already seen, Guevara believed that the early 1960s offered a unique
historical juncture, one reason being the widespread sympathy and support for socialist ideas and goals. In "On the Budgetary Finance System," Guevara writes, "Socialist
ideas have touched the consciousness of all the world's peoples," while in "The Meaning of Socialist Planning" he remarks, "in today's age of imperialism, consciousness
acquires world dimensions."[64] In a word, the world was "turning toward socialism" as
a result, at least in part, of the effect of "the development of all the world's productive forces," together with "the steady advance" of "a world socialist system," which
"influences the consciousness of peoples at all levels."[65] To the extent that this was the
case, socialist ideas had assumed considerable power to influence economic development—the power to mobilize people to devote themselves to maximizing productivity—which they lack in normal times and circumstances. Which is to say, the unusual
prevalence of socialist consciousness was, if Guevara's assessment was correct, *an objective condition* favoring the accelerated development of the productive forces. Yet, if
this was the case, then the appeal to consciousness was in fact an appeal an objective
conditions and hence not a form of voluntarism at all. (One finds an analogous idea
in the young Marx's well-known statement that "material force must be overthrown
by material force; but theory also becomes a material force as soon as it has gripped
the masses."[66]) So, in claiming that the dominance or currency of "socialist ideas"—
that is, a socialist consciousness—made it possible to "advance ahead of the particular
state of the productive forces in any given country,"[67] Guevara is merely saying that
the power and importance of subjective factors has become an objective condition
that favors the efforts of those trying to establish socialism.[68]

It is worth noting that in other texts, Guevara supplements these considerations
with some reflections defending the somewhat controversial notion that it is possible
for ideas to steer and shape the development of the forces of production. According
to the classical Marxist model of social causation and change, in a given social formation the "forces of production" (machinery, tools, land, labor-power, etc.) shape the
"relations of prodution" (property relations, structures regulating control over the
forces of production), which in turn determine a society's "superstructure" (its political institutions, legal notions, and philosophical, moral, and aesthetic ideas, etc.).
Developing, in effect, a line of thought first expressed by Engels in letters from the
1890s, Guevara emphasizes, in the draft introduction for his planned book on Marxist political economy, that it is possible for elements of the superstructure to "react

back" upon—that is, exert an influence on—the relations of production.[69] And the relations of production can, in turn, shape, or react back upon, the forces of production and should be modified so as to do so: it had been necessary, Guevara writes in 1962, to "confront the complex task of developing the new model of social relations of production in industry, so as to make these relations serve as an accelerator in the planned expansion of the productive forces."[70]

In any case, it is important to underscore that even as Guevara maintains that the currency of "socialist consciousness" has in some sense turned consciousness into an objective condition, he stresses, as we have just seen, that it is a matter of "forc[ing] the pace of events, but forcing it within what is objectively possible." This remark attests to Guevara's respect for the objective limitations on progress toward socialism while also belying the accusations of unbridled voluntarism: revolutionary zeal alone is not sufficient for Guevara.[71] On the other hand, we should also bear in mind in this connection that Guevara assumed that the objective conditions for revolution, as more conventionally conceived, already existed in all of Latin America,[72] such that "socialist consciousness" was, so to speak, an *additional* objective condition for radical social transformation, over and above the other conditions.

Finally, it should be noted that Guevara maintains that, even assuming the utmost acceleration of the development of the productive forces, the building of socialism and communism will still be a highly protracted process. Indeed, in a December 1961 speech, Guevara tells administrators at the Ministry of Industries that many of them will not live to see communism, either because they will die a natural death before it has been achieved or because of the actions of "foreign invaders."[73] If building socialism (and communism) would require a lengthy period of time, it was not merely because it would take Cuba years to educate and train all of the technical personnel needed to run the socialist economy.[74] An additional problem, and one that I have already discussed, had to do with the effects of capitalist socialization, which could hardly be overcome, or undone, overnight. For example, Guevara held, as already noted, that Cuba would have to continue using material incentives for some time for the simple reason that capitalism had offered this as the only motivation for people to work, and one had no choice but to start with Cubans as they were: as Guevara would say during one of his bimonthly meetings with colleagues from the Ministry of Industries, "who told you that the Revolution is made with angels or that kind of people[?]" The revolution "would not be necessary" if people were like that.[75] In short, Guevara's realism and sobriety regarding the timeframe for building socialism (and eventually communism) also make it difficult to sustain the accusation of voluntarism regarding his belief in the possibility of substantially accelerating socioeconomic development.

As for the second way in which one might assume that Guevara's thought embodies a kind of voluntarism—namely, his assumption that it is possible to establish a socialist ethos before the creation of those conditions of abundance that would spontaneously tend to engender and sustain such an ethos—it is well to recall a point made in the last chapter. There I noted that Guevara holds that the relations of production need not correspond to the forces of production during the period of transition. According to Guevara, it is a mistake to "mechanically" apply "the concept of necessary correspondence between relationships [i.e., relations] of production and development of the productive forces, which is of universal validity, into the 'microcosm' of the relationships of production in concrete aspects of a specific country during the period of transition."[76] In this regard, Guevara agrees with "the classic Marxist theorists," who, Ernest Mandel reminds us, maintain that "there is no *integral correlation* among the mode of production, the relationships of production, the mode of exchange, and the mode of distribution" during the transition from capitalism to socialism.[77] This local nonalignment or noncorrespondence between the forces and relations of production also implied more autonomy for the superstructure, since, just as the relations of production would be less subject to determination by the forces of production, so the superstructure would develop more independently of the relations of production. Thus, the ideas that, as just noted, could "react back" upon the development of the relations of production were also developing more independently of them, and Guevara assumes that it might be possible to accelerate this development of ideas, to accelerate the transformation of people's "mentality," too.[78] Indeed, developments in Cuba appeared to confirm as much. As Guevara would claim in 1963, "a total change in the consciousness of the masses [has occurred] in a few years of revolutionary work."[79] It is fair to say, therefore, that Guevara rejects to a certain extent the orthodox Marxist view as formulated, for instance, by Trotsky, which holds that "socialism does not aim at creating a socialist psychology as a prerequisite to socialism but at creating socialist conditions of life as a prerequisite to socialist psychology."[80]

While some might regard Guevara's perspective on this question as representing a somewhat voluntaristic position, it would seem more reasonable to view it as a reaction against, and deliberate modification of, an excessively mechanistic version of Marxism, which Engels himself had already warned against in the letters to which I just alluded. Indeed, as Mandel has suggested, what Guevara propounds is best understood as an intermediate position between voluntarism and a rather crudely mechanistic Marxism.[81] In other words, one need not assume that the repudiation of a mechanistic Marxism necessarily entails the embrace of voluntarism. There may be a third alternative, and one can plausibly argue that this is precisely the position that Guevara defends. (Given the very widespread unpopularity, and scant intellectual appeal, of highly mechanistic conceptions of Marxism, one would expect Guevara's critics to welcome his rejection of a mechanistic interpretation of Marxist theory.) To be sure, it may be the case that Guevara's position tends toward voluntarism rather than establishing a simple intermediate position between the two poles of voluntarism and a mechanistic Marxism. Yet, even if that turns out to be the case, his position as regards the creation of a socialist ethos hardly amounts to an instance of extreme voluntarism.

It is my contention, then, that accusations of voluntarism are largely unwarranted in Guevara's case. If I am right, one might reasonably wonder why this accusation against Guevara or, to use a more neutral term, "description" of his thought is as common as it is. There are, I believe, several factors that lead some commentators to substantially overstate the voluntarist tendencies in Guevara's thought. I have already mentioned a couple of relevant factors, such as a tendency to conclude that, in rejecting a rigidly mechanistic understanding of Marxist theory, Guevara must inevitably opt for a variety of voluntarism, or the failure to bear in mind that Guevara believed, rightly or wrongly, that the early 1960s constituted a unique historical juncture with regard to the objective possibilities for revolution. Another factor is the very selective reading of Guevara's works—that is, the tendency to ascribe certain views or positions to Guevara on the basis of a very limited sample of his articles, speeches, and other communications. Even assuming that it is true that, as one commentator argues, "Socialism and Man in Cuba" "emphasises the subjective over the objective," it does not necessarily follow that this is true of Guevara's work as a whole, let alone that we should classify Guevara's Marxism as voluntarist.[82] (It is, incidentally, especially odd to suggest that "Socialism and Man in Cuba" represents a voluntarist outlook, considering that Guevara states explicitly in this essay that "what we must create is the human being of the twenty-first century." Guevara wrote this work in 1965 and was therefore thinking in terms of a social transformation that would take decades—not the sort of timeframe one normally associates with voluntarism.) Yet another factor that leads many to mistakenly conclude that Guevara defends a robust voluntarism has to do with Guevara's insistence on the importance of the moral dimension of social transformation, for to emphasize a "subjective" element such as this will smack of "voluntarism" to many. Finally, we must not overlook the fact that when referring to "revolution" in the sense of "conquest of power" Guevara sometimes uses language that lends itself to a voluntarist interpretation and that this, too, may mislead some readers. In one of his final interviews, for example, Guevara remarks, "But what is most important is not the 'objective conditions' but the subjective conditions—that is, in the final analysis, the determination of the revolutionary movement. The revolution is not an apple that falls when it is ripe! You have to make it fall, and it was precisely this that was our historic role, especially Fidel Castro's."[83] Whether or not this emphasis on the "subjective conditions" amounts to a form of voluntarism in conceptualizing the means of taking power—and Guevara holds, once again, that his view merely represents a rejection of the mechanistic conception of social transformation that, for example, led Latin American Communist Parties to eschew revolutionary actions[84]—it is a mistake to conclude that Guevara holds exactly the same view with regard to the building of socialism following a revolutionary seizure of power.

GUEVARA'S CONTINUING RELEVANCE

The late Fernando Martínez Heredia once described two ways of defending Guevara that in reality render him utterly irrelevant. The first defense consists in maintaining that Guevara was a very good, most selfless, heroic, generous man, and well-nigh inimitable, but one who was a man of the 1960s, and hence of no relevance to history after that period. The other defense holds that Guevara was quite beyond his time—so far beyond it, in fact, that he belongs to a time that has yet to arrive, and indeed will never arrive (the advent of a utopia of solidarity and freedom, the millennium). In short, according to one "defense" it is impossible to detach Guevara from the 1960s, while according to the other Guevara belongs to a time that has no point of contact with our own. Both defenses, or interpretations, of Guevara thus turn him into a figure who is altogether irrelevant to our time.[85]

As should be quite obvious from my remarks throughout this book, I do not subscribe to either of these views of Guevara. I do not believe that Guevara was a utopian thinker whose ideas have no relevance for our world, and neither do I think that Guevara's ideas were only applicable in the 1960s or lack sense when divorced from the framework of that decade. To say that many of Guevara's theses and commitments remain valuable and relevant today, however, is hardly to claim that we can ignore subsequent historical developments in approaching, and attempting to appropriate, Guevara's ideas. The world has changed a great deal since Guevara's death half a century ago, needless to say. The political changes have been immense—for example, the Soviet Union and Soviet Bloc no longer exist, and we associate the great anticolonial movements with an increasingly distant past—and social and cultural transformations have been no less far-reaching: computers and the Internet have revolutionized everyday life, while the "new social movements" (such as the environmental movement, the feminist movement, and the LGBTQ movement) thoroughly reshaped cultural sensibilities. Cuba has of course also undergone momentous changes since Guevara's death. As Pedro Vuskovic and Belarmino Elgueta remind us, Guevara's years in Cuba, from 1959 to 1966, coincided with the revolution's infancy[86]; those years radically transformed the country, but subsequent policy choices and political developments (e.g., 1968's Revolutionary Offensive in Cuba, an increasing dependence on the Soviet Union, the emergence of new national liberation struggles in Africa and Latin America, and the collapse of the Soviet Bloc countries) also led to thoroughgoing transformations of Cuban society.

However, despite the profound changes that have taken place in the world, it is not difficult to find many striking similarities between Guevara's time and our own. Poverty, oppression, domination, social exclusion, exploitation, and massive social inequalities are still commonplace throughout the world. Underdevelopment still exists, as does imperialism. This is, ultimately, the reason why, in spite of the dramatic changes that have occurred in our world and despite the fact that Guevara developed his theories and policies in the midst of a very specific historical process (the title of the first edition of his "collected works," *El Che en la Revolución cubana*, or *Che in the Cuban Revolution*, was quite apt), many of Guevara's ideas remain relevant today. In short, we continue to face most of the problems that Guevara confronted more than fifty years ago, and many of the basic positions and commitments that he advocated in addressing these problems seem eminently sensible today. These positions and commitments include egalitarianism, social solidarity, internationalism, Latin

Americanism, anti-imperialism, dedication to education, and support for an alternative framework for international economic relations. And, not least important, if perhaps less obvious, anticapitalism and revolution. As for anticapitalism, Guevara both warns us against attempts "to build socialism with capitalist motivations," as he puts it in his last published interview,[87] and urges us to be bolder, more ambitious, and more imaginative in thinking about alternatives to capitalism. As for revolution, the fact that Guevara's own theory of guerrilla warfare would oblige him to reject this strategy for contemporary Latin America, as we saw in chapter 3, by no means implies that radical social transformations—in a word, revolutions—are no longer necessary. As Juan Valdés Paz has written in making the case for Guevara's continuing relevance, "in our [Latin] American societies making the revolution tends to be necessary in order to carry out reforms—that is, for the really existing order to be reformed. Hence the premises of mobilizing the masses by means of struggle, supplanting the power of dominant sectors, and confronting American hegemony seem to continue being the conditions of a minimal program for transformation in Latin America."[88] In sum, Guevara's thought is a valuable resource for the theorization of what has come to be called "twenty-first-century socialism."

Of course, to claim that Guevara's thought remains highly relevant to radical social theory today is not to claim that there are no significant omissions in Guevara's works. Like many other important Latin American Marxist thinkers (e.g., José Carlos Mariátegui, Aníbal Ponce, or Ludovico Silva), Guevara died quite young, and during his relatively short life as a major political actor—little more than a decade—he had to devote his time and energy to many different tasks. Consequently, he lacked the time to develop many of his ideas in a systematic manner, and this is one reason that Guevara's writings may appear somewhat inadequate to those who take an interest in contemporary socialist theory. Another reason has to do with the fact that Guevara scarcely addresses a few of the themes that have become the focus of much radical social theory today, and that seem central to the future development of such theory. For example, Guevara says very little about the topic of race. Guevara was, without a doubt, staunchly antiracist; there are several passages in his works, and anecdotes from his life that attest to his concern with racism and adherence to antiracism.[89] (Interestingly, Guevara crossed out the line corresponding to "race" on the form that he filled out for the Cuban armed forces, as though this information were superfluous.[90]) Moreover, as Luis Vitale has observed, Guevara's extensive travels throughout Latin America prior to joining the Cuban revolutionaries probably afforded him an understanding of the interconnections between class and ethnicity that was missing among much of the Latin American left after Mariátegui,[91] and Guevara's own reading of Mariátegui was probably decisive in this regard as well. On the other hand, Guevara praises the great analyst of racism and colonialism Frantz Fanon in his *Apuntes filosóficos*,[92] and Fanon's classic *The Wretched of the Earth* was published in Cuba at Guevara's request.[93] Furthermore, Guevara may have even held some ideas on racism similar to those of Fanon.[94] Still, Guevara's works offer no extended treatment of the theme of race and racism. One finds even less in Guevara on another question central to contemporary radical social theory—namely the question of patriarchy. To be sure, Guevara defends the complete equality of men and women—"women still have to learn that they are just as good [*valen exactamente igual*] as a man in everything"[95]—and expresses the belief that mechanization will eventually eliminate men's physical advantages for some physically demanding jobs.[96] In addition, his conception of the new human being is, despite Guevara's preference for the term "new man"—which is, in any case, quite unremarkable, given the era in which he lived—hardly a distinctively "masculine" ideal: recall that Guevara emphasizes the values of equality and social duty. Yet one finds almost nothing in Guevara's works that deals more directly with the basic questions raised by feminism.

Yet, while these lacunae are certainly significant, what left-wing commentators have most emphasized in considering the "omissions" in Guevara's works is Guevara's lack of interest in the question of democracy, and the mechanisms of "socialist democracy" in particular. We find a typical statement of this concern in Oliver Besancenot and Michael Löwy's *Che Guevara: His Revolutionary Legacy*. "Che Guevara," they write, "never worked out a theory of the role of democracy in the transition to socialism. Perhaps this is the greatest lacuna in his work." They continue, "The main limit of his thought in this area is an inadequate analysis of the relation between democracy and planning."[97] Löwy has faulted Guevara on similar grounds—that is, for not addressing questions about who does the planning and sets priorities, and so on, elsewhere[98]—and others have likewise criticized Guevara for failing to reflect on issues relating to democracy.[99]

It is certainly true that Guevara never offers us more or less systematic statements on the questions mentioned by Besancenot and Löwy, and to this extent one may fairly say that Guevara neglects the question of democracy, and in particular the procedural aspects of a healthy democratic socialism. At the same time, many of Guevara's comments, a few of which were cited in chapter 5, indicate that he was indeed concerned with fostering democractic participation in decision making; "a plan that lacks the participation of the masses," says Guevara in 1961, "is a plan that is always threatened with defeat."[100] Indeed, Besancenot and Löwy themselves, just a few pages after underscoring Guevara's failure to develop the necessary theory of democracy during the transition period, suggest that toward the end of his life Guevara was in fact concerned with the problem of "socialist democracy" and "democratic socialist planning."[101] Furthermore, it seems clear that Guevara was committed to political democracy as he understood it (i.e., in fairly conventional Marxist terms), and he plainly identified socialism with democracy.[102] Perhaps Guevara could have devoted more time and thought to the question of democracy. But given the fact that his very considerable political responsibilities and commitments scarcely left him time to write on other topics he considered of great importance (such as revolutionary strategy, political economy, or guerrilla warfare), and the fact that he died before reaching the age of forty, one could reasonably wonder whether it is entirely fair to take Guevara to task for failing to reflect on questions pertaining to democracy.

"BE LIKE CHE"

During his speech at the mass public tribute to Guevara held in Havana nine days after Guevara's execution, Fidel Castro said, "If we wish to express what we want the men of future generations to be, we must say, 'Let them be like Che!'"[103] Castro's exhortation introduced the phrase that would subsequently become one of the most emblematic slogans of the Cuban Revolution: "Be like Che." At first glance, this slogan may strike us as quite unreasonable, and we might well conclude, as Margaret Randall has observed, that adopting this slogan "raised the bar to unattainable heights."[104] After all, not many people could possibly maintain Guevara's grueling work schedule. Not many could assume so many occupational and political roles with the same facility: Guevara was variously a physician, photographer, soldier, military official, banker, journalist, industrial analyst, government minister, diplomat, military strategist, management theorist, economic planner, and revolutionary theoretician . . . among other things. Not many people could achieve Guevara's self-discipline or commitment to self-improvement. (For example, after the triumph of the Cuban Revolution, Guevara spent about five years studying mathematics,[105] in addition to his wide reading and intensive study in all of the areas in which he assumed official responsibilities—the National Bank, the Ministry of Industries, etc.)

At the same time, there are plainly some ways in which we can and should strive to "be like Che." We can, for instance, adopt the substantive commitments that I mentioned in the previous section and have sought to explain and defend in the present study. To the extent that we do so and succeed in making our actions consistent with our beliefs, we shall not only have demonstrated that it is indeed possible to "be like Che," but will also have contributed, however modestly, to making the world a better place.

Notes

TIMELINE

1. The book appears to have been first published in April 1960, but it is difficult to obtain exact information on the date of publication.

2. The book seems to have appeared in May or June 1964.

3. It is unclear when Guevara left Tanzania, but it was probably in February, or early March, 1966. Accordingly, one cannot say with certainty when he reached Prague, either.

INTRODUCTION

Wherever possible, I have used existing English-language translations of Guevara's works. In a couple of cases I have used two different English-language translations of the same text, either for comparative purposes or because of the need for maximum accuracy in the English rendering of Guevara's words. When the published English translation provides an abridged or otherwise incomplete version of Guevara's original text, I often cite from both the translation and the original, and both sources have been included in the bibliography.

In the case of works that have not been previously translated into English, references are to Guevara's Spanish-language text, and any translation provided, whether in the body of the text or in an endnote, is my own. In citing pieces included in *El Che en la Revolución cubana* and *Escritos y discursos*, I use the titles that appear on the initial page of each selection, for the titles that appear in the tables of contents for these volumes are often inordinately long, as they also contain information bearing on such things as a text's date of publication and, in the case of *El Che en la Revolución cubana*, the location in which a talk took place or a speech was delivered. In any case, since I include the volume number for all of the works from these collections, page numbers make it very easy to locate all of Guevara's Spanish-language texts to which I refer.

Finally, references are given in accordance with the standard conventions for capitalization in the language in which the title is cited.

1. Guevara's full name was Ernesto Guevara de la Serna, but in Spanish-speaking countries only the first surname is used in most contexts. According to Jon Lee Anderson, it was Ñico López, one of the Cuban exiles whom Guevara met in Guatemala in the early 1950s, who first gave him the nickname "El Che Argentino" (*Che Guevara: A Revolutionary Life* [London: Bantam Books, 1997], 129), and this would eventually become simply "Che." The origin of this nickname was Guevara's habitual usage, typical of Argentines, of the expression *che*, which can be roughly translated as "listen," "hey," "man," or "mate," depending on the context.

2. Ambrosio Fornet, "La década prodigiosa: Un testimonio personal," in *Narrar la nación: Ensayos en blanco y negro* (Havana: Letras Cubanas, 2011), 353; see also "Political Sovereignty and Economic Independence," found in Ernesto Che Guevara, *Che Guevara Reader*, ed. David Deutschmann (Melbourne: Ocean Press, 2003), 101.

3. Rafael Hernández et al., "1968: Una mirada retrospectiva," in *Último jueves: Los debates de Temas* (Havana: Ediciones ICAIC and Revista *Temas*, 2010), 4:109; see also Adolfo Sánchez Vázquez's "La gran lección del Che," found in Juan Almeida et al., *Che siempre* (Donostia [San Sebastián], Sp.: Tercera Prensa-Hirugarren Prentsa, S.L., 1997), 123.

4. Fernando Martínez Heredia, "El Che Guevara: Los sesenta y los noventa," in *El corrimiento hacia el rojo* (Havana: Editorial Letras Cubanas, 2001), 244; see also Martínez Heredia's interview by Néstor Kohan, "Cuba y el pensamiento crítico," found in Fernando Martínez Heredia, *A viva voz* (Havana: Editorial de Ciencias Sociales, 2010), 23.

5. "The Che of popular culture is much more a man of action than ideas" (Margaret Randall, *Che on My Mind* [Durham and London: Duke University Press, 2013], 36).

6. *Collier's Encyclopedia*, 1992 ed., s.v. "Guevara, Che."

7. *Merriam-Webster's Collegiate Dictionary*, 10th edition.

8. Randall, *Che*, 47. Fidel Castro describes Guevara in very similar terms in "In Tribute to Che," in *Reminiscences of the Cuban Revolutionary War*, by Ernesto Che Guevara, trans. Victoria Ortiz (Harmondsworth, UK: Penguin Books, 1969), 22; see also Alan Bullock, "Guevara de la Serna, Ernesto (Che)," in *Twentieth-Century Culture: A Biographical Companion*, ed. Alan Bullock and R. B. Woodings (New York: Harper and Row Publishers, 1983), 293.

9. Samuel Farber's recent *The Politics of Che Guevara: Theory and Practice* (Chicago: Haymarket Books, 2016) is a case in point: the book contains no references, for example, to *El Che en la Revolución cubana*.

10. David Miller, ed., *Blackwell Encyclopaedia of Political Thought* (Oxford and Cambridge, MA: Blackwell Publishers, 1991); Tom Bottomore, ed., *A Dictionary of Marxist Thought*, 2nd ed. (Oxford and Malden, MA: Blackwell Publishers, Ltd., 1991). Equally surprising, David McLellan barely mentions Guevara in a chapter on Marxism in Latin America in his authoritative *Marxism after Marx*, 4th ed. (Basingstoke, UK: Palgrave Macmillan, 2007). It is worth noting, on the other hand, that in his anthology *The Marxists* (C. Wright Mills, ed. [New York: Dell Publishing Co., Inc., 1962]), C. Wright Mills did include some brief selections from Guevara (from, among other works, "Notes for the Study of the Ideology of the Cuban Revolution," found in Ernesto Che Guevara, *Che: Selected Works of Ernesto Guevara*, ed. Rolando E. Bonachea and Nelson P. Valdés [Cambridge, MA, and London: The MIT Press, 1969]).

11. See, for example, Michael Löwy, *The Marxism of Che Guevara: Philosophy, Economics, Revolutionary Warfare*, 2nd ed. (Lanham, MD, and Boulder: Rowman & Littlefield Publishers, 2007).

12. See, for example, Mike González, *Che Guevara and the Cuban Revolution* (London and Sydney: Bookmarks, 2004); or see Farber, *Politics*.

13. It is significant that Guevara makes a point of referring to his Marxism in his "farewell" letter to his parents (Ernesto Che Guevara to [His] Parents (1965), in Guevara, *Che Guevara Reader*, 384).

14. From John Gerassi's introduction to Ernesto Che Guevara, *Venceremos! The Speeches and Writings of Che Guevara*, ed. John Gerassi (London: Panther Books Ltd., 1969), 51.

15. In 1997, Fernando Martínez Heredia actually proposed that we pay tribute to Guevara by changing the expression *new man* to *new person* (from his interview with Jesús Arencibia Lorenzo, "Expresión viva de la herejía cubana," found in Martínez Heredia, *A viva voz*, 291).

16. For the earlier development of Guevara's political thought, and particularly in relation to its historical context, see María del Carmen Ariet García, *El pensamiento político de Ernesto Che Guevara* (Mexico City: Ocean Sur, 2010), 15–62.

17. Luiz Bernardo Pericás maintains that Guevara's thought underwent a rapid change between the start of the Cuban Revolution and Guevara's guerrilla campaign in Bolivia (*Che Guevara y el debate económico en Cuba*, trans. Rodolfo Alpízar Castillo [Buenos Aires: Ediciones Corregidor, 2011], 219). Yet Pericás goes on to explain that what changed was the nature of Guevara's Marxism, which was superficial and derivative in January 1959 but had become far more nuanced, dynamic, and "heterodox" by the end of 1966 (ibid.). If this is all that is meant by "changes" in Guevara's political thought, then I do not disagree with Pericás.

18. Vicente R. Martínez Llebrez and Luis. A. Sabadí Castillo, *Concepción de la calidad en el pensamiento del Che* (Havana: Editorial de Ciencias Sociales, 2006), 61.

19. From Guevara's "Speech to Medical Students and Health Workers," found in Guevara, *Che Guevara Reader*, 113; 114.

20. I discuss the criticisms mentioned here in chapters 3 and 5.

21. The only exception would seem to be an article that Guevara published just one week before Castro's momentous announcement—"Cuba: Historical Exception or Vanguard in the Anticolonial Struggle?" found in Guevara, *Che Guevara Reader*, 130. Yet even in this text the identification of the Cuban Revolution with socialism remains somewhat ambiguous.

22. From Guevara's "Working Class and the Industrialization of Cuba," found in Guevara, *Che: Selected Works*, 237ff., 241, 239. Guevara does use the word "capitalist" on page 238 of this essay, but this is the one exception.

23. "Guerrilla Warfare: A Method," found in Guevara, *Che Guevara Reader*, 74–75; 77.

24. "El papel de la ayuda exterior en el desarrollo de Cuba," found in Guevara, *El Che en la Revolución cubana*, 3:81, 96, 99.

25. "Speech to the Latin American Youth Congress," found in Guevara, *Che Guevara Reader*, 232, 234; and see "Notes for the Study of the Ideology of the Cuban Revolution," ibid., 122, 123. The sheer vagueness of the latter essay makes it misleading to say, as does Paco Ignacio Taibo II, that it is Guevara's "first public declaration" of his Marxism (*Ernesto Guevara, también conocido come el Che*, 4th ed. [Barcelona: Editorial Planeta, 1997], 394).

26. To be sure, three months before the declaration, during a January 1961 television appearance, Guevara had stated that "on arriving in the Soviet Union, one senses that it is the place where socialism was born and senses that socialism is a just system" ("Conferencia Televisada," found in Guevara, *El Che en la Revolución cubana*, 3:51). But such a statement hardly amounts to a self-identification with socialism, let alone Marxism.

27. "Memoria Anual 1961–1962," found in Guevara, *El Che en la Revolución cubana*, 6:675. This text is in fact undated but was apparently written in 1962. See also Ernesto Che

Guevara, "Conferencia ofrecida por el Comandante Guevara a los estudiantes de la carrera de Economía de la Universidad de Oriente," *Utopías, Nuestra Bandera* 184, no. 1 (2000): 172.

28. "On Economic Planning in Cuba," found in Guevara, *Venceremos!*, 207, 222, 224; 208; 210.

29. One particularly noteworthy occasion in this regard was the speech Guevara delivered at the United Nations in December 1964 ("At the United Nations," from Guevara, *Che Guevara Reader*, 327; 334. See also Sam Russell, "The Americans Still Want to Come Here," *Daily Worker*, December 4, 1962, 2; and see Guevara's "En relación con la II zafra del pueblo," found in Guevara, *El Che en la Revolución cubana*, 4:63; 64). Incidentally, Fidel Castro would publicly define himself as a "Marxist-Leninist" for the first time on December 1, 1961 (Sergio Guerra and Alejo Maldonado, *Historia de la revolución cubana* [Tafalla, Sp.: Txalaparta, 2009], 191).

30. Fernando Martínez Heredia, *Las ideas y la batalla del Che* (Havana: Ciencias Sociales and Ruth Casa Editorial, 2010), 221.

31. Part of this letter, "A modo de Prólogo: Algunas reflexiones sobre la transición socialista," has been included as a foreword of sorts to Ernesto Che Guevara, *Apuntes críticos a la economía política*, ed. María del Carmen Ariet García (Melbourne: Ocean Sur, 2006).

32. Ernesto Che Guevara, *Congo Diary: Episodes of the Revolutionary War in the Congo* (North Melbourne, Au.: Ocean Press, 2011); Ernesto Che Guevara, *The Bolivian Diary* (Melbourne and New York: Ocean Press, 2006); Guevara, *Apuntes críticos*; Ernesto Che Guevara, *Apuntes filosóficos*, ed. María del Carmen Ariet García (Mexico City: Ocean Sur, 2012). The latter two volumes assemble notes from 1965 to 1967, along with some previously published material and selections from the texts that are the subject of Guevara's notes.

33. Frederick Engels, "Karl Marx's Funeral," in *Marx and Engels Collected Works* (New York: International Publishers, 1989), 24:468.

CHAPTER 1

1. In *The End of the State*, Andrew Levine writes that this transformation "is, of course, psychological" (London: Verso, 1987, 162). Given recent advances in biotechnology, it is surely less obvious today that what one has in mind is a psychological transformation.

2. See Joseph H. Carens, *Equality, Moral Incentives, and the Market: An Essay in Utopian Politico-Economic Theory* (Chicago and London: The University of Chicago Press, 1981), 103–108, and especially the citation from Alfred Kuhn on 104–105.

3. Ibid., 104.

4. The thesis says that the human essence "is the ensemble of the social relations" (Karl Marx, "Theses on Feuerbach," in *Marx and Engels Collected Works* (New York: International Publishers, 1976), 5:4. For a passage in which Marx equates history with "a continuous transformation of human nature," see *Poverty of Philosophy*, 192. For discussion of Marx's view of human nature, see Norman Geras, *Marx and Human Nature* (London: Verso, 1983), and Vernon Venable, *Human Nature: The Marxian View* (London: Dennis Dobson Ltd., 1946).

5. One of the most familiar general statements of this idea appears in the *Communist Manifesto*: "Does it require deep intuition to comprehend that man's ideas, views, and conception, in one word, man's consciousness, changes with every change in the conditions of his material existence, in his social relations, and in his social life?" (Karl Marx and Frederick Engels, *Manifesto of the Communist Party*, in *Marx and Engels Collected Works* [New York: International Publishers, 1976], 6:503).

6. The working class "will have to pass . . . through a series of historic processes, transforming circumstances and men," in the course of "work[ing] out their own emancipation" (Karl Marx, *The Civil War in France*, in *Marx and Engels Collected Works* [New York: International Publishers, 1986], 22:335). See also Karl Marx and Frederick Engels, *The German Ideology*, where the authors write that "the alteration of men on a mass scale is necessary" (in *Marx and Engels Collected Works* [New York: International Publishers, 1976], 5:53).

7. See, for example, Karl Marx, *A Contribution to the Critique of Political Economy, Part One*, in *Marx and Engels Collected Works* (New York: International Publishers, 1987), 29:264; and see Frederick Engels, *Anti-Dühring*, in *Marx and Engels Collected Works* (New York: International Publishers, 1987), 25:270.

8. For example, Georg Lukács writes, "When the forces of production are governed by society in general, this brings about a radical transformation of man and his relation to his labor and to his fellow men" (*The Process of Democratization*, trans. Susanne Bernhardt and Norman Levine [Albany: State University of New York Press, 1991], 156).

9. See *Russian Revolution*, 306, and "The Socialization of Society," 348, both in Rosa Luxemburg, *The Rosa Luxemburg Reader*, ed. Peter Hudis and Kevin B. Anderson (New York: Monthly Review Press, 2004). In the latter essay, Luxemburg argues that socialism actually requires "a complete inner rebirth of the proletarian" (ibid.).

10. See, for example, Herbert Marcuse, *An Essay on Liberation* (Boston: Beacon Press, 1969), especially chapters 1 and 2.

11. Manuel Sacristán helpfully draws attention to this aspect of Lukács's later thought. See "Nota necrológica sobre Lukács," 229, and "Sobre el 'marxismo ortodoxo' de György Lukács," 248, both in Manuel Sacristán Luzón, *Sobre Marx y marxismo: Panfletos y materiales*, ed. Juan-Ramón Capella (Barcelona: Icaria Editorial, S.A., 1983).

12. Levine, *End*, 162.

13. As Levine puts it, "in the sense Rousseau anticipated and Kant made explicit, they [people] must become more moral: more inclined to assess alternative courses of action as pure personalities adopting the standpoint of generality, not empirically distinct selves bent on improving their own positions" (ibid.).

14. Engels, *Anti-Dühring*, 88.

15. C. B. Macpherson analyzes possessive individualism in *The Political Theory of Possessive Individualism: Hobbes to Locke* (Oxford and New York: Oxford University Press, 1962).

16. Germán Sánchez is surely correct in claiming that this "aspect of Che's ethicoeconomic thought . . . has been especially mutilated, distorted, criticized, and treated superficially" (*Che sin enigmas* [Mexico City: Ocean Sur, 2007], 114–15).

17. As Guevara, following convention, uses *hombre* (man) in all of the relevant passages as a term for "human being," use of nonsexist terminology in no way changes the meaning of his ideas (and some of the translations that I shall be using actually do employ inclusive terminology in translating this word into English).

18. N. Bychkova, R. Lavrov, and V. Lubisheva, eds., *Communist Morality* (Moscow: Progress Publishers, n.d.). This anthology contains selections from Marx, Engels, Lenin, Khrushchev, and others. One of the figures referring to the new man most insistently and explicitly is Mikhail Kalinin (see 118, 121–25, and 128–29).

19. See, for example, Randall, *Che*, 36; Delia Luisa López, in Martha Pérez-Rolo et al., "El socialismo y el hombre en Cuba: Una mirada en los 90," *Temas* 11 (1997): 108; and Roberto Fernández Retamar's "Leer al Che," found in his *Cuba defendida* (Buenos Aires: Nuestra América Editorial, 2004), 153. Guevara himself was of the same opinion, according

to Orlando Borrego. After reviewing the seven-volume edition of his works (articles, speeches, interviews, etc.) published in 1966, Guevara remarked that "Socialism and Man in Cuba" struck him as his most finished piece (Orlando Borrego, *Che: El camino del fuego*, 2nd ed. [Havana: Imagen Contemporánea, 2011], 378).

20. From Cathy Ceibe's interview with Fernando Martínez Heredia, "Para el Che, la ética y la política eran inseparables," found in Martínez Heredia, *A viva voz*, 294; and see his interview with Néstor Kohan, "Cuba y el pensamiento crítico," found in *A viva voz*, 23. See also Martínez Heredia, *Las ideas*, 214.

21. See, for example, Adolfo Sánchez Vázquez, "El socialismo y el Che," in *Filosofía, praxis y socialismo* (Buenos Aires: Tesis 11 Grupo Editor, 1998), 116; Ludovico Silva, "El hombre del siglo XXI: La memoria futura del Che Guevara," in *En busca del socialismo perdido: Las bases de la Perestroika y la Glasnost* (Caracas: Editorial Pomaire Venezuela, S.A., 1991), 93; and Fernando Martínez Heredia's "Prólogo: Los apuntes filosóficos del Che," the preface to Guevara, *Apuntes filosóficos*,14.

22. McLellan, *Marxism*, 435.

23. For the one other occasion on which Guevara uses this expression a few times, see "Selección de Actas de reuniones efectuadas en el Ministerio de Industrias: 2 de octubre de 1964," found in Guevara, *Apuntes críticos*, 346 and 347. Considering how seldom Guevara actually uses this term, or expression, it is rather misleading to say that "he wrote a lot about what he called the 'New Man'" (Hilda Barrio and Gareth Jenkins, *The Che Handbook* [London: MQ Publications, Ltd., 2003], 252).

24. For some examples of Guevara's acceptance of this usage, see, for example, "Volunteer Labor," found in Guevara, *Che: Selected Works*, 307; "Delegados en el Congreso Obrero," found in Guevara, *El Che en la Revolución cubana*, 3:514; and "Resumen Plenaria de Industrias en Stgo. de Cuba," found in Guevara, *El Che en la Revolución cubana*, 5:279. I discuss some aspects of Guevara's conception of socialism and communism in chapter 4.

25. See, for example, Maurice Halperin, *The Taming of Fidel Castro* (Berkeley, Los Angeles, and London: University of California Press, 1981), 265; Kelly Ainsworth, "Ernesto (Che) Guevara de la Serna," in *Biographical Dictionary of Marxism*, ed. Robert A. Gorman (Westport, CT: Greenwood Press, 1986), 125; and Gerassi's introduction to Guevara, *Venceremos!*, 42, 45, 46, and 49. By contrast, Löwy (*Marxism*, 18) and Donald C. Hodges (*The Bureaucratization of Socialism* [Amherst: The University of Massachusetts Press, 1981], 165) correctly point out that what Guevara has in mind is a "communist human being."

26. "Socialism and Man in Cuba," found in Guevara, *Che Guevara Reader*, 217.

27. Ibid., 221.

28. Anderson provides this abbreviated title in English; the full Spanish title that he gives is "Socialismo y El Hombre Nuevo en Cuba"—"Socialism and the new man in Cuba" (*Revolutionary*, 636). For Anderson's assumption that Guevara's goal is a "new socialist man," see ibid., 502, 597, and 604.

29. "Socialism and Man in Cuba," found in Guevara, *Che Guevara Reader*, 218.

30. "A modo de Prólogo: Algunas reflexiones sobre la transición socialista," in Guevara, *Apuntes críticos*, 18.

31. "Socialism and Man in Cuba," found in Guevara, *Che Guevara Reader*, 223; see also 227.

32. "En el programa de TV 'Información Pública,'" in Guevara, *El Che en la Revolución cubana*, 5:36.

33. "At the Afro-Asian Conference in Algeria," in Guevara, *Che Guevara Reader*, 341.

34. Carta a León Felipe, 21 de agosto de 1964, in Guevara, *El Che en la Revolución cubana*, 1:452.

35. Andrew Levine argues that "transforming human nature is the central political task for socialist societies in the transition to communism" (*End*, 6). Guevara would agree.

36. For example, Hodges claims that "the essence of the new man is voluntary labor" (*Bureaucratization*, 165), while Pericás argues that the three practices that I mention are the basic aspects of the "idea" of the new man, at least in practical terms (*Che*,168).

37. For a philosophical defense of radical egalitarianism, see Kai Nielsen, *Equality and Liberty* (Totowa, NJ: Rowman and Allanheld, 1985). For an analysis of the principle of equal consideration of interests, see Stanley I. Benn, "Egalitarianism and the Equal Consideration of Interests," in *Equality* (Nomos IX), ed. J. Roland Pennock and John W. Chapman (New York: Atherton Press, 1967), 61–78.

38. For some examples, see the chapter titled "La equidad" in Mayra Mendoza Gil, ed., *Para vivir como tú vives: Anecdotario del Che* (Havana: Editora Política, 2006).

39. See, for example, "In Cuba Imperialism Was Caught Sleeping, but Now It Is Awake," found in Ernesto Che Guevara, *Che Guevara Talks to Young People*, Mary-Alice Waters, ed. (New York: Pathfinder Press, 2000), 66; see also "Conferencia Televisada," found in Guevara, *El Che en la Revolución cubana*, 3:45.

40. "En la primera reunión nacional de producción," in Guevara, *El Che en la Revolución cubana*, 3:394–95.

41. "Graduación del curso de administradores," in Guevara, *El Che en la Revolución cubana*, 3: 556.

42. "Inauguración fábrica de bujías," in Guevara, *El Che en la Revolución cubana*, 5:155.

43. "Youth Must March in the Vanguard," in Guevara, *Che Guevara Talks to Young People*, 128. For other expressions of this idea, see, for example, "On the Budgetary Finance System," in Guevara, *Che Guevara Reader*, 209 and 210; and see "Graduación en la escuela de administradores 'Patricio Lumumba,'" in Guevara, *El Che en la Revolución cubana*, 4:321.

44. "Socialism and Man in Cuba," in Guevara, *Che Guevara Reader*, 225.

45. My understanding of Guevara's reasoning in this connection is indebted to Peter Singer, *How Are We to Live? Ethics in an Age of Self-Interest* (Melbourne: The Text Publishing Company, 1993), ch. 11.

46. The original statement appears in José Martí, "Discurso en el *Liceo Cubano*, Tampa (Con todos y para el bien de todos)," in *Obras Completas*, 2nd ed. (Havana: Editorial de Ciencias Sociales, 1975), 4:270; I cite the translation provided in Löwy, *Marxism*, 24. For some of the passages in which Guevara cites Martí's dictum, see "A Party of the Working Class," in Guevara, *Che Guevara Reader*, 177; "Honoring José Martí," in Guevara, *Che: Selected Works*, 211; "Technology and Society," in ibid., 303; and "Con el periodista uruguayo Carlos Granda," in Guevara, *El Che en la Revolución cubana*, 5:272.

47. "Asamblea de trabajadores portuarios," in Guevara, *El Che en la Revolución cubana*, 4:17; "The Working Class and the Industrialization of Cuba," in Guevara, *Che: Selected Works*, 242. The quoted passage comes from the latter text, which is a speech that Guevara delivered before the Cuban Revolution was overtly socialist.

48. For some relevant texts, see "Volunteer Labor," in Guevara, *Che: Selected Works*, 307; "Youth Must March in the Vanguard," in Guevara, *Che Guevara Talks to Young People*, 128; "Reunión bimestral, febrero 22 de 1964," in Guevara, *El Che en la Revolución cubana*, 6:454; and "The Cadre: Backbone of the Revolution," in Guevara, *Che Guevara Reader*, 157.

49. The term in Spanish, *conciencia*, can mean either "consciousness" or "conscience." Guevara's usage of *conciencia* almost invariably corresponds to "consciousness."

50. See, for example, "Entrega de premios," in Guevara, *El Che en la Revolución cubana*, 5:67; "On Creating a New Attitude," in Guevara, *Venceremos!*, 475 (mistranslated as "conscience");

"Clausura del Consejo de la CTC," in Guevara, *El Che en la Revolución cubana*, 4:137; and "Clausura de la Asamblea de Producción de la Gran Habana," in ibid., 3:456.

51. See, for example, "En relación con la II zafra del pueblo," in Guevara, *El Che en la Revolución cubana*, 4:62; and "Clausura de la Asamblea de Producción de la Gran Habana," in ibid., 3:461.

52. Orlando Borrego, preface to *El Che en la Revolución cubana*, vol. 1. Guevara's countless references to "consciousness" are, incidentally, reminiscent of Lenin's discussion of consciousness in Vladimir I. Lenin, *What Is to Be Done? Burning Questions of Our Movement*, in *Collected Works*, vol. 5 (London: Lawrence and Wishart, 1961), above all chapter 2.

53. "Socialism and Man in Cuba," in Guevara, *Che Guevara Reader*, 217.

54. See, for example, "Asamblea de trabajadores portuarios," in Guevara, *El Che en la Revolución cubana*, 4:17, 19; and "Reunión bimestral, marzo 10 de 1962," in ibid., 6:183.

55. "Memoria Anual 1961–1962," in ibid., 6:689.

56. "Socialism and Man in Cuba," in Guevara, *Che Guevara Reader*, 219.

57. "Entrevista concedida a Jean Daniel en Argelia," in Guevara, *El Che en la Revolución cubana*, 4:469–70.

58. See, for example, Carta a Robert Starkie, 12 de junio de 1961, in ibid., 1:408; "Inauguración fábrica de bujías," in ibid., 5:154; "Tactics and Strategy of the Latin American Revolution," Guevara, in *Che Guevara Reader*, 304; "On the Alliance for Progress," in Guevara, *Venceremos!*, 268; and "El papel de los estudiantes de tecnología y el desarrollo industrial del país," in Guevara, *El Che en la Revolución cubana*, 4:191.

59. Augusto Salazar Bondy, "La quiebra del capitalismo," in *Entre escila y caribdis* (Lima: Instituto Nacional de Cultura, 1973), 155.

60. For two brief commentaries that lend support to this interpretation, see Juan Valdés Paz's "Notas para un epílogo," the epilogue in Manuel Monereo, *Con su propia cabeza: El socialismo en la obra y la vida del Che* (Barcelona: El ViejoTopo, 2001), 124–25; and Delia Luisa López García, "Che Guevara: Una aproximación a su ideario," in *Che: el hombre del siglo XXI* (Havana: University of Havana and Editorial Félix Varela, 2001), 123.

61. See, for example, Frederick Engels, "Principles of Communism," in *Marx and Engels Collected Works* (New York: International Publishers, 1976), 6:342.

62. See, for example, Karx Marx, *The Eighteenth Brumaire of Louis Bonaparte*, in *Marx and Engels Collected Works* (New York: International Publishers, 1979), 11:104, 106; "Moralising Criticism and Critical Morality: A Contribution to German Cultural History; Contra Karl Heinzen," in *Marx and Engels Collected Works* (New York: International Publishers, 1976), 6:319; and *A Contribution to the Critique*, 29:261 and 263.

63. See, for example, Karl Marx, *The Poverty of Philosophy*, in *Marx and Engels Collected Works* (New York: International Publishers, 1976), 6:162, 174, 202; see also *Capital: A Critique of Political Economy, Vol. 1*, in *Marx and Engels Collected Works* (New York: International Publishers, 1996), 35:14.

64. "Debourgeoisification" as used here should not be equated with "proletarianization" (whether understood as the loss of middle-class social status or the conscious adoption of a progressive working-class political outlook), if only because "proletarianization" as conventionally understood occurs within the context of a capitalist economy.

65. "Entrega de premios a ganadores en la emulación de Círculo de Estudios," in Guevara, *El Che en la Revolución cubana*, 4:73–74.

66. "A New Culture of Work," in Guevara, *Che Guevara Reader*, 146. "What we are dealing with here is a communist society . . . just as it *emerges* from capitalist society, which is thus in

every respect, economically, morally, and intellectually, still stamped with the birth-marks of the old society from whose womb it emerges" (Karl Marx, "Critique of the Gotha Programme," in *Marx and Engels Collected Works* [New York: International Publishers, 1989], 24:85, emphasis in the original). "We can only build communism out of the material created by capitalism . . . and which—as far as concerns the human material in the apparatus—is therefore inevitably imbued with the bourgeois mentality. That is what makes the building of communist society difficult" (Vladimir I. Lenin, "A Little Picture in Illustration of Big Problems," in *Collected Works* [Moscow: Progress Publishers, 1965], 28:388; see also his *"Left-Wing" Communism: An Infantile Disorder*, in *Collected Works* [Moscow: Progress Publishers, 1966], 31:50).

67. "Reunión bimestral, diciembre 21 de 1963," in Guevara, *El Che en la Revolución cubana*, 6:423; see also "Socialism and Man in Cuba," in Guevara, *Che Guevara Reader*, 216.

68. For Guevara's commitment to a classless society, see, for example, "Graduación del curso de administradores," in Guevara, *El Che en la Revolución cubana*, 3:553. See also "A los obreros más destacados durante el año 1962," in ibid., 4:336.

69. "In Cuba Imperialism Was Caught Sleeping, but Now It Is Awake," in Guevara, *Che Guevara Talks to Young People*, 65.

70. "Youth Must March in the Vanguard," in ibid., 122.

71. "Discusión colectiva; decisión y responsabilidades únicas," in Guevara, *El Che en la Revolución cubana*, 1:108; see also "Entrega de premios de la emulación socialista," in ibid., 5:240; and "On Economic Planning in Cuba," in Guevara, *Venceremos!*, 220.

72. One of the few commentators to appreciate this is Ludovico Silva. See "El hombre," 101.

73. Marx, *Capital: A Critique of Political Economy, Vol. 1*, 17. I have modified the translation, replacing "receipt" with "recipe." This is the English word used in other translations of this passage, and the nineteenth-century meaning of *"Rezepte,"* the German term used by Marx.

74. "Tasks of Communist Education," in Leon Trotsky, *Problems of Everyday Life and Other Writings on Culture and Science* (New York: Monad Press, 1973), 107.

75. For an influential statement of a Marxist view on this topic, and one first presented around the time that Guevara was developing his ideas, see Isaac Deutscher, "On Socialist Man," in *Marxism in Our Time*, ed. Tamara Deutscher (London: Jonathan Cape Ltd., 1971).

76. Leon Trotsky, *Literature and Revolution*, trans. Rose Strunsky (Ann Arbor: University of Michigan Press, 1960), 256.

77. "To Be a Young Communist," in Guevara, *Che Guevara Reader*, 167.

78. Borrego, *Camino*, 114.

79. "A New Culture of Work," in Guevara, *Che Guevara Reader*, 146; "En el seminario sobre planificación en Argelia," in Guevara, *El Che en la Revolución cubana*, 4:464; Guevara, "Conferencia ofrecida," 155.

80. Farber, *Politics*, xix, 76, and 18. As we shall see, many of Farber's claims regarding Guevara's thought prove wholly untenable. I briefly discuss some of the basic flaws in Farber's account of Guevara's thought in my review of his *The Politics of Che Guevara: Theory and Practice (International Journal of Cuban Studies* 9, no. 1 [2017]: 155–57).

81. This seems to be, for example, what Kenneth Minogue holds in his early commentary on Guevara. Minogue states, correctly, that the new human being will possess "a highly developed social consciousness" but then adds, "This means, presumably, that the category of the private will disappear from his thinking" ("Che Guevara," in *The New Left: Six Critical Essays*, ed. Maurice Cranston [London, Sydney, and Toronto: The Bodley Head, Ltd., 1970], 32). See also Eugenio del Río, "Influencia de Che Guevara en la Europa occidental de los años setenta," in *Disentir, resistir: Entre dos épocas* (Madrid: Talasa Ediciones, S.L., 2001), 27.

82. "Socialism and Man in Cuba," in Guevara, *Che Guevara Reader*, 212; 220.

83. "Only within the community has each individual the means of cultivating his gifts in all directions; hence personal freedom becomes possible only within the community"; and "the real intellectual wealth of the individual depends entirely on the wealth of his real connections" (Marx and Engels, *The German Ideology*, 78 and 51). Jon Elster provides a useful statement of the more general point: "Marx conceived communism as a synthesis of capitalist and pre-capitalist societies, reconciling the individualism of the former and the communitarian character of the latter" (*Making Sense of Marx* ([Cambridge: Cambridge University Press, 1985], 523).

84. Robert M. Bernardo, cited in Miguel Martinez-Saenz, "Che Guevara's New Man: Embodying a Communitarian Attitude," *Latin American Perspectives* 31, no. 6 (2004): 24.

85. Karl Marx and Frederick Engels, *The Holy Family; or Critique of Critical Criticism*, in *Marx and Engels Collected Works* (New York: International Publishers, 1975), 4:130–31; see also Karl Marx, "Critical Marginal Notes on the Article 'The King of Prussia and Social Reform, by a Prussian,'" in *Marx and Engels Collected Works* (New York: International Publishers, 1975), 3:198. For an additional passage in which Guevara claims that personal interest should be a reflection of social interest, see "X preguntas sobre las enseñanzas de un libro famoso," in Guevara, *Apuntes críticos*, 173. Löwy correctly notes (*Marxism*, 19) that the new human being will transcend many of the tensions, or antagonisms (e.g., between particular interests and general interests, or the individual and the community), that we associate with capitalist society.

86. "On Production Costs and the Budgetary System," found in Bertram Silverman, ed., *Man and Socialism in Cuba: The Great Debate* (New York: Atheneum, 1973), 121.

87. Karl Marx, *Outlines of the Critique of Political Economy (Rough Draft of 1857–1858)*, in *Marx and Engels Collected Works* (New York: International Publishers, 1987), 29:91.

88. I discuss this topic in the next chapter.

89. "On Socialist Competition and Sugar Production," in Guevara, *Venceremos!*, 337.

90. Marx and Engels, *Manifesto*, 499; see also 500.

91. Frederick Engels, *Ludwig Feuerbach and the End of Classical German Philosophy*, in *Marx and Engels Collected Works* (New York: International Publishers, 1990), 26:381; *Anti-Dühring*, 87.

92. Marx, *A Contribution to the Critique*, 263–64.

93. Engels, *Anti-Dühring*, 88.

94. See, for example, "Reunión bimestral, septiembre 12 de 1964," in Guevara, *El Che en la Revolución cubana*, 6:521.

95. Ernest Mandel, "El debate económico en Cuba durante el periodo 1963–1964," in *El Gran Debate*, ed. David Deutschmann and Javier Salado (Melbourne and New York: Ocean Press, 2006), 315.

96. Georg Lukács, *Record of a Life*, ed. István Eörsi, trans. Rodney Livingstone (London: Verso Editions, 1983), 172. For one passage in which Guevara also stresses that socialism is a merely "transitory state," see "Selección de Actas de reuniones efectuadas en el Ministerio de Industrias: 2 de octubre de 1964," in Guevara, *Apuntes críticos*, 337.

97. Ibid., 342.

98. See, for example, "On the Budgetary Finance System," in Guevara, *Che Guevara Reader*, 195; and see also "Youth Must March in the Vanguard," in Guevara, *Che Guevara Talks to Young People*, 122. I return to this question in chapter 6.

99. Guevara is, in any case, hardly alone among Marxists in attaching great importance to moral transformation. As the young Lukács wrote, "the transition from the old society to the new implies, *not merely an economic and institutional, but also and at the same time a moral transformation*" (from "The Moral Mission of the Communist Party," found in Georg Lukács,

Tactics and Ethics, 1919–1929, trans. Michael McColgan [London and New York: Verso, 2014], 66; emphasis in the original).

100. Quoted in Andrew Sinclair, ed., *Viva Che! The Strange Death and Life of Che Guevara* (Stroud, UK: Sutton Publishing Limited, 2006), 118.

101. Leopoldo Zea's "El Che y el hombre nuevo," found in Almeida et al., *Che siempre*, 153.

102. For example, Manuel Galich's "Che: Encarnación del hombre nuevo," in ibid., 177; Marta Harnecker's "Marta, viento cálido," an interview by Iosu Perales, found in Iosu Perales, ed., *Querido Che* (Madrid: Editorial Revolución, S.A.L., 1987), 73; Borrego, *Camino*, 225; Carlos Rafael Rodríguez, "Sobre el hombre nuevo," in *Letra con filo* (Havana: Editorial de Ciencias Sociales, 1983), 2:566; and Hilda Gadea's "A Ernesto Che Guevara," found in Almeida et al., *Che siempre*, 173.

103. Francisco Fernández Buey, "Ernesto 'Che' Guevara, ayer y hoy," introduction to *Escritos revolucionarios*, by Ernesto Che Guevara, ed. Francisco Fernández Buey (Madrid: Libros de la Catarata, 1999), 17.

104. Ernesto Che Guevara, "La conferencia de prensa del nueve de agosto en el Playa Hotel," in *Para dar vuelta el mate: 1961, Ernesto Che Guevara en Uruguay*, ed. Asdrúbal Pereira Cabrera (Havana: Editora Política, 2012), 1:350. Orlando Borrego confirms that until the end of 1962, Guevara's workday normally lasted until 2 or 3 in the morning, and some of his colleagues remained at work until Guevara left. In early 1963, mindful of the toll that this routine was taking on him and his colleagues, Guevara proposed that they work no later than *1 a.m.* (Orlando Borrego, *Che: Recuerdos en ráfaga* [Havana: Editorial de Ciencias Sociales, 2004], 17). As Fidel Castro rightly said of Guevara at the massive tribute to Guevara in Havana shortly after his assassination, "for him there were no days of rest, for him there were no hours of rest!" (Castro, "In Tribute," 23).

105. For some examples of this commitment, see Helen Yaffe, *Che Guevara: The Economics of Revolution* (Basingstoke, UK: Palgrave Macmillan, 2009), 71.

106. "Entrega de premios a ganadores en la emulación de Círculo de Estudios," in Guevara, *El Che en la Revolución cubana*, 4:80.

107. "At the Afro-Asian Conference in Algeria," in Guevara, *Che Guevara Reader*, 342.

108. Fidel Castro, "Las ideas del Che son de una vigencia absolua y total," in *El pensamiento económico de Ernesto Che Guevara*, by Carlos Tablada (Panama City: Ruth Casa Editorial, 2005), 85.

109. Guevara, *Bolivian Diary*, 208.

CHAPTER 2

The present chapter incorporates a small amount of material from my essay "'Socialism and Man in Cuba' Revisited," *International Critical Thought* 5, no. 3 (2015).

1. Found in Guevara, *Che Guevara Reader*, 220 and 221.

2. Cited in Ralph Miliband, *Socialism for a Sceptical Age* (London and New York: Verso, 1995), 135.

3. In this connection, see Melvin L. Kohn and Carmi Schooler, *Work and Personality: An Inquiry Into the Impact of Social Stratification* (Norwood, NJ: Ablex Publishing Corporation, 1983). In light of his comprehensive review of the social-science literature on work, Robert E. Lane concludes that "working activities are the best agents of well-being . . . and the best sources of cognitive development, a sense of personal control, and self-esteem available in

economic life, better than a higher standard of living, and, I believe, better than what is offered by leisure" (Robert E. Lane, *The Market Experience* [Cambridge: Cambridge University Press, 1991], 335).

4. John Stuart Mill, *Principles of Political Economy*, in *Collected Works of John Stuart Mill*, ed. J. M. Robson (Toronto: University of Toronto Press, 1965), 2:212.

5. One reason that work is so important to Marxism is that it is centrally connected with equality, community, and self-realization, which are, as G. A. Cohen has pointed out, the "values . . . integral to the Marxist belief structure" (G. A. Cohen, *Self-Ownership, Freedom, and Equality* [New York and Cambridge: Cambridge University Press, 1995], 5).

6. For a classic statement of this view, see Marx and Engels, *German Ideology*, 31–32; see also Engels, *Anti-Dühring*, 277–78.

7. Karl Marx, "On the Hague Congress," in *Marx and Engels Collected Works* (New York: International Publishers, 1988), 23:255.

8. "A New Culture of Work," found in Guevara, *Che Guevara Reader*, 150; see also "Memoria Anual 1963: Conclusiones," found in Guevara, *El Che en la Revolución cubana*, 6:714.

9. Karl Marx, *Outlines of the Critique of Political Economy (Rough Draft of 1857–1858)*, in *Marx and Engels Collected Works* (New York: International Publishers, 1986), 28:530. Guevara describes the way in which work is generally perceived under capitalism as "a sad duty" ("To Be a Young Communist," found in Guevara, *Che Guevara Reader*, 164).

10. "Socialism and Man in Cuba," found in ibid., 220; see also "To Be a Young Communist," found in ibid., 163; "Youth Must March in the Vanguard," found in Guevara, *Che Guevara Talks to Young People*, 128; and "Speech to Medical Students and Health Workers," found in Guevara, *Che Guevara Reader*, 118. For brief statements of Marx's view, see, for example, *Outlines*, 28:530; and "Draft of an Article on Friedrich List's Book *Das Nationale System der Politischen Oekonomie*," in *Marx and Engels Collected Works* (New York: International Publishers, 1975), 4:278.

11. "Socialism and Man in Cuba," found in Guevara, *Che Guevara Reader*, 221–22; see also 220; "The Working Class and the Industrialization of Cuba," found in Guevara, *Che: Selected Works*, 238; and "On Creating a New Attitude," found in Guevara, *Venceremos!*, 469: "what enslaves man is not work but rather his failure to possess the means of production."

12. "Socialism and Man in Cuba," found in Guevara, *Che Guevara Reader*, 219. Guevara was, incidentally, also mindful of the alienation caused by lack of work, a major problem at the beginning of the Cuban Revolution, given the high levels of unemployment in Cuba prior to 1959. In this connection, see, for example, "Encuentro Nacional Azucarero," found in Guevara, *El Che en la Revolución cubana*, 3:108; and "Inauguración 2da. etapa fábrica de alambre de púas," found in ibid., 5:173.

13. As Rosa Luxemburg succinctly puts it, "If we establish in this way a nation of workers, where everybody works for everyone, for the public good and benefit, then work itself must be organized quite differently" ("The Socialization of Society," found in Luxemburg, *The Luxemburg Reader*, 347). For one of Guevara's explicit references to a new organization of work, see "XI Congreso Nacional Obrero," found in Guevara, *El Che en la Revolución cubana*, 3:535.

14. "Reunión bimestral, marzo 10 de 1962," found in ibid., 6:211; "Socialism and Man in Cuba," found in Guevara, *Che Guevara Reader*, 220; see also "Discurso en la inauguración de la planta beneficiadora de caolín, Isla de Pinos," found in Guevara, *Escritos y discursos*, 8:84.

15. See, for example, "Fragmento de la entrevista concedida al periódico *El-Taliah* (*La Vanguardia*) de El Cairo, abril de 1965," found in Guevara, *Apuntes críticos*, 424; and "Reunión bimestral, julio 14 de 1962," found in Guevara, *El Che en la Revolución cubana*, 6:276. For

Marxist statements on the obligation to work, see, for example, Marx and Engels, *Manifesto*, 505; Frederick Engels, "Introduction to Karl Marx's *Wage Labour and Capital*," in *Marx and Engels Collected Works* (New York: International Publishers, 1990), 27:201; Vladimir I. Lenin, "How to Organise Competition," in *Collected Works* (Moscow: Progress Publishers, 1972), 26:414; and Leon Trotsky, *Terrorism and Communism* (Ann Arbor: The University of Michigan Press, 1961), 135.

16. "Sobre las normas de trabajo y la escala salarial," in Guevara, *El Che en la Revolución cubana*, 4:597.

17. "On the Budgetary Finance System," in Guevara, *Che Guevara Reader*, 210; see also 209 and 197.

18. "A los obreros premiados por haberse destacado en la producción," found in Guevara, *El Che en la Revolución cubana*, 3:336.

19. "XI Congreso Nacional Obrero," found in ibid., 3:528–29.

20. "A New Culture of Work," found in Guevara, *Che Guevara Reader*, 146 and 150; "Entrega de premios a obreros más destacados julio," found in Guevara, *El Che en la Revolución cubana*, 4:262; "Volunteer Labor," found in Guevara, *Che: Selected Works*, 308. (the relevant Spanish word is translated here as "necessity").

21. "En la Universidad de Montevideo," found in ibid., 3:336.

22. "On the Budgetary Finance System," in Guevara, *Che Guevara Reader*, 211; see also "The Cadre: Backbone of the Revolution," found in ibid., 157, where Guevara refers to a stage in which "the advance of socialist consciousness begins making work and total devotion to the cause of the people into a necessity."

23. "XI Congreso Nacional Obrero," found in Guevara, *El Che en la Revolución cubana*, 3:535; "On Creating a New Attitude," found in Guevara, *Venceremos!*, 469.

24. "A los funcionarios y empleados del Ministerio de Industrias," in Guevara, *El Che en la Revolución cubana*, 3:480.

25. "To Be a Young Communist," found in Guevara, *Che Guevara Reader*, 161; see also "Inauguración 2da. etapa fábrica de alambre de púas," found in Guevara, *El Che en la Revolución cubana*, 5:155.

26. "Socialism and Man in Cuba," found in Guevara, *Che Guevara Reader*, 220.

27. "On the Budgetary Finance System," in ibid., 199 (emphasis in the original); see also "X preguntas sobre las enseñanzas de un libro famoso," found in *Apuntes críticos*, 170. For discussion of the production norms and, above all, salary scale, see Yaffe, *Economics*, 95ff.

28. Vladimir I. Lenin, "A Great Beginning: Heroism of the Workers in the Rear; 'Communist Subbotniks,'" in *Collected Works*, vol. 29 (Moscow: Progress Publishers, 1965). Guevara's *Apuntes filosóficos*, 236, makes it clear that he was familiar with Lenin's text, but Guevara appears to have first read the essay long after he had himself begun advocating and practicing voluntary labor.

29. Yaffe, *Economics*, 216.

30. The closest thing to an official definition and justification of voluntary labor, the August 1964 communiqué on the subject that Guevara drafted together with three collaborators, does not state that physical labor alone counts as voluntary labor ("On Creating a New Attitude," found in Guevara, *Venceremos!*, 477). Still, Guevara clearly regarded physical labor as the most valuable type of voluntary labor, as the information in the following sentence indicates. In connection with this point, see also Borrego, *Camino*, 115, and Ángel Arcos Bergnes, *Evocando al Che* (Havana: Editorial de Ciencias Sociales, 2007), 169.

31. Tirso W. Sáenz, *El Che ministro: Testimonio de un colaborador* (Havana: Ciencias Sociales, 2005), 234.

32. Borrego, *Camino*, 115.

33. "Youth Must March in the Vanguard," found in Guevara, *Che Guevara Talks to Young People*, 128. For texts in which Guevara remarks that the economic value of voluntary labor is not the important consideration, see "On Creating a New Attitude," found in Guevara, *Venceremos!*, 469 and 474; and "Volunteer Labor," found in Guevara, *Che: Selected Works*, 305.

34. "On Creating a New Attitude," found in Guevara, *Venceremos!*, 480; "Entrega de premios a ganadores de la emulación de Círculo de Estudios," found in Guevara, *El Che en la Revolución cubana*, 4:246.

35. "Reunión bimestral, marzo 10 de 1962," found in ibid., 6:183. For some other statements of the same idea, see, for example, "Volunteer Labor," found in Guevara, *Che: Selected Works*, 305; "On Creating a New Attitude," found in Guevara, *Venceremos!*, 469; and "Entrega de premios a ganadores de la emulación de Círculo de Estudios," found in Guevara, *El Che en la Revolución cubana*, 4:249. Luiz Bernardo Pericás maintains that Guevara initally attached relatively little importance to the "educational" aspects of voluntary labor (as opposed to its economic benefits) but that this changed over time (Pericás, *Che*, 192). This interpretation is, in my view, untenable.

36. "Youth Must March in the Vanguard," found in Guevara, *Che Guevara Talks to Young People*, 128; see also "Entrega de premios a ganadores de la emulación de Círculo de Estudios," found in Guevara, *El Che en la Revolución cubana*, 4:249.

37. "Reunión bimestral, diciembre 5 de 1964," in ibid., 6:563. Elena Díaz and Delia Luisa López are two commentators who rightly point out that voluntary labor is, for Guevara, an expression of nonalienated labor ("Ernesto Che Guevara: Aspectos de su pensamiento ético," in *Pensar al Che*, ed. Alfredo Prieto González [Havana: Editorial José Martí, 1989], 2:191).

38. Marx, "Gotha," 87.

39. "Homenaje a macheteros del MININD," in Guevara, *El Che en la Revolución cubana*, 5:169; "Clausura de la Asamblea de Producción de la Gran Habana," found in ibid., 3:449.

40. "Durante trabajo voluntario en la textilera 'Camilo Cienfuegos,'" in ibid., 4:260; "Our Industrial Tasks," in Guevara, *Venceremos!*, 289.

41. "Reunión bimestral, septiembre 12 de 1964," found in Guevara, *El Che en la Revolución cubana*, 6:522; "Entrega de premios a ganadores de la emulación de Círculo de Estudios," found in ibid., 4:245.

42. The other elements were production, training, and worker emulation ("Entrega de premios a ganadores de la emulación de Círculo de Estudios," found in ibid., 4:235).

43. "Plenaria Nacional Azucarera [b]," in ibid., 4:354 and 360; "Clausura del Consejo de la CTC," in ibid., 3:127. In the same title, see also "Homenaje a trabajadores y técnicos más destacados en el año 1962," 4:422; and "Entrega de premios a ganadores de la emulación de Círculo de Estudios," 4:75.

44. "On Creating a New Attitude," found in Guevara, *Venceremos!*, 476. (This phrase comes from a communiqué written jointly by Guevara and three of his colleagues.) See also Carta a Luis Corvea, 14 de marzo de 1964, found in Guevara, *El Che en la Revolución cubana*, 1:442; "Entrevista a la revista *Economía mundial y relaciones internacionales*," in ibid., 5:117; and "Volunteer Labor," found in Guevara, *Che: Selected Works*, 305.

45. Arcos Bergnes, *Evocando*, 229–30.

46. See, for example, Luis Báez, "No te puedes separar de Fidel," interview by Pedro de La Hoz, in *Como el primer día*, ed. Pedro de La Hoz (Havana: Editorial Letras Cubanas, 2008), 47; Korda [Alberto Díaz Gutiérrez], "La foto que ha recorrido el mundo," interview by Alicia Elizundia, in *Bajo la piel del Che*, ed. Alicia Elizundia (Havana: Ediciones *La Memoria*, Centro

Cultural *Pablo de la Torriente Brau*, 2005), 139; and "Un montón de memorias," found in Fernández Retamar, *Cuba defendida*, 165.

47. "Conferencia en el salón de actos del Ministerio de Industrias," found in Guevara, *El Che en la Revolución cubana*, 5:397.

48. "Fragmento de la entrevista concedida al periódico *El-Taliah* (*La Vanguardia*) de El Cairo, abril de 1965," found in Guevara, *Apuntes críticos*, 431; see also "On the Budgetary Finance System," in Guevara, *Che Guevara Reader*, 194: "In our view, direct material incentives and consciousness are contradictory terms." Elsewhere in the same essay, Guevara refers to "the individualistic way of thinking that direct material incentives instill in consciousness" as "acting as a brake on the development of man as a social being" (ibid., 201).

49. "Socialism and Man in Cuba," found in ibid., 217; see also Ernesto Che Guevara to José Medero Mestre, February 26, 1964, in ibid., 377.

50. "Graduación en la escuela de administradores 'Patricio Lumumba,'" found in Guevara, *El Che en la Revolución cubana*, 4:320; "Entrega de premios a ganadores de la emulación de Círculo de Estudios," found in ibid., 4:70.

51. "On Party Militancy," found in Guevara, *Venceremos!*, 343; "Con los visitantes latinoamericanos," found in Guevara, *El Che en la Revolución cubana*, 4:482; "Reunión bimestral, octubre 12 de 1963," found in ibid., 6:388.

52. Ernesto Che Guevara to José Medero Mestre, February 26, 1964, in Guevara, *Che Guevara Reader*, 377.

53. See also "Graduación en la escuela de administradores 'Patricio Lumumba,'" found in Guevara, *El Che en la Revolución cubana*, 4:320.

54. "Delegados obreros extranjeros asistentes al 1ro. de mayo," in ibid., 4:177; "Graduación en la escuela de administradores 'Patricio Lumumba,'" found in ibid., 4:325; "Discurso en el acto de graduación de la escuela de administradores 'Patricio Lumumba,'" found in Guevara, *Escritos y discursos*, 8:181–82.

55. "On the Budgetary Finance System," in Guevara, *Che Guevara Reader*, 194; see also "Selección de Actas de reuniones efectuadas en el Ministerio de Industrias: 2 de octubre de 1964," found in Guevara, *Apuntes críticos*, 348.

56. "Reunión bimestral, enero 20 de 1962," in Guevara, *El Che en la Revolución cubana*, 6:146; "Selección de Actas de reuniones efectuadas en el Ministerio de Industrias: 2 de octubre de 1964," found in Guevara, *Apuntes críticos*, 371, 348; "Reunión bimestral, febrero 22 de 1964," found in Guevara, *El Che en la Revolución cubana*, 6:438.

57. "Reunión bimestral, enero 20 de 1962," in ibid., 6:146–47.

58. For an explicit statement of this idea, see "A los obreros premiados por haberse destacado en la producción," found in ibid., 3:72–73; see also "Entrega de premios a ganadores de la emulación de Círculo de Estudios," found in ibid., 4:70; and "Selección de Actas de reuniones efectuadas en el Ministerio de Industrias: 2 de octubre de 1964," found in Guevara, *Apuntes críticos*, 370.

59. This is one of the ideas that Guevara emphasizes in "Socialism and Man in Cuba": "As I have already said, in moments of great peril it is easy to muster a powerful response with moral incentives. Retaining their effectiveness, however, requires the development of a consciousness in which there is a new scale of values" (found in Guevara, *Che Guevara Reader*, 217).

60. "Memoria Anual 1961–1962," found in Guevara, *El Che en la Revolución cubana*, 6:689.

61. "Reunión bimestral, enero 20 de 1962," found in ibid., 6:147.

62. "X preguntas sobre las enseñanzas de un libro famoso," found in Guevara, *Apuntes críticos*, 170 and 172.

63. I discuss topics mentioned in this paragraph in chapter 5.

64. Roberto Massari, *Che Guevara: Grandeza y riesgo de la utopía*, 2nd ed., trans. José María Pérez (Tafalla, Sp.: Txalaparta, 1992), 233.

65. See Lenin, "Great Beginning."

66. Guevara makes the same point in "Selección de Actas de reuniones efectuadas en el Ministerio de Industrias: 2 de octubre de 1964," found in Guevara, *Apuntes críticos*, 370.

67. Karl Marx, *Capital: A Critique of Political Economy, Vol. 3*, in *Marx and Engels Collected Works* (New York: International Publishers, 1998), 37:812. John Roemer provides a useful, brief characterization of the Marxist view of self-realization as "the development and application of an individual's talents in a way that gives meaning to life. This is a specifically Marxist conception of human flourishing." He adds that self-realization is "a process of self-transformation that requires struggle in a way that eating a fine meal does not" (John E. Roemer, *A Future for Socialism* [Cambridge, MA: Harvard University Press, 1994], 11).

68. He seems to mean something like "general essential interests," to use one of Albert Weale's characterizations of "needs" (Albert Weale, "Needs and Interests," in *Concise Routledge Encyclopedia of Philosophy* [London and New York: Routledge, 2000], 620), or "urgent rational preferences," to use a formulation provided by Richard Arneson (Richard J. Arneson, "Is Work Special? Justice and the Distribution of Employment," *American Political Science Review* 84, no. 4 [1990]: 1133).

69. "Socialism and Man in Cuba," found in Guevara, *Che Guevara Reader*, 220.

70. "On Creating a New Attitude," found in Guevara, *Venceremos!*, 469.

71. "A New Culture of Work," found in Guevara, *Che Guevara Reader*, 146 and 150. In the original, Guevara uses the word *necesidad*, which can be translated as either "need" or "necessity." Of course, "necessity" suggests an even more vital, critical requirement than "need"; indeed, *Merriam-Webster's Collegiate Dictionary*, 10th edition, defines "necessity" as "an urgent need or desire."

72. Karl Marx, "Comments on James Mill, Élémens d'économie politique," in *Marx and Engels Collected Works* (New York: International Publishers, 1975), 3:227–28.

73. For one of the few occasions in which Guevara refers to work as a nonmoral need, see "Volunteer Labor," found in Guevara, *Che: Selected Works*, 308.

74. Marx, "Gotha," 87.

75. "Reunión bimestral, marzo 10 de 1962," found in Guevara, *El Che en la Revolución cubana*, 6:211; "Acto conmemorativo del asesinato de Antonio Guiteras," found in ibid., 3:192. See also "Youth Must March in the Vanguard," found in Guevara, *Che Guevara Talks to Young People*, 128.

76. "Reunión bimestral, enero 20 de 1962," in Guevara, *El Che en la Revolución cubana*, 6:149.

77. See also "Curso de adiestramiento para funcionarios y empleados del Ministerio de Industrias," found in ibid., 3:229.

78. "To Be a Young Communist," found in Guevara, *Che Guevara Reader*, 164.

79. References to works that discuss these aspects of US policy toward Cuba are provided at the beginning of chapter 5.

80. "To Be a Young Communist," found in Guevara, *Che Guevara Reader*, 163.

81. See Karl Marx, *Economic and Philosophic Manuscripts of 1844*, in *Marx and Engels Collected Works* (New York: International Publishers, 1975), 3:274. Marx discusses estrangement, i.e., "alienation," more generally in 3:270–82.

82. "Socialism and Man in Cuba," found in Guevara, *Che Guevara Reader*, 213.

83. It is perhaps also worth noting here that Guevara acknowledges in an October 1961 talk that "people do not like voluntary labor very much" ("A los funcionarios y empleados del Ministerio de Industrias," in Guevara, *El Che en la Revolución cubana*, 3:480).

84. Incidentally, Lenin seems to agree with the proposition that voluntary labor is "the genuine expression of the communist attitude toward work." He writes, "Communist labour in the narrower and stricter sense of the term is labour performed gratis for the benefit of society . . . voluntary labour . . . it is labour performed without expectation of reward . . . because of a conscious realisation (that has become a habit) of the necessity of working for the common good" (Vladimir I. Lenin, "From the Destruction of the Old Social System to the Creation of the New," in *Collected Works* [Moscow: Progress Publishers, 1965], 30:517). See also Lenin, "Great Beginning," 427; and Lenin, "Report on Subbotniks Delivered to a Moscow City Conference of the R.C.P. (B.), December 20, 1919," in *Collected Works* (Moscow: Progress Publishers, 1965), 30:286–87.

85. "Volunteer Labor," found in Guevara, *Che: Selected Works*, 307.

86. Karl Marx, *Economic Manuscript of 1861–1863*, in *Marx and Engels Collected Works* (New York: International Publishers, 1988), 30:267. Trotsky summarizes the standard Marxist view of the division of labor well when he observes that "the reconciliation of physical and mental labor . . . is the only thing that can lead to the harmonious development of man" ("A Few Words on How to Raise a Human Being," found in Trotsky, *Problems of Everyday Life*, 136).

87. "XI Congreso Nacional Obrero," found in Guevara, *El Che en la Revolución cubana*, 3:547; see also "On Creating a New Attitude," found in Guevara, *Venceremos!*, 470; "Clausura del Consejo," found in Guevara, *El Che en la Revolución cubana*, 3:136; and "A los obreros más destacados," found in ibid., 4:344. In light of passages such as these (and Guevara's commitment to egalitarianism), it makes little sense to claim, as does Samuel Farber, that Guevara "ignored the hierarchical division of labor" (Farber, *Politics*, 67–68).

88. "A New Culture of Work," found in Guevara, *Che Guevara Reader*, 147.

89. Regarding this policy, see "Plan especial de integración al trabajo," found in Guevara, *El Che en la Revolución cubana*, 6:724–25; "Entrega de premios a ganadores de la emulación de Círculo de Estudios," found in ibid., 4:249; and Borrego, *Camino*, 352–53.

90. See, for example, "Reunión bimestral, julio 11 de 1964," in Guevara, *El Che en la Revolución cubana*, 6:511; and "Entrega de premios a ganadores de la emulación de Círculo de Estudios," found in ibid., 4:250.

91. Marx, *Civil War*, 334–35.

CHAPTER 3

1. See, for example, "Cuba: Historical Exception or Vanguard in the Anticolonial Struggle?" found in Guevara, *Che Guevara Reader*, esp. 132–33 and 136–37; "Interview with *Libération*," in Guevara, *Che Guevara Speaks*, 139–40; and "'Pueblo de Bolivia; Pueblos de América' (Una primera proclama inconclusa del Che)," in Guevara, *El Che en Bolivia: Documentos y testimonios: Los otros diarios*, ed. Carlos Soria Galvarro Terán (La Paz: La Razón, 2005), 2:188.

2. "Interview with Jorge Masetti," found in Guevara, *Che: Selected Works*, 364; Anderson, *Revolutionary*, 151.

3. Ernesto Che Guevara, "Cuba Will Continue to Call Things by Their Right Names. Reply to General Assembly Debate, December 11, 1964," in *To Speak the Truth: Why Washington's*

"Cold War" against Cuba Doesn't End, by Fidel Castro and Ernesto Che Guevara (New York: Pathfinder Press, 1992), 147; Ernesto Che Guevara to Fidel Castro, 1965, found in Guevara, *Che Guevara Reader*, 387. One finds a very similar statement in "Inauguración de la INPUD," found in Guevara, *El Che en la Revolución cubana*, 5:205.

4. *Merriam-Webster's Collegiate Dictionary*, 10th edition.

5. Ronald Barker, "Internationalism," in *Dictionary of Theories*, ed. Jennifer Bothamley (London, Detroit, and Washington, DC: Gale Research International Ltd., 1993), 282.

6. Karl Marx, "Inaugural Address of the Working Men's International Association," in *Marx and Engels Collected Works* (New York: International Publishers, 1985), 20:13. The translation of the *Manifesto* included in the English-language edition of Marx and Engels's *Collected Works* uses the words "working men" rather than "proletarians" (Marx and Engels, *Manifesto*, 519). But the word used in the original German version of the *Manifesto* is "proletarians" (*Proletarier*).

7. Monty Johnstone's "Internationalism" entry to Bottomore, *Dictionary of Marxist Thought*, 260.

8. Vladimir I. Lenin, "The Petrograd City Conference of the R.S.D.L.P. (Bolsheviks)," in *Collected Works* (Moscow: Progress Publishers, 1964), 24:160; Vladimir I. Lenin, "The Tasks of the Proletariat in Our Revolution (Draft Platform for the Proletarian Party)," in *Collected Works* (Moscow: Progress Publishers, 1964), 24:75.

9. Vladimir I. Lenin, "Preliminary Draft Theses on the National and the Colonial Questions (For the Second Congress of the Communist International)," in *Collected Works* (Moscow: Progress Publishers, 1966), 31:148.

10. "A Party of the Working Class," found in Guevara, *Che Guevara Reader*, 176; "Conmemoración de la muerte del General Antonio Maceo," found in Guevara, *El Che en la Revolución cubana*, 4:288. A more conventional definition of "proletarian internationalism" is provided by Jozef Wilczynski: "The solidarity of the workers in different countries among whom it is postulated there can be no conflicts once their common interests are clearly perceived and who constitute a single class united by their struggle against the bourgeoisie and imperialism" ("Proletarian Internationalism," in Jozef Wilczynski, *An Encyclopedic Dictionary of Marxism, Socialism and Communism* [Berlin and New York: De Gruyter, 1981], 466).

11. Guevara, "La conferencia de prensa," 350.

12. "En la asamblea de los tabacaleros," found in Guevara, *El Che en la Revolución cubana*, 2:330.

13. Jorge Ricardo Masetti, *Los que luchan y los que lloran, y otros escritos inéditos* (Buenos Aires: Nuestra América, 2006), 82; Guevara, "La conferencia de prensa," 354.

14. See, for example, Guevara's April 1954 letter to his mother cited in Anderson, *Revolutionary*, 142, and his self-identification during his dialogue with a Bolivian army officer shortly before being executed (ibid., 735).

15. Taibo, *Ernesto*, 498.

16. Guevara often refers to himself as a Cuban and/or part of the Cuban people. For a few noteworthy instances of this self-identification, see Guevara, "La conferencia de prensa," 350; Ernesto Che Guevara, Carta a Miguel A. Quevedo, Director de la Revista *Bohemia*, 23 de mayo de 1959, in *Che desde la memoria*, ed. Víctor Casaus (Havana, Melbourne, and New York: Centro de Estudios Che Guevara and Ocean Press, 2004), 210; and Guevara, "Cuba will Continue," 147.

17. "Create Two, Three, Many Vietnams (Message to the Tricontinental)," 357, and "At the United Nations," 336, both found in Guevara, *Che Guevara Reader*.

18. See, for example, Roberto Fernández Retamar, *Entrevisto* (Havana: Ediciones Unión, 1982), 121–22; and see Silva, "El hombre," 93.

19. Sinclair, *Viva Che!*, 184.

20. "Social Ideals of the Rebel Army," from Guevara, *Che Guevara Reader*, 95.

21. "Inmortalidad del Che," Manuel Piñeiro Losada interviewed by Luis Suárez Salazar, from Manuel Piñeiro Losada, *Barbarroja: Selección de testimonios y discursos del Comandante Manuel Piñeiro Losada*, ed. Luis Suárez Salazar (Havana: Ediciones Tricontinental-Simar S.A., 1999), 111. See also Fidel Castro, "Discurso pronunciado por el Comandante Fidel Castro Ruz, primer ministro del Gobierno Revolucionario y primer secretario del PCC, en el Acto Clausura," in *Tricontinental/1966* (Havana: Secretaría General de la O.S.P.A.A.A.A.L., 1966), 156; and see Anderson, *Revolutionary*, 657.

22. Guevara, *Bolivian Diary*, 190; Anderson, *Revolutionary*, 703.

23. See, for example, Anderson, *Revolutionary*, 688 and 709.

24. "At the Afro-Asian Conference in Algeria," from Guevara, *Che Guevara Reader*, 342 and 341; see also 344.

25. Ibid., 347.

26. Guevara, "Conferencia ofrecida," 169.

27. See, for example, "The Philosophy of Plunder Must Cease," from Guevara, *Che Guevara Reader*, 320–21.

28. "At the Afro-Asian Conference in Algeria," found in ibid., 340.

29. José Carlos Mariátegui, *Ideología y política*, in *Mariátegui total* (Lima: Empresa Editora Amauta S.A., 1994), 1:197.

30. "Interview with *Libération*," in Guevara, *Che Guevara Speaks*, 139–40.

31. Anastas Mikoyan, "Más vale ver una vez que escuchar cien," interview by Norberto Fuentes, in *Posición Uno*, by Norberto Fuentes (Havana: Ediciones Unión, 1982), 171.

32. "Create Two, Three, Many Vietnams (Message to the Tricontinental)," from Guevara, *Che Guevara Reader*, 358.

33. See, for example, "Discurso en el acto de graduación de la escuela de administradores 'Patricio Lumumba,'" from Guevara, *Escritos y discursos*, 8:180.

34. Guevara, "Conferencia ofrecida," 180.

35. McLellan, *Marxism*, 259.

36. Vladimir I. Lenin, *Imperialism, the Highest Stage of Capitalism: A Popular Outline*, in *Collected Works*, vol. 22 (Moscow: Progress Publishers, 1964).

37. Guevara, *Congo*, 15.

38. Significantly, Guevara contributed a brief note regretting Baran's passing—as well as an editorial on his death from *Nuestra Industria Económica* (a journal published by Guevara's Ministry of Industries)—to a memorial volume on Baran's life and work (Paul M. Sweezy and Leo Huberman, eds., *Paul A. Baran [1910–1964]: A Collective Portrait* [New York: Monthly Review Press, 1965], 107–108). For Guevara's comments on Baran's *Political Economy of Growth*, see Guevara, *Apuntes filosóficos*, 299–301. For some examples of Guevara's allusions to the concept of dependency theory, see, for example, "The Philosophy of Plunder Must Cease," found in Guevara, *Che Guevara Reader*, 311–12; "A los compañeros argentinos," found in Guevara, *El Che en la Revolución cubana*, 4:216; and "On Creating a New Attitude," found in Guevara, *Venceremos!*, 470.

39. Guevara, *Congo*, 230.

40. Vladimir I. Lenin, "Imperialism and the Split in Socialism," in *Collected Works* (Moscow: Progress Publishers, 1964), 23:115 and 114; emphasis in the original.

41. "X preguntas sobre las enseñanzas de un libro famoso," from Guevara, *Apuntes críticos*, 74.

42. "A modo de Prólogo: Algunas reflexiones sobre la transición socialista," found in ibid., 15.

43. Guevara, "Conferencia ofrecida," 169 and 159. And see "X preguntas sobre las enseñanzas de un libro famoso," found in Guevara, *Apuntes críticos*, 93; see also pages 67, 73, and 96 from this same essay, and "Socialism and Man in Cuba," 215.

44. Ibid., 93. Page 70 of this text contains interesting remarks on the same phenomenon.

45. "Create Two, Three, Many Vietnams (Message to the Tricontinental)," found in Guevara, *Che Guevara Reader*, 362; see also "Entrega de premios a.ganadores en la emulación de Círculo de Estudios," found in Guevara, *El Che en la Revolución cubana*, 4:77; and see "Fidel's Trip to New York," in Guevara, *Che Guevara Speaks*, in which Guevara calls the United States "the most barbaric nation on earth" (22).

46. "Volunteer Labor," found in Guevara, *Che: Selected Works*, 305–6.

47. Ibid., 309.

48. "Tactics and Strategy of the Latin American Revolution," found in Guevara, *Che Guevara Reader*, 299; "Guerrilla Warfare: A Method," found in ibid., 83.

49. "At the United Nations," found in ibid., 337. Bolívar famously remarked, "The United States seems destined to plague us with miseries in the name of liberty" (as cited in George Black, *The Good Neighbor: How the United States Wrote the History of Central America and the Caribbean* [New York: Pantheon Books, 1988], 71).

50. "Inauguración de la INPUD," found in Guevara, *El Che en la Revolución cubana*, 5:206; "Discurso en el Banco Nacional," found in Guevara, *Escritos y discursos*, 4:66.

51. Lenin, *Imperialism*, 298.

52. Ernesto Che Guevara to [His] Parents, found in Guevara, *Che Guevara Reader*, 384.

53. "Guerrilla Warfare: A Method," found in ibid., 73; see also "Tactics and Strategy of the Latin American Revolution," found in ibid., 297.

54. "En la Universidad de Montevideo," found in Guevara, *El Che en la Revolución cubana*, 3:339–40.

55. "Presentación del número especial de la revista *Tricontinental* dedicada a Ernesto Che Guevara, el 27 de septiembre de 1997," in Piñeiro Losada, *Barbarroja*, 106; William Gálvez Rodríguez, *El guerrillero heroico: Che en Bolivia* (Arrigorriaga, Sp.: Status Ediciones, S.L., 2003), 332; Oliver Besancenot and Michael Löwy, *Che Guevara: His Revolutionary Legacy*, trans. James Membrez (New York: Monthly Review Press, 2009), 64; and Néstor Kohan, "Por la revolución mundial" (http://www.rebelion.org/noticia.php?id=124579). Guevara apparently wrote this essay in the fall of 1966.

56. "Create Two, Three, Many Vietnams (Message to the Tricontinental)," found in Guevara, *Che Guevara Reader*, 358; see also Guevara's remarks in Eduardo Galeano, "El Che Guevara: Cuba como vitrina o catapulta," in *Nosotros decimos no: Crónicas (1963/1988)* (Madrid: Siglo XXI de España Editores, S.A., 1989), 60. For Guevara's reasons for holding that peaceful methods of struggle are likely to prove ineffective in Latin America, see "Tactics and Strategy of the Latin American Revolution," found in Guevara, *Che Guevara Reader*, 295–98.

57. Löwy, *Marxism*, 67. Elsewhere in the same text Löwy attributes to Guevara a "deep and unshakable conviction that only the road of armed struggle can lead to the emancipation of the oppressed peoples of Latin America (and of the whole world)" (79).

58. "Discurso a las milicias en Pinar del Río," found in Guevara, *Escritos y discursos*, 5:77; Deena Stryker, *Cuba 1964: When the Revolution Was Young* (Lexington, KY: Big Picture Publishers, 2013), 171.

59. "Discurso a las milicias en Pinar del Río," found in Guevara, *Escritos y discursos*, 5:77.

60. "The Philosophy of Plunder Must Cease," found in Guevara, *Che Guevara Reader*, 312; "Inauguración de la planta de sulfometales 'Patricio Lumumba,'" found in Guevara, *El Che en la Revolución cubana*, 3:490.

61. "Discurso a las milicias en Pinar del Río," found in Guevara, *Escritos y discursos*, 5:74; "Inauguración combinado industrial de Santiago de Cuba," found in Guevara, *El Che en la Revolución cubana*, 5:295; and "Inauguración de la planta de sulfometales 'Patricio Lumumba,'" found in ibid., 3:489.

62. "Faced with the dilemma of choosing between the people or imperialism, the weak national bourgeoisies choose imperialism and definitively betray their country. In this part of the world the possibility is almost totally gone for there to be a peaceful transition to socialism" ("A Party of the Working Class," found in Guevara, *Che Guevara Reader*, 170).

63. "Guerrilla Warfare: A Method," found in ibid., 82; see also Guevara, *Congo*, 235.

64. "Inauguración de la INPUD," found in Guevara, *El Che en la Revolución cubana*, 5:205. In his 1962 essay "Tactics and Strategy of the Latin American Revolution," Guevara actually goes so far as to say that "we must follow the road of liberation even though it may cost millions of atomic war victims" (found in Guevara, *Che Guevara Reader*, 304). This essay was first published after Guevara's death, in 1968. It is worth bearing this in mind, along with the fact that, as Rolando E. Bonachea and Nelson P. Valdés point out, "according to the Cuban government this article was written during the missile crisis of October 1962" (unnumbered editorial footnote in Guevara, *Che: Selected Works*, 77).

65. "Cuba: Historical Exception or Vanguard in the Anticolonial Struggle?" found in Guevara, *Che Guevara Reader*, 142; "Mobilizing the Masses for the Invasion," found in Guevara, *Che Guevara Speaks*, 34. See also "Inauguración de la planta de sulfometales 'Patricio Lumumba,'" found in Guevara, *El Che en la Revolución cubana*, 3:490.

66. "Asamblea de trabajadores portuarios," found in ibid., 4:8; "Inauguración combinado industrial de Santiago de Cuba," found in ibid., 5:295; "At the Afro-Asian Conference in Algeria," found in Guevara, *Che Guevara Reader*, 349.

67. This slogan is part of the title of the English translation that I cite ("Create Two, Three, Many Vietnams [Message to the Tricontinental]"), but in the original Spanish version of the essay it appears below the title, in the space where one would normally place an epigraph.

68. "Create Two, Three, Many Vietnams (Message to the Tricontinental)," found in Guevara, *Che Guevara Reader*, 358.

69. See, for example, "Inauguración fábrica de bujías," found in Guevara, *El Che en la Revolución cubana*, 5:155 and 156; "Mobilizing the Masses for the Invasion," found in Guevara, *Che Guevara Speaks*, 33; "Inauguración de la escuela de capacitación técnica para obreros," found in Guevara, *El Che en la Revolución cubana*, 4:87; and Russell, "Americans," 2.

70. "Asamblea de trabajadores portuarios," found in Guevara, *El Che en la Revolución cubana*, 4:8.

71. "Inauguración combinado industrial de Santiago de Cuba," found in ibid., 5:295 and 296; "Create Two, Three, Many Vietnams (Message to the Tricontinental)," found in Guevara, *Che Guevara Reader*, 360; "Interview with Josie Fanon," found in Guevara, *Che: Selected Works*, 401.

72. Found in Guevara, *Che Guevara Reader*, 225.

73. One might recall in this connection Max Weber's observation from a century ago: in politics, Weber remarked, "it is *not* true that good can follow only from good and evil only from evil, but that often the opposite is true" (Max Weber, "Politics as a Vocation," in *From*

Max Weber: Essays in Sociology, trans. and ed. H. H. Gerth and C. Wright Mills [New York: Oxford University Press, 1946], 123; emphasis in the original; see also 121).

74. "Conferencia en Dar-Es-Salam," found in Guevara, *El Che en la Revolución cubana*, 5: 355; "Conferencia en el salón de actos del Ministerio de Industrias," found in ibid., 5:388.

75. Ibid., 388. One commentator who rightly underscores this consideration is Manuel Monereo, in *Con su propia cabeza*, 36.

76. Löwy, *Marxism*, 100.

77. According to Harry Villegas Tamayo, "Pombo," who had been one of Guevara's bodyguards and fought with him in both the Congo and Bolivia, Guevara criticized Debray's rendering of the foco theory (contained in Debray's *Revolution in the Revolution?*) at length in Bolivia. The notebooks in which Villegas recorded Guevara's comments were kept by the Bolivian Army (Néstor Kohan, *De ingenieros al Che: Ensayos sobre el marxismo argentino y latinoamericano* [Buenos Aires: Editorial Biblos, 2000], 273, n. 63).

78. "The Essence of Guerrilla Struggle," in Guevara, *Che Guevara Reader*, 64.

79. "Conferencia Televisada," found in Guevara, *El Che en la Revolución cubana*, 3:43.

80. Guevara, *Congo*, 235.

81. "Guerrilla Warfare: A Method," found in Guevara, *Che Guevara Reader*, 80.

82. Ibid., 78–79. Guevara presents similar arguments, citing the first two of these considerations, in "Tactics and Strategy of the Latin American Revolution," found in ibid., 302.

83. "Communiqué No. 5 to the Bolivian Miners," in Guevara, *Bolivian Diary*, 276.

84. Bertrand Russell, "Peace through Resistance to U.S. Imperialism," in *Readings in U.S. Imperialism*, ed. K. T. Fann and Donald C. Hodges (Boston: Porter Sargent Publisher, 1971), xvi.

85. For an impassioned denunciation of the barbarism of imperialism, see, in addition to the "Message to the Tricontinental," "Inauguración combinado industrial de Santiago de Cuba," found in Guevara, *El Che en la Revolución cubana*, 5:293.

86. Taibo, *Ernesto*, 619.

87. "The Essence of Guerrilla Struggle," found in Guevara, *Che Guevara Reader*, 65. In a similar vein, Guevara writes in *Guerrilla Warfare* that the "guerilla fighter" only "initiates the fight" "once peaceful means are exhausted" (Ernesto Che Guevara, *Guerrilla Warfare*, trans. J. P. Morray [New York: Vintage Books, 1961], 32).

88. "The Essence of Guerrilla Struggle," in Guevara, *Che Guevara Reader*, 65.

89. K. S. Karol, "Why Quadros Fell," *New Statesman*, September 1, 1961, 265.

90. "The Essence of Guerrilla Struggle," in Guevara, *Che Guevara Reader*, 67; Guevara, *Congo*, 216; "The Cuban Revolution's Influence in Latin America," found in Guevara, *Che Guevara Reader*, 283.

91. Ernesto Che Guevara, "Qué es un 'guerrillero,'" in *Obras 1957–1967* (Havana: Casa de Las Américas, 1970), 1:156.

92. Monereo, *Con su propia cabeza*, 49–50, 114. One place in which Guevara refers to the increasing popularity of socialist ideas is his account of his intervention in the Congo: "We are strongly assisted by the present conditions of humanity, the development of socialist ideas" (Guevara, *Congo*, 237).

93. "Reunión bimestral, enero 20 de 1962," found in Guevara, *El Che en la Revolución cubana*, 6:149.

94. Monereo, *Con su propia cabeza*, 49–50; Daniel Bensaïd's "Che: A Thinker of Acts," afterword to Besancenot and Löwy, *Che Guevara*, 116; John Gerassi's introduction to Guevara, *Venceremos!*, 45, 50.

95. "Cuba: Historical Exception or Vanguard in the Anticolonial Struggle?" found in Guevara, *Che Guevara Reader*, 138–39.

96. "A los compañeros argentinos," found in Guevara, *El Che en la Revolución cubana*, 4:220; "At the Afro-Asian Conference in Algeria," found in Guevara, *Che Guevara Reader*, 340.

97. "Guerrilla Warfare: A Method," found in ibid., 74.

98. Ibid., 70.

99. Armando Hart Dávalos's "El Che: Una cultura de liberación," found in Almeida et al., *Che siempre*, 14. Hart wrote this essay in the late 1990s.

CHAPTER 4

1. Sinclair, *Viva Che!*, 114.

2. Francisco Fernández Buey's preface to Monereo, *Con su propia cabeza*, 11.

3. The position that I criticize here has recently been defended by Samuel Farber, who maintains that Guevara's "theory of guerrilla warfare and the conditions to conduct this kind of struggle" is his "most significant contribution to revolutionary thought and practice" (*Politics*, 36).

4. "A New Culture of work," found in Guevara, *Che Guevara Reader*, 145.

5. For example, see Guevara's "On the Concept of Value," found in Silverman, *Man and Socialism in Cuba*, 237; "En la Universidad de Montevideo," found in Guevara, *El Che en la Revolución cubana*, 3:339–40; "On the Alliance for Progress," found in Guevara, *Venceremos!*, 268; Guevara's "The Meaning of Socialist Planning," found in Silverman, *Man and Socialism in Cuba*, 100–101; and "El papel de los estudiantes de tecnología y el desarrollo industrial del país," found in Guevara, *El Che en la Revolución cubana*, 4:191.

6. "At the Afro-Asian Conference in Algeria," found in Guevara, *Che Guevara Reader*, 342 (*hombre*—"man"—is translated here as "human being").

7. "Entrega de premios de la emulación socialista," found in Guevara, *El Che en la Revolución cubana*, 5:252; "Graduación en la escuela de administradores 'Patricio Lumumba,'" found in ibid., 4:320; "Reunión bimestral, septiembre 28 de 1962," in ibid., 6:317.

8. See, for example, Carta a Robert Starkie, 12 de junio de 1961, found in ibid., 1:408; "Inauguración fábrica de bujías," found in ibid., 5:154; and Ernesto Che Guevara to José Medero Mestre, February 26, 1964, found in Guevara, *Che Guevara Reader*, 377.

9. "On Economic Planning in Cuba," found in Guevara, *Venceremos!*, 222 ("consciousness" is translated as "conscience"); "X preguntas sobre las enseñanzas de un libro famoso," found in Guevara, *Apuntes críticos*, 142.

10. "Reunión bimestral, febrero 22 de 1964," found in Guevara, *El Che en la Revolución cubana*, 6:436; "Selección de Actas de reuniones efectuadas en el Ministerio de Industrias: 2 de octubre de 1964," found in Guevara, *Apuntes críticos*, 370.

11. "Reunión bimestral, febrero 22 de 1964," found in Guevara, *El Che en la Revolución cubana*, 6:453. Guevara's remarks are reminiscent of a passage from the young Lukács: "The ultimate objective of communism is the construction of a society in which freedom of morality will take the place of legal compulsion in the regulation of all behaviour" (see "The Role of Morality in Communist Production," found in Lukács, *Tactics and Ethics*, 48).

12. "On Production Costs and the Budgetary System," found in Silverman, *Man and Socialism in Cuba*, 121; see also "Selección de Actas de reuniones efectuadas en el Ministerio de Industrias: 2 de octubre de 1964," found in Guevara, *Apuntes críticos*, 337.

13. "On the Budgetary Finance System," found in Guevara, *Che Guevara Reader*, 211; "Selección de Actas de reuniones efectuadas en el Ministerio de Industrias: 2 de octubre de 1964," found in Guevara, *Apuntes críticos*, 363; "Sobre las normas de trabajo y la escala salarial," found in Guevara, *El Che en la Revolución cubana*, 4:600; "Asamblea de trabajadores portuarios," found in ibid., 4:16.

14. See, for example, "Graduación en la escuela de administradores 'Patricio Lumumba,'" found in ibid., 4:320; "Inauguración de la fábrica de galletas 'Albert Kuntz,'" found in ibid., 4:4; "Entrega de premios de la emulación socialista," found in ibid., 5:251; "On Production Costs and the Budgetary System," found in Silverman, *Man and Socialism in Cuba*, 121; and "The Cuban Economy: Its Past and Its Present Importance," found in Guevara, *Che: Selected Works*, 145.

15. I borrow this distinction from Cohen, *Self-Ownership*, introduction and chapter 5.

16. "Discurso en la inauguración de la planta beneficiadora de caolín, Isla de Pinos," found in Guevara, *Escritos y discursos*, 8:84.

17. "Technology and Society," found in Guevara, *Che: Selected Works*, 299; "Delegados en el Congreso Obrero," found in Guevara, *El Che en la Revolución cubana*, 3:514; Carta a Luis Corvea, 14 de marzo de 1964, found in ibid., 1:442.

18. Farber, *Politics*, 77–78; see also 11 and 118.

19. Ibid., 78. Hodges also seems to defend this view in *Bureaucratization* (161ff.).

20. Marx, "Gotha," 87.

21. For example, "Sobre las normas de trabajo y la escala salarial," found in Guevara, *El Che en la Revolución cubana*, 4:599; "Graduación de 400 alumnos de las escuelas populares," found in ibid., 4:549; "Delegados en el Congreso Obrero," found in ibid., 3:514; "Clausura de la Asamblea de Producción de la Gran Habana," found in ibid., 3:455; "A los obreros más destacados durante el año 1962," found in ibid., 4:341; and "Entrega de premios de la emulación socialista," found in ibid., 5:70.

22. Farber, *Politics*, 78.

23. Ernesto Che Guevara to [His] Children (1965), in Guevara, *Che Guevara Reader*, 383.

24. "The Sin of the Revolution," in Guevara, *Venceremos!*, 191; Guevara, "La conferencia de prensa," 349.

25. Löwy, *Marxism*, xxviii.

26. Marx, *Civil War*, 328.

27. "The Cuban Revolution's Influence in Latin America," found in Guevara, *Che Guevara Reader*, 284.

28. "Cuba: Historical Exception or Vanguard in the Anticolonial Struggle?" found in ibid., 136; emphasis in the original.

29. "A los compañeros argentinos," found in Guevara, *El Che en la Revolución cubana*, 4:217.

30. "Conferencia Televisada," found in ibid., 3:43–44; see also "Inauguración de la IN-PUD," found in ibid., 5:206; and see "Cuba: Historical Exception or Vanguard in the Anticolonial Struggle?" found in Guevara, *Che Guevara Reader*, 141.

31. "En la visita del Gral. Líster," in Guevara, *El Che en la Revolución cubana*, 3:207. In fact, Guevara "never tired of telling his Cuban comrades that in Guatemala Arbenz had fallen because he had not purged his armed forces of disloyal elements" (Anderson, *Revolutionary*, 389).

32. There seem to have been slightly over fifty executions while Guevara was in charge of the military tribunals (Yaffe, *Economics*, 292–93, n. 5; and Felipa de las Mercedes Suárez Ra-

mos, "Tribunales revolucionarios: Monumento a la justicia," *Trabajadores*, January 19, 2014, http://www.trabajadores.cu/20140119/tribunales-revolucionarios-monumento-la-justicia/). The far higher estimates for the number of executions in 1959 that one finds, for example, in Anderson's biography of Guevara (*Revolutionary*, 419) and Lars Schoultz's more recent *That Infernal Little Cuban Republic: The United States and the Cuban Revolution* ([Chapel Hill: The University of North Carolina Press, 2009], 87) presumably refer to Cuba as a whole.

33. "En respaldo de la Declaración de La Habana," in Guevara, *El Che en la Revolución cubana*, 2:334; "Entrevista en el INRA," in ibid., 2:116. According to Carlos Franqui, a national survey conducted at the time of the tribunals found that more than 90 percent of Cubans approved of the trials and executions (Taibo, *Ernesto*, 344).

34. Guevara, "Cuba Will Continue," 152. Elsewhere Guevara emphasizes that the executions in the immediate aftermath of the rebels' triumph were "done openly before the public opinion of the continent and with a clear conscience" ("The OAS Conference at Punta del Este," in Guevara, *Che Guevara Reader*, 252).

35. "Guerrilla Warfare: A Method," found in ibid., 76.

36. See, for example, "On Economic Planning in Cuba," found in Guevara, *Venceremos!*, 223.

37. "Fidel's Trip to New York," found in Guevara, *Che Guevara Speaks*, 21; "Acto en el Palacio de los Sindicatos de la URSS," found in Guevara, *El Che en la Revolución cubana*, 2:419; "Interview with Laura Bergquist (#1)," found in Guevara, *Che: Selected Works*, 387. Guevara summarizes his general thesis concisely in a speech delivered in August 1961: "It is an agrarian, antifeudal, and anti-imperialist revolution that under the imperatives of its internal evolution and of the external aggressions became transformed into a socialist revolution and that declares itself as such before all the Americas: a socialist revolution" ("The OAS Conference at Punta del Este," found in Guevara, *Che Guevara Reader*, 251).

38. "Guerrilla Warfare: A Method," in ibid., 76. The view that Guevara defends is vividly expressed by Rosa Luxemburg, who refers to "the basic lesson of every great revolution, the law of its being, which decrees: either the revolution must advance at a rapid, stormy, and resolute tempo, break down all barriers with an iron hand and place its goals ever farther ahead, or it is quite soon thrown backward behind its feeble point of departure and suppressed by counter-revolution" (*Russian Revolution*, 287; see also 289).

39. Masetti, *Los que luchan*, 129.

40. Guevara, *Guerrilla Warfare*, 34–35; see also "Speech to the Latin American Youth Congress," found in Guevara, *Che Guevara Reader*, 233; and see "What We Have Learned and What We Have Taught," found in ibid., 61–62.

41. Ibid., 62; and see "Discurso en el Banco Nacional," found in Guevara, *Escritos y discursos*, 4:61.

42. "Memoria Anual 1961–1962," found in Guevara, *El Che en la Revolución cubana*, 6:674.

43. "Speech to the Latin American Youth Congress," found in Guevara, *Che Guevara Reader*, 234; see also 232.

44. "Entrevista con estudiantes norteamericanos," in Guevara, *El Che en la Revolución cubana*, 4:473; see also "Con los visitantes," 490 and "At the Afro-Asian Conference in Algeria," found in Guevara, *Che Guevara Reader*, 342.

45. In what follows, I shall be referring to some of Guevara's own comments that confirm as much. But many of the works that deal with Guevara's life prior to the Cuban Revolution demonstrate that he had a Marxist, communist outlook before he first set foot in Cuba. Jon

Lee Anderson's biography of Guevara, for example, makes this very clear; see, for example, Anderson, *Revolutionary*, 156, 166, 172, 181, 191, 198, 202, and 565.

46. Cited in Gálvez Rodríguez, *Che en Cuba*, 293.

47. "Discurso en Minas del Frío," found in Guevara, *Escritos y discursos*, 7:57; "Interview with Laura Bergquist (#2)," found in Guevara, *Che: Selected Works*, 398.

48. I cite from the English transcript prepared by Walter Lippmann and available at http://www.walterlippmann.com/che-032264.html. The audio of the interview, apparently in the form in which it aired in March 1964, complete with English voiceover translation, is available at https://www.youtube.com/watch?v=I3wAQG6HUGQ.

49. The joke has a number of different variants. Guevara himself tells the joke during an August 1963 meeting with Latin American visitors to Cuba ("Con los visitantes latinoamericanos," found in Guevara, *El Che en la Revolución cubana*, 4:485).

50. "Notes for the Study of the Ideology of the Cuban Revolution," found in Guevara, *Che Guevara Reader*, 122.

51. Guevara, Carta a Miguel A. Quevedo, 210. When asked during a television interview less than a month earlier whether he was a communist, Guevara responded, "If you think that what we do for the people is communism, then we are communists; if you ask me if I am a member of the Partido Socialista Popular [Cuba's Communist Party], then I would answer no" ("Interview by Telemundo Televisión," found in Guevara, *Che: Selected Works*, 377).

52. Gerónimo Álvarez Batista, *Che: Una nueva batalla* (Havana: Editorial Pablo de la Torriente, 1994), 108.

53. "Tactics and Strategy of the Latin American Revolution," found in Guevara, *Che Guevara Reader*, 303; "A los compañeros argentinos," found in Guevara, *El Che en la Revolución cubana*, 4:218; "Cuba: Historical Exception or Vanguard in the Anticolonial Struggle?" found in Guevara, *Che Guevara Reader*, 136; "Entrevista para la televisión suiza," in Guevara, *El Che en la Revolución cubana*, 5:124.

54. "The Cuban Revolution's Influence in Latin America," found in Guevara, *Che Guevara Reader*, 276; "The OAS Conference at Punta del Este," found in ibid., 273; "Interview by Telemundo Televisión," found in Guevara, *Che: Selected Works*, 378; "Graduación del primer grupo de soldados," found in Guevara, *El Che en la Revolución cubana*, 2:34.

55. For Guevara's responses, see Guevara, "Cuba Will Continue," 146 and 153; and see Guevara, Interview with *Face the Nation*, CBS Television Network, December 13, 1964, transcript available online at https://guevaristas.org/2016/07/15/interview-of-che-guevara-on-cbs-face-the-nation-transcriptvideo/.

56. Guevara, "Cuba Will Continue," 146.

57. "The OAS Conference at Punta del Este," found in Guevara, *Che Guevara Reader*, 273; see also Guevara, "La conferencia de prensa," 349. For a statement in favor of noninterference from the period in which Guevara did not yet openly acknowledge his Marxism, see "Entrevista con un periodista de Guatemala," found in Guevara, *El Che en la Revolución cubana*, 2:132.

58. Fernando López Muiño, "Vivencias con el Che: Viaje desde Cuba a Punta del Este," in *El debut continental de un estadista: Ernesto Che Guevara en Punta del Este, 1961*, ed. Carlos D. González Torres (Havana: Editora Política, 2001), 49.

59. This is the criterion mentioned by William Gálvez, a general in the Cuban military and author of several books on Guevara (William Gálvez Rodríguez, "Um exemplo superior," interview by Viriato Teles, in *A utopia segundo Che Guevara*, by Viriato Teles (Porto: Campo das Letras, 2005), 161–62.

60. "Discurso en el acto de graduación de la escuela de administradores 'Patricio Lumumba,'" found in Guevara, *Escritos y discursos*, 8:183.

61. "Reunión bimestral, enero 20 de 1962," found in Guevara, *El Che en la Revolución cubana*, 6:148.

62. "A los ganadores de la emulación de alfabetización," found in ibid., 3:500.

63. Monereo, *Con su propia cabeza*, 33.

64. Guevara's "The Meaning of Socialist Planning," found in Silverman, *Man and Socialism in Cuba*, 103; see also 101.

65. Guevara, *Congo*, 236.

66. Hal Draper, *The "Dictatorship of the Proletariat" from Marx to Lenin* (New York: Monthly Review Press, 1987), 26.

67. Harold J. Laski, *Harold J. Laski on the Communist Manifesto* (New York: New American Library, 1967), 64.

68. "A los obreros más destacados durante el año 1962," found in Guevara, *El Che en la Revolución cubana*, 4:336.

69. See, for example, "Informe de la Empresa Consolidada de la Electricidad," found in ibid., 6:53.

70. "Clausura del Consejo de la CTC," found in ibid., 4:122.

71. See "X preguntas sobre las enseñanzas de un libro famoso," found in Guevara, *Apuntes críticos*, 109. For the relevant passage from the "Critique of the Gotha Programme," see Marx, "Gotha," 95.

72. "Socialism and Man in Cuba," found in Guevara, *Che Guevara Reader*, 219.

73. "On Party Militancy," found in Guevara, *Venceremos!*, 341.

74. "The Working Class and the Industrialization of Cuba," found in Guevara, *Che: Selected Works*, 241–43.

75. "Socialism and Man in Cuba," found in Guevara, *Che Guevara Reader*, 219.

76. According to Fernando Martínez Heredia, this statement was a source of scandal in the years following the publication of "Socialism and Man in Cuba" (Martínez Heredia, "El Che Guevara," 255–56). Samuel Farber's recent gloss on this statement (*Politics*, 81) confirms that it remains a source of scandal in some quarters.

77. "The Role of Morality in Communist Production," found in Lukács, *Tactics and Ethics*, 51.

78. Guevara, "La conferencia de prensa," 353. Guevara also noted on this occasion that people who did not have a favorable attitude toward the government were allowed to visit Cuba (ibid., 357–58).

79. "Technology and Society," found in Guevara, *Che: Selected Works*, 299.

80. "Entrevista con estudiantes norteamericanos," found in Guevara, *El Che en la Revolución cubana*, 4:478; Guevara, "La conferencia de prensa," 345.

81. "Technology and Society," found in Guevara, *Che: Selected Works*, 299. For one expression of Guevara's encouragement of robust discussion, see Guevara's "On the Concept of Value," found in Silverman, *Man and Socialism in Cuba*, 238.

82. Fidel Castro, "Discurso pronunciado como conclusión de las reuniones con los intelectuales cubanos, Biblioteca Nacional 'José Martí,'" in *Habla Fidel: 25 discursos en la Revolución*, ed. Pedro Álvarez Tabío (Havana: Oficina de Publicaciones del Consejo de Estado, 2008), 205. (The latter part of Castro's dictum is often mistranslated, substituting "outside" for "against"; for a recent example of this, see Farber, *Politics*, 57.) Trotsky, incidentally, proposes a very similar "policy" in his *Literature and Revolution* (14).

83. See, for example, "Reunión bimestral, diciembre 5 de 1964," found in Guevara, *El Che en la Revolución cubana*, 6:577.

84. "Reunión bimestral, agosto 10 de 1963," found in ibid., 6:368 and 370.

85. For the circular, see "On Ideological Investigations," found in Guevara, *Che: Selected Works*, 71. Regarding Guevara's defense of Trotskyists, see Roberto Acosta Hechavarría, "An Interview with Roberto Acosta Hechavarría," interview by Tano Nariño, trans. Gary Tennant and John Sullivan, in "The Hidden Pearl of the Caribbean," *Revolutionary History* 7, no. 3 (2000): 246; and see Gary Tennant, "The Reorganised Partido Obrero Revolucionario (Trotskista) and the 1959 Revolution," in "The Hidden Pearl of the Caribbean," *Revolutionary History* 7, no. 3 (2000): 192 and 195. Concerning the incident involving the printing of *The Permanent Revolution*, see Ernesto Che Guevara, "An Interview with 'Che' Guevara, Cuban Minister of Industries, 14 September 1961," interview by Maurice Zeitlin, in *Cuba: An American Tragedy*, ed. Robert Scheer and Maurice Zeitlin (Harmondsworth, UK: Penguin Books, Ltd., 1964), 341.

86. Guerra and Maldonado, *Historia*, 183.

87. Guevara's biographer Paco Ignacio Taibo II points out that between February and August 1962 alone there were 716 acts of sabotage organized by the CIA (Taibo, *Ernesto*, 438).

88. For a recent overview of the effects of the embargo, see Salim Lamrani, *The Economic War against Cuba*, trans. Larry Oberg (New York: Monthly Review Press, 2013).

89. "En la Universidad de Montevideo," found in Guevara, *El Che en la Revolución cubana*, 3:340.

90. "Technology and Society," found in Guevara, *Che: Selected Works*, 299. On the intensification of the class struggle after the triumph of the revolution, see ibid., 300; and see Guevara, *Apuntes filosóficos*, 175; see also "Socialism and Man in Cuba," found in Guevara, *Che Guevara Reader*, 221. Lenin mentions the postrevolutionary intensification of the class struggle in "Theses on the Fundamental Tasks of the Second Congress of the Communist International": "The proletariat's conquest of political power does not put a stop to its class struggle against the bourgeoisie; on the contrary, it renders that struggle most widespread, intense and ruthless" (in *Collected Works* [Moscow: Progress Publishers, 1966], 31:189).

91. "Acto conmemorativo del asesinato de Antonio Guiteras," found in Guevara, *El Che en la Revolución cubana*, 3:188.

92. "A las milicias a su regreso de las trincheras," found in ibid., 3:63.

93. Ernesto Che Guevara, "Cuba and the U.S.," interview by Leo Huberman, *Monthly Review* 13, no. 5 (1961), http://monthlyreview.org/1961/09/01/cuba-and-the-u-s/. Guevara says something similar in his interview with Maurice Zeitlin: "Our task is to enlarge, as much as is possible, democracy within the revolution and to liquidate the counterrevolution as soon as possible" (Guevara, "An Interview with 'Che,'" 340).

94. Such as Rosa Luxemburg: "All this resistance [from "the imperialist capitalist class"] must be broken step by step, with an iron fist and ruthless energy. The violence of the bourgeois counterrevolution must be confronted with the revolutionary violence of the proletariat" ("What does the Spartacus League Want?" found in Luxemburg, *Rosa Luxemburg Reader*, 352–53).

95. For a typical example, see "Entrevista en el INRA," found in Guevara, *El Che en la Revolución cubana*, 2:116.

96. "Technology and Society," found in Guevara, *Che: Selected Works*, 300.

97. See, for example, "Reunión bimestral, enero 20 de 1962," found in Guevara, *El Che en la Revolución cubana*, 6:155; "Guerrilla Warfare: A Method," found in Guevara, *Che Guevara Reader*, 80.

98. "Clausura de la Asamblea de Producción de la Gran Habana," found in Guevara, *El Che en la Revolución cubana*, 3:455; "Technology and Society," found in Guevara, *Che: Selected*

Works, 300; see also "Informe de la Empresa Consolidada de la Electricidad," found in Guevara, *El Che en la Revolución cubana*, 6:53.

99. "The Cuban Revolution's Influence in Latin America," found in Guevara, *Che Guevara Reader*, 291.

100. See, for example Michael Löwy's foreword to Pericás, *Che*, 9. And also see the following: Löwy, *Marxism*, 77–78, n. 15; Donald C. Hodges, *The Latin American Revolution: Politics and Strategy from Apro-Marxism to Guevarism* (New York: W. Morrow, 1974), 167–69, 171, 174; Pericás, *Che*, 218; Massari, *Che Guevara*, 116; and Rolando E. Bonachea and Nelson P. Valdés's introduction to Guevara, *Che: Selected Works*, 20.

101. All of the passages cited in this paragraph come from Leon Trotsky's *Permanent Revolution*, found in Leon Trotsky, *"The Permanent Revolution" and "Results and Prospects"* (New York: Pathfinder Press, 1970), 132–33, 276, and 278–79; emphasis in the original.

102. "A los obreros más destacados durante el año 1962," which is found in Guevara, *El Che en la Revolución cubana*, 4:336, seems to suggest as much.

103. See Marx, *A Contribution to the Critique*, 263.

104. See Trotsky, *"Permanent Revolution"*, chap. 6. And, for some relevant passages from Guevara, see "A los obreros más destacados durante el año 1962," found in Guevara, *El Che en la Revolución cubana*, 4:336; "Clausura de la Asamblea de Producción de la Gran Habana," found in ibid., 3:459; and "Memoria Anual 1961–1962," found in ibid., 6:674. Regarding the change of mentality, see "Technology and Society," found in Guevara, *Che: Selected Works*, 302.

105. See, for example, "Delegados obreros extranjeros asistentes al 1ro. de mayo," found in Guevara, *El Che en la Revolución cubana*, 4:182; "Entrevista a la revista *Economía mundial y relaciones internacionales*," found in ibid., 5:116; "The Philosophy of Plunder Must Cease," found in Guevara, *Che Guevara Reader*, 323; and "On the Cuban Experience," found in Guevara, *Venceremos!*, 372.

106. "Guerrilla Warfare: A Method," found in Guevara, *Che Guevara Reader*, 79 and 82.

107. "Conferencia en el salón de actos del Ministerio de Industrias," found in Guevara, *El Che en la Revolución cubana*, 5:388. For an earlier—November 1961—statement regarding the importance of "helping our brother nations who are fighting for their liberation," see "Delegados en el Congreso Obrero," found in ibid., 3:514.

108. Guevara, "Pueblo de Bolivia; Pueblos de América," 188.

109. From "Trotskyism," Tamara Deutscher's contribution to Bottomore, *Dictionary of Marxist Thought*, 547. As Jozef Wilczynski puts it, "permanent revolution" "is sometimes taken as synonymous with Trotskyism" (from "Permanent Revolution," found in Wilczynski, *Encyclopedic Dictionary of Marxism*, 430).

110. Anderson, *Revolutionary*, 596; Pericás, *Che*, 206; and Massari, *Che Guevara*, 112–13. Massari implies that those who made the accusations may not really have been students (113).

111. Roberto Massari says that as late as December 1964—essentially the end of Guevara's life and work in Cuba—Guevara had read practically nothing by Trotsky (*Che Guevara*, 114).

112. Guevara, "Conferencia ofrecida," 156; "Reunión bimestral, diciembre 5 de 1964," found in Guevara, *El Che en la Revolución cubana*, 6:566; "A modo de introducción: Carta de Che a Armando Hart," found in Guevara, *Apuntes filosóficos*, 25.

113. Guevara, *Apuntes filosóficos*, 347.

114. Guevara, "La conferencia de prensa," 340–41.

115. "Entrevista con estudiantes norteamericanos," found in Guevara, *El Che en la Revolución cubana*, 4:478; "Reunión bimestral, diciembre 5 de 1964," found in ibid., 6:566. The Revolution's Technical Advisory Councils (Consejos Técnicos Asesores) were apparently

one target of Cuban Trotskyists' criticism. For Guevara's rejection of this criticism, see "La economía en Cuba," found in ibid., 3:171.

116. Guevara, *Apuntes filosóficos*, 345.

117. "Entrevue avec 'Che' Guevara," *Quatrième Internationale* 14 (1961), 92; Borrego, *Camino*, 249. The "Entrevue" article tells us a bit about the Uruguayan Trotskyists' view of the Cuban Revolution in 1961 but very little about what Guevara said at his meeting with them.

CHAPTER 5

1. Alan Bullock's pronouncement represents a typical expression of the widespread misconception that Guevara had scant interest in the mechanics of a viable socialism: "He was more attracted by the liberation of the Third World, especially his native Latin America, than by making socialism work" ("Guevara," 293).

2. Volume 6 of *El Che en la Revolución cubana*, whose contents I have already cited on numerous occasions, includes a fairly extensive selection of reports and other documents produced by Guevara in his capacity as head of the Ministry of Industries.

3. K. S. Karol, *Guerrillas in Power: The Course of the Cuban Revolution*, trans. Arnold Pomerans, (New York: Hill and Wang, 1970), 47.

4. "On the Cuban," found in Guevara, *Venceremos!*, 364; see also "Plenaria Nacional Azucarera [b]," found in Guevara, *El Che en la Revolución cubana*, 4:311–12.

5. "At the United Nations," found in Guevara, *Che Guevara Reader*, 335. For information on terrorist activities against Cuba, see Keith Bolender, *Voices from the Other Side: An Oral History of Terrorism against Cuba* (London and New York: Pluto Press, 2010); Jesús Arboleya Cervera, *El otro terrorismo: Medio siglo de política de los Estados Unidos hacia Cuba* (Havana: Editorial de Ciencias Sociales, 2009); Salim Lamrani, ed., *Superpower Principles: U.S. Terrorism against Cuba* (Monroe, ME: Common Courage Press, 2005); Fabián Escalante Font, *Operación exterminio: 50 años de agresiones contra Cuba* (Havana: Editorial de Ciencias Sociales, 2010); and the illustrated history edited by Juan Carlos Rodríguez Cruz, *Cuba, la historia no contada* (Havana: Editorial Capitán San Luis, 2003).

6. "La necesidad de este libro," found in Guevara, *Apuntes críticos*, 31.

7. "Reunión bimestral, diciembre 21 de 1963," found in Guevara, *El Che en la Revolución cubana*, 6:423; see also "La conferencia para el comercio y desarrollo en Ginebra," found in ibid., 1:84.

8. "Discurso en el acto de graduación de la escuela de administradores 'Patricio Lumumba,'" found in Guevara, *Escritos y discursos*, 8:174. For data on literacy in Cuba on the eve of the Cuban Revolution, see Yaffe, *Economics*, 72.

9. Yaffe, *Economics*, 139.

10. "Con el periodista uruguayo Carlos Granda," found in Guevara, *El Che en la Revolución cubana*, 5:269.

11. "Against Bureaucratism," found in Guevara, *Che Guevara Reader*, 181.

12. C. B. Macpherson, "Elegant Tombstones: A Note on Friedman's Freedom," in *Democratic Theory: Essays in Retrieval* (Oxford: Clarendon Press, 1973), 151–52.

13. See, for example, Guevara, "Conferencia ofrecida," 172; "Volunteer Labor," found in Guevara, *Che: Selected Works*, 307; "Meaning," found in Silverman, *Man and Socialism*, 101; and "Socialism and Man in Cuba," found in Guevara, *Che Guevara Reader*, 221.

14. Lukács, *Process*, 127.

15. "Meaning," found in Silverman, *Man and Socialism*, 101.

16. Ibid., 98–99. According to Marxist theory, the relations of production of a given mode of production (for example, feudalism) initially promote the development of—and in this sense "correspond to"—the forces of production, while in a later phase they hinder or inhibit the forces' continued development. The appearance of the latter phase indicates the need for new relations of production and thus the need for revolution as well.

17. "Plan tentativo," found in Guevara, *Apuntes críticos*, 25.

18. Guevara, "Conferencia ofrecida," 155–56 and 173–74; see also "Selección de Actas de reuniones efectuadas en el Ministerio de Industrias: 2 de octubre de 1964," found in Guevara, *Apuntes críticos*, 339 (the transcript of a meeting held two months earlier).

19. "What We Have Learned and What We Have Taught," found in Guevara, *Che Guevara Reader*, 61.

20. "Social Ideals of the Rebel Army," found in ibid., 95.

21. "Acto del 1o. de mayo en Santiago de Cuba," found in Guevara, *El Che en la Revolución cubana*, 2:50.

22. "At the United Nations," found in Guevara, *Che Guevara Reader*, 326; "Colonialism Is Doomed," found in Guevara, *Che: Selected Works*, 335.

23. "Conferencia en el salón de actos del Ministerio de Industrias," found in Guevara, *El Che en la Revolución cubana*, 5:397.

24. "Inicio de la campaña de honradez y honestidad en la COA," found in ibid., 2:106; "The Working Class and the Industrialization of Cuba," found in Guevara, *Che: Selected Works*, 231 and 238. The latter lecture ends with a reference to the goal of unity not included in the English translation; see "Programa TV 'Cuba Avanza,'" found in Guevara, *El Che en la Revolución cubana*, 2:265.

25. "Reunión bimestral, diciembre 5 de 1964," found in ibid., 6:578.

26. Ibid., 578 and 579.

27. "Reunión bimestral, julio 14 de 1962," found in Guevara, *El Che en la Revolución cubana*, 6:272; "Terminación de la primera etapa de las escuelas populares," found in ibid., 4:332. For a rather different Marxist argument to the effect that unions should cease to exist in the postrevolutionary society, see Anton Pannekoek, "World Revolution and Communist Tactics," in *Pannekoek and Gorter's Marxism*, ed. D. A. Smart (London: Pluto Press, 1978), 114–16.

28. "Reunión bimestral, julio 11 de 1964," found in Guevara, *El Che en la Revolución cubana*, 6:509; Guevara, "An Interview with 'Che,'" 344; "Reunión bimestral, diciembre 5 de 1964," found in Guevara, *El Che en la Revolución cubana*, 6:579.

29. "Entrevista filmada para la TV canadiense," found in ibid., 4:379; "Create Two, Three, Many Vietnams (Message to the Tricontinental)," found in Guevara, *Che Guevara Reader*, 353.

30. Ernesto Che Guevara to [His] Children (1965), found in ibid., 383.

31. "Socialism and Man in Cuba," found in ibid., 213.

32. Ernesto Che Guevara to [His] Children (1965), found in ibid., 383; and Arcos Bergnes, *Evocando*, 101.

33. As another of Guevara's close collaborators, Óscar Fernández Mel, puts it, Guevara's "life revolved around the Revolution" (interview with Doctor Óscar Fernández Mel, found in Barrio and Jenkins, *Che Handbook*, 264).

34. "Reunión bimestral, febrero 22 de 1964," found in Guevara, *El Che en la Revolución cubana*, 6:453.

35. "It would be truly utopian to think that ninety miles away from American territory you can make a social revolution that completely changes the structure of the country, that changes

the relations of production, that inaugurates a new era . . . and that it can all be done without sacrifices" ("En la Universidad de Montevideo," found in ibid., 3:327).

36. "En relación con la II zafra del pueblo," found in ibid., 4:61; see also "Curso de adiestramiento para funcionarios y empleados del Ministerio de Industrias," found in ibid., 3:229; "Graduación del curso de administradores," found in ibid., 3:558; "Technology and Society," found in Guevara, *Che: Selected Works*, 302; "A New Culture of Work," found in Guevara, *Che Guevara Reader*, 148; and "Volunteer Labor," found in Guevara, *Che: Selected Works*, 305.

37. Guevara, "Cuba and the U.S."

38. "To Be a Young Communist," found in Guevara, *Che Guevara Reader*, 159; "The Cadre: Backbone of the Revolution," found in ibid., 157.

39. "Discusión colectiva; decisión y responsabilidades únicas," found in Guevara, *El Che en la Revolución cubana*, 1:113.

40. "In Cuba Imperialism Was Caught Sleeping, but Now It Is Awake," found in Guevara, *Che Guevara Talks to Young People*, 64; "Graduación del curso de administradores," found in Guevara, *El Che en la Revolución cubana*, 3:558; "Reunión bimestral, febrero 22 de 1964," found in ibid., 6:453.

41. "Reunión bimestral, julio 14 de 1962," found in ibid., 6:258.

42. "Reunión bimestral, diciembre 5 de 1964," found in ibid., 6:571; "Socialism and Man in Cuba," found in Guevara, *Che Guevara Reader*, 226.

43. "Honoring José Martí," found in Guevara, *Che: Selected Works*, 211. Guevara made these remarks before Fidel Castro had proclaimed the socialist orientation of the Cuban Revolution.

44. See chapter 1, note 108.

45. Guevara, "La conferencia de prensa," 350.

46. "The Cadre: Backbone of the Revolution," found in Guevara, *Che Guevara Reader*, 157.

47. "Entrega de premios a ganadores en la emulación de Círculo de Estudio," found in Guevara, *El Che en la Revolución cubana*, 4:79 and 80; see also "Reunión bimestral, enero 20 de 1962," found in ibid., 6:152.

48. "Memoria Anual 1961–1962," found in ibid., 6:684; see also "Inauguración plenaria provincial de la CTC de Camaguey," found in ibid., 5:164.

49. See, for example, Castro, "Las ideas," 89; and Borrego, *Camino*, 280.

50. Guevara mentions the importance of moral compulsion in "Memoria Anual 1961–1962," found in Guevara, *El Che en la Revolución cubana*, 6:684; and he briefly explains his understanding of the term in "On Party Militancy," found in Guevara, *Venceremos!*, 349.

51. "Volunteer Labor," found in Guevara, *Che: Selected Works*, 305.

52. "Youth Must March in the Vanguard," found in Guevara, *Che Guevara Talks to Young People*, 128; "Reunión bimestral, enero 20 de 1962," found in Guevara, *El Che en la Revolución cubana*, 6:149.

53. Herbert Marcuse evokes the essence of prefiguration, without using the term, when he writes that "the images and values of a future free society must appear in the personal relationships within the unfree society" (*Counterrevolution and Revolt* [Boston: Beacon Press, 1972], 49).

54. From "Marta, viento cálido," Marta Harnecker's interview by Iosu Perales, found in Perales, *Querido Che*, 74.

55. "The Cadre: Backbone of the Revolution," found in Guevara, *Che Guevara Reader*, 154 and 155. Regarding discipline, see, too, "A New Culture of Work," found in ibid., 146–47.

56. Guevara, *Guerrilla Warfare*, 132.

57. Sáenz, *El Che ministro*, 225.

58. Arcos Bergnes, *Evocando*, 252.

59. Ibid., 250. Helen Yaffe mentions the specific examples of "adjusting inventories . . . [and] carrying out unauthorised investments" (*Economics*, 218).

60. "Reunión bimestral, enero 20 de 1962," found in Guevara, *El Che en la Revolución cubana*, 6:166.

61. "Reunión bimestral, septiembre 12 de 1964," found in Guevara, *El Che en la Revolución cubana*, 6:530.

62. Arcos Bergnes, *Evocando*, 252.

63. "Reunión bimestral, enero 20 de 1962," found in Guevara, *El Che en la Revolución cubana*, 6:165.

64. Arcos Bergnes, *Evocando*, 253–54; Borrego, *Camino*, 70.

65. Orlando Borrego, "Álvaro Vargas Llosa Jr.: Un vástago al descubierto," *Rebelión*, November 21, 2005, http://www.rebelion.org/noticia.php?id=23017; Arcos Bergnes, *Evocando*, chap. 14.

66. Jorge G. Castañeda, *Compañero: The Life and Death of Che Guevara*, trans. Marina Castañeda (New York: Vintage Books, 1998), 178.

67. González, *Che Guevara*, 123. Alfredo Muñoz-Unsain fosters a similar misconception with his brief, ill-informed reference to Guanahacabibes in his posthumously circulated memoir (Alfredo Muñoz-Unsain, "Cuba, sociedad anónima: Memorias parciales de un corresponsal en La Habana," unpublished manuscript, http://www.juangasparini.com/libros-especiales/cuba-sociedad-anonima/, 41–42).

68. Farber, *Politics*, 74. In his biography of Guevara, *Che: La vida por un mundo mejor* (Barcelona: Plaza y Janés, 2003), Pacho O'Donnell likewise offers a very misleading account of Guanahacabibes, which he describes as a "concentration camp" (261).

69. "Reunión bimestral, julio 14 de 1962," found in Guevara, *El Che en la Revolución cubana*, 6:276; "XI Congreso Nacional Obrero," found in ibid., 3:534, 546; "Reunión bimestral, septiembre 12 de 1964," found in ibid., 6:522; "A los obreros más destacados durante el año 1962," found in ibid., 4:336. See also "Selección de Actas de reuniones efectuadas en el Ministerio de Industrias: 2 de octubre de 1964," found in Guevara, *Apuntes críticos*, 339.

70. For example, "Clausura del Consejo de la CTC," found in Guevara, *El Che en la Revolución cubana*, 4:124; "Reunión bimestral, febrero 22 de 1964," found in ibid., 6:441; and "On the Budgetary Finance System," found in Guevara, *Che Guevara Reader*, 199.

71. "Our Industrial Tasks," found in Guevara, *Venceremos!*, 286 ("consciousness" would be a far better translation than "conscience" here).

72. "Intervención en una reunión," found in Guevara, *El Che en la Revolución cubana*, 4:95. See, too, Guevara's comments in "Reunión bimestral, febrero 22 de 1964," found in ibid., 6:444.

73. "Entrega de premios de la emulación socialista," found in ibid., 5:240; "XI Congreso Nacional Obrero," found in ibid., 3:539.

74. "A los obreros premiados por haberse destacado en la producción," found in ibid., 3:75 (from a speech two months prior to the announcement that the Cuban Revolution was a socialist revolution).

75. "XI Congreso Nacional Obrero," found in ibid., 3:531; see also 540.

76. "A los ganadores de la emulación de alfabetización," found in ibid., 3:502.

77. "Graduación de 400 alumnos de las escuelas populares," found in ibid., 4:550.

78. "Discurso en el acto de graduación de la escuela de administradores 'Patricio Lumumba,'" found in Guevara, *Escritos y discursos*, 8:174. For discussion of specific policies for, and methods of, training, see Yaffe, *Economics*, chap. 4.

79. "Graduación del curso de administradores," found in Guevara, *El Che en la Revolución cubana*, 3:557; "Discusión colectiva; decisión y responsabilidades únicas," found in ibid., 1:109. See also "Reunión bimestral, febrero 22 de 1964," found in ibid., 6:446; and "A New Culture of Work," found in Guevara, *Che Guevara Reader*, 147.

80. "Convención nacional de los consejos técnicos asesores," found in Guevara, *El Che en la Revolución cubana*, 3:69; "Our Industrial Tasks," found in Guevara, *Venceremos!*, 291.

81. "Graduación en la escuela de administradores 'Patricio Lumumba,'" found in Guevara, *El Che en la Revolución cubana*, 4:324; see also "En la primera reunión nacional de producción," found in ibid., 3:384.

82. Guevara, "'Pueblo de Bolivia; Pueblos de América,'" 188.

83. "Discurso en 'El Pedrero,'" found in Guevara, *Escritos y discursos*, 4:26.

84. "Graduación del curso de administradores," found in Guevara, *El Che en la Revolución cubana*, 3:552.

85. See, for example, Guevara, *Bolivian Diary*, 61.

86. Borrego, *Camino*, 378.

87. Farber, *Politics*, 107; 68.

88. González, *Che Guevara*, 164 and 151.

89. Farber, *Politics*, 90.

90. "A New Old Che Guevara Interview," found in Guevara, *Che: Selected Works*, 369. For a recent work that shows how the working class did in fact play an important part in the triumph of the Cuban Revolution, see Stephen Cushion, *A Hidden History of the Cuban Revolution: How the Working Class Shaped the Guerrillas' Victory* (New York: Monthly Review Press, 2016).

91. González, *Che Guevara*, 101.

92. "Create Two, Three, Many Vietnams (Message to the Tricontinental)," found in *Che Guevara Reader*, 354.

93. See, for example, "Interview by Telemundo Televisión," found in Guevara, *Che: Selected Works*, 382; "Acto de la Federación de Trabajadores de La Industria Textil," found in Guevara, *El Che en la Revolución cubana*, 2:178; "The OAS Conference at Punta del Este" in *Che Guevara Reader*, 251–52; "Reunión bimestral, julio 11 de 1964," found in Guevara, *El Che en la Revolución cubana*, 6:491; and "Editorial ('Nuestra Industria Tecnológica')," found in Guevara, *El Che en la Revolución cubana*, 6:720.

94. As for Marx, see, for example, Marx, *Civil War*, 335; and "Gotha," 95. One relevant passage from Lenin can be found in "The Socialist Revolution and the Right of Nations to Self-Determination": "The socialist revolution is not one single act, not one single battle on a single front; but a whole epoch of intensified class conflicts, a long series of battles on all fronts, that is, battles around all the problems of economics and politics, which can culminate only in the expropriation of the bourgeoisie" (in *Collected Works* [Moscow: Progress Publishers, 1964], 22:144).

95. González, *Che Guevara*, 102; Farber, *Politics*, xix. Löwy, by contrast, notes that Guevara does espouse the principle proletarian self-emancipation (*Marxism*, 15).

96. This at least seems to be the gist of one of his well-known remarks on the Paris Commune: see Marx, *Civil War*, 335.

97. On the most general level, the principle holds that "the emancipation of the working classes must be conquered by the working classes themselves" (Karl Marx, "Provisional Rules

of the Association," in *Marx and Engels Collected Works* [New York: International Publishers, 1985], 20:14). Marx and Engels underscore the paramount importance of this principle in their "Circular Letter to August Bebel, Wilhelm Liebknecht, Wilhelm Bracke and Others" (in *Marx and Engels Collected Works* [New York: International Publishers, 1989], 24:269).

98. "Entrega de premios a los 45 obreros más destacados del Ministerio de Industrias," found in Guevara, *El Che en la Revolución cubana*, 4:152.

99. See "El papel de la ayuda exterior en el desarrollo de Cuba," found in ibid., vol. 3; and "Sobre las normas," found in ibid., vol. 4.

100. See "En relación con la II zafra del pueblo," found in ibid., vol. 4; and "Plenaria Nacional Azucarera [a]," found in ibid., vol. 4.

101. See, for example, "The Cuban Economy: Its Past and Its Present Importance," found in Guevara, *Che: Selected Works*; "Our Industrial Tasks," found in Guevara, *Venceremos!*; "Tareas Generales para 1963," found in Guevara, *El Che en la Revolución cubana*, vol. 6; and "En el programa de TV 'Información Pública,'" found in ibid., vol. 5.

102. "En el seminario," found in ibid., 4:455–56.

103. "Con los visitantes," found in ibid., 4:485–86; "The Cuban Economy: Its Past and Its Present Importance," found in Guevara, *Che: Selected Works*, 141–42. For some revealing statistics on the importance of sugar in the Cuban economy on the eve of the revolution, see Yaffe, *Economics*, 172.

104. Guevara, *Congo*, 16; see also "Reunión bimestral, enero 20 de 1962," found in Guevara, *El Che en la Revolución cubana*, 6:170.

105. Muñoz-Unsain's comment forms part of the interview fragments included in Enrique Arrosagaray, *Rodolfo Walsh en Cuba: Agencia Prensa Latina, militancia, ron y criptografía* (Buenos Aires: Catálogos, 2004), 161. See also Aurelio Alonso, "El pensamiento revolucionario es invariablemente crítico," interview by Pedro de La Hoz, in *Como el primer día*, ed. Pedro de La Hoz (Havana: Editorial Letras Cubanas, 2008), 24.

106. "Reunión bimestral, agosto 10 de 1963," found in Guevara, *El Che en la Revolución cubana*, 6:356ff.

107. See, for example, "A New Culture of Work," found in Guevara, *Che Guevara Reader*, 148; "Our Industrial Tasks," found in Guevara, *Venceremos!*, 287; and "Entrega de premios de la emulación socialista," found in Guevara, *El Che en la Revolución cubana*, 5:237 and 239.

108. Monereo, *Con su propia cabeza*," 84 and 62.

109. "Entrega de premios de la emulación socialista," found in Guevara, *El Che en la Revolución cubana*, 5:146; see also Guevara's "On Production Costs and the Budgetary System," found in Silverman, *Man and Socialism*, 119.

110. See, for example, "Inauguración de la fábrica de galletas 'Albert Kuntz,'" found in Guevara, *El Che en la Revolución cubana*, 4:5; "Asamblea de trabajadores portuarios," found in ibid., 4:12; and "En relación con la II zafra del pueblo," found in ibid., 4:46 and 50.

111. "Discurso a las milicias en Pinar del Río," found in Guevara, *Escritos y discursos*, 5:76.

112. "Entrega de premios de la emulación socialista," found in Guevara, *El Che en la Revolución cubana*, 5:252.

113. "Our Industrial Tasks," found in Guevara, *Venceremos!*, 289.

114. Ibid.; see also "Inauguración fábrica de bujías," found in Guevara, *El Che en la Revolución cubana*, 5:159.

115. "Clausura del Consejo de la CTC," found in ibid., 4:134–35; "Intervención en una reunión," found in ibid., 4:108.

116. "En la primera reunión nacional de producción," found in ibid., 3:393.

117. "A New Culture of Work," found in Guevara, *Che Guevara Reader*, 148; "En la primera reunión nacional de producción," found in Guevara, *El Che en la Revolución cubana*, 3:394.

118. Silverman, *Man and Socialism*, collects the most important contributions to this debate. For a discussion of Guevara's positions in the debate, see Yaffe, *Economics*, chap. 3.

119. Preface to Silverman, *Man and Socialism*, viii.

120. Miguel Cossío, one of the participants in the debate, defines the law of value as "the general law of the distribution of labor in mercantile societies . . . [which] expresses that commodities must be exchanged according to the quantity of social necessary labor expended on their production" ("Contribution to the Debate on the Law of Value," found in Silverman, *Man and Socialism*, 243).

121. Yaffe, *Economics*, 53.

122. "On Production," found in Silverman, *Man and Socialism*, 113.

123. "Fragmento de la entrevista concedida al periódico *El-Taliah* (*La Vanguardia*) de El Cairo, abril de 1965," found in Guevara, *Apuntes críticos*, 429. See also "Reunión bimestral, diciembre 5 de 1964," found in Guevara, *El Che en la Revolución cubana*: "for me, the law of value is equivalent to capitalism" (6:577).

124. Guevara's "On the Concept of Value," found in Silverman, *Man and Socialism*, 236. For one passage in which Guevara acknowledges that the law of value continued to operate in Cuba, see "On the Budgetary Finance System," found in Guevara, *Che Guevara Reader*, 201.

125. Ibid., 202.

126. Guevara, "Conferencia ofrecida," 165.

127. "Delegados obreros extranjeros asistentes al 1ro. de mayo," found in Guevara, *El Che en la Revolución cubana*, 4:182; "XI Congreso Nacional Obrero," found in ibid., 3:534; "Reunión bimestral, enero 20 de 1962," found in ibid., 6:154.

128. "Plan especial de integración al trabajo," found in ibid., 6:724. In the passage cited, Guevara is referring to enterprises within his ministry, but one could just as well apply this image to the economy as a whole.

129. "On the Budgetary Finance System," found in Guevara, *Che Guevara Reader*, 206; Guevara's "On Production Costs and the Budgetary System," found in Silverman, *Man and Socialism*, 115.

130. Guevara's "On the Concept of Value," found in ibid., 237.

131. Guevara's "On Production Costs and the Budgetary System," found in ibid., 115; Guevara's "On the Concept of Value," found in ibid., 237–38.

132. "On the Budgetary Finance System," found in Guevara, *Che Guevara Reader*, 192.

133. Ibid. See also Guevara's "Banking, Credit, and Socialism," found in Silverman, *Man and Socialism*, 304.

134. Guevara's "On Production Costs and the Budgetary System," found in ibid., 120; see also 118.

135. "Entrega de premios," found in Guevara, *El Che en la Revolución cubana*, 5:70; see also "Reunión bimestral, febrero 22 de 1964," found in ibid., 6:436.

136. "Reunión bimestral, octubre 12 de 1963," found in ibid., 6:387.

137. "On the Budgetary Finance System," found in Guevara, *Che Guevara Reader*, 192.

138. For a useful overview of the differences between the two systems, see Yaffe, *Economics*, 48. Yaffe also provides a helpful summary of Guevara's budgetary finance system (ibid., 261–62).

139. Guevara, "Conferencia ofrecida," 155; see also 165. And see "Selección de Actas de reuniones efectuadas en el Ministerio de Industrias: 2 de octubre de 1964," found in Guevara, *Apuntes críticos*, 370.

140. "Discurso en el acto de graduación de la escuela de administradores 'Patricio Lumumba,'" found in Guevara, *Escritos y discursos*, 8:180, 183–84; "Selección de Actas de reuniones efectuadas en el Ministerio de Industrias: 2 de octubre de 1964," found in Guevara, *Apuntes críticos*, 356.

141. "On the Budgetary Finance System," found in Guevara, *Che Guevara Reader*, 192.

142. "Discurso en el acto de graduación de la escuela de administradores 'Patricio Lumumba,'" found in Guevara, *Escritos y discursos*, 8:183.

143. "La necesidad de este libro," found in Guevara, *Apuntes críticos*, 31.

144. "X preguntas sobre las enseñanzas de un libro famoso," found in ibid., 125.

145. "La necesidad de este libro," found in ibid., 31; "Selección de Actas de reuniones efectuadas en el Ministerio de Industrias: 2 de octubre de 1964," found in ibid., 345.

146. "X preguntas sobre las enseñanzas de un libro famoso," found in ibid., 125; Luis Báez, *Más esperanza que fe: Revelaciones de Roberto Fernández Retamar* (Havana: Casa Editora Abril, 2006), 103. See also "Interview by Al-Tali-'ah," found in Guevara, *Che: Selected Works*, 412.

147. Gerassi's introduction to Guevara, *Venceremos!*, 47.

148. "Reunión bimestral, octubre 12 de 1963," found in Guevara, *El Che en la Revolución cubana*, 6:389–90.

149. "La necesidad de este libro," found in Guevara, *Apuntes críticos*, 31.

150. For some criticism of Guevara's analysis and explanation of the failure of the Soviet model, together with an appreciation of his perspicacity in gauging the scope of the crisis in Soviet-style socialism, see Monereo, *Con su propia cabeza*, 114–16.

151. See, for example, "Entrega de premios a los 45 obreros más destacados del Ministerio de Industrias," found in Guevara, *El Che en la Revolución cubana*, 4:157; "En la escalinata de la Universidad de La Habana," found in ibid., 3:523; "Inauguración 2da. etapa combinado del lápiz," found in ibid., 5:186; and "Volunteer Labor," found in Guevara, *Che: Selected Works*, 305, where the Spanish word is translated as "lighthouse."

152. Guevara, *Guerrilla Warfare*, 123; see also 133.

153. Guevara, "Delegados en el Congreso Obrero," found in Guevara, *El Che en la Revolución cubana*, 3:513; "Entrega de premios," found in ibid., 5:75.

154. "Inauguración de la escuela de capacitación técnica para obreros," found in ibid., 4:85; see also "Convención nacional de los consejos técnicos asesores," found in ibid., 3:69.

155. Engels, "Introduction," 201.

156. Ibid.

CHAPTER 6

1. See, for example, A. Belden Fields, *Trotskyism and Maoism: Theory and Practice in France and the United States* (Brooklyn: Autonomedia, 1988), 59.

2. For example, Besancenot and Löwy, *Che Guevara*, 33 and 34; Massari, *Che Guevara*, 116; Alonso Aguilar Monteverde's "Mi imagen del Che," found in Almeida, et al., *Che siempre*, 39; Pericás, *Che*, 199; Peter McLaren's "The Future of the Past," foreword to Löwy, *Marxism*; and Flávio Koutzii's "Che: O contexto histórico e a história do contexto," found in Flávio

Koutzii and José Corrêa Leite, eds., *Che 20 anos depois* (São Paulo: Editora Busca Vida, Ltda.: 1987), 62.

3. "Socialism and Man in Cuba," found in Guevara, *Che Guevara Reader*, 226.

4. "Selección de Actas de reuniones efectuadas en el Ministerio de Industrias: 2 de octubre de 1964," found in Guevara, *Apuntes críticos*, 327.

5. Ricardo Napurí, "Thirty Years since the Death of Ernesto Guevara: An Interview with Ricardo Napurí," interview by José Bermúdez and Luis Castelli, trans. Alejandra Ríos and Philip Marchant, in "The Hidden Pearl of the Caribbean," *Revolutionary History* 7, no. 3 (2000): 268. Napurí does not mention the year, but it would seem to be 1960. Napurí's anecdote suggests that Roberto Massari may overstate the extent of Guevara's unfamiliarity with Trotsky's works in 1964 (see my earlier note in chapter 4, note 111).

6. See the anecdote mentioned in Yaffe, *Economics*, 81.

7. Anderson, *Revolutionary*, 585 and 596. The Argentine Communist Party held a similar view (ibid., 581).

8. Farber, *Politics*, 16–17; Massari, *Che Guevara*, 203. I personally heard Guevara's politics characterized and defended as "anarchist" during a panel at the 2000 Socialist Scholars Conference in New York City.

9. Luis Vitale, *De Martí a Chiapas: Balance de un siglo* (Santiago, Cl.: Ed. Síntesis y CELA, 1995), chap. 7.

10. "On the Budgetary Finance System," found in Guevara, *Che Guevara Reader*, 211.

11. Hodges, *Latin American Revolution*, 168.

12. Ibid., 169. Löwy reaches a similar conclusion (*Marxism*, 77–78, n. 15).

13. "Reunión bimestral, diciembre 5 de 1964," found in Guevara, *El Che en la Revolución cubana*, 6:567.

14. "Cuba: Historical Exception or Vanguard in the Anticolonial Struggle?" found in *Che Guevara Reader*, 136; "X preguntas sobre las enseñanzas de un libro famoso," found in Guevara, *Apuntes críticos*, 93–94. See also "Conferencia televisada," found in Guevara, *El Che en la Revolución cubana*, 3:43.

15. Taibo claims that Guevara's views on Trotsky and Trotskyism began to change slowly following his November 1964 trip to the Soviet Union (*Ernesto*, 497). While this seems to be the case, it does not mean that Guevara ever came to hold a generally positive view of Trotsky.

16. Cited in Anderson, *Revolutionary*, 191. On at least one occasion in Mexico, Guevara called his daughter Hilda "my little Mao" (ibid., 202).

17. "A New Old Che Guevara Interview," found in Guevara, *Che: Selected Works*, 368.

18. Anderson, *Revolutionary*, 579–80.

19. Ibid., 584.

20. Guevara, "Conferencia ofrecida," 176.

21. Pericás rightly notes as much (*Che*, 204), and Castañeda makes essentially the same point (*Compañero*, 86).

22. As regards his early admiration for Stalin, see, for example, the letter cited in Castañeda, *Compañero*, 62. Guevara recommends the reading of Stalin's works in "Conferencia ofrecida," 176, and, more implicitly, in "A modo de introducción: Carta de Che a Armando Hart," found in Guevara, *Apuntes filosóficos*, 24.

23. Farber, *Politics*, 16.

24. "X preguntas sobre las enseñanzas de un libro famoso," found in Guevara, *Apuntes críticos*, 214.

25. Guevara, "Conferencia ofrecida," 174.

26. Monereo, *Con su propia cabeza*, 115; Besancenot and Löwy, *Che Guevara*, 74–75.

27. Karol, *Guerrillas*, 47; see also Karol's "Cuba's Road to Communism," *New Statesman*, May 19, 1961, 778.

28. From Gerassi's introduction to Guevara, *Venceremos!*, 45.

29. See, for example, Díaz and López, "Ernesto Che Guevara," 145; Besancenot and Löwy, *Che Guevara*, chap. 1; Aguilar Monteverde's "Mi imagen del Che," found in Almeida et al., *Che siempre*, 39; Valdés Paz's epilogue, "Notas," in Monereo, *Con su propia cabeza*, 123; José Dirceu's "O resgate do humanismo pelo marxismo," found in Koutzii and Corrêa Leite, *Che 20 anos depois*, 223; and Clive W. Kronenberg, "Manifestations of Humanism in Revolutionary Cuba: Che and the Principle of Universality," *Latin American Perspectives* 36, no. 2 (2009).

30. "Revolutionary humanism" is the term preferred by Löwy (*Marxism*, 8), María del Carmen Ariet García (*El pensamiento político*, 143), Massari (*Che Guevara*, 203), and Luis Suárez Salazar ("Che: Artista de la lucha revolucionaria," in *Pensar al Che*, vol. 1, ed. Alfredo Prieto González [Havana: Editorial José Martí, 1989], 142), among others. For one commentator who prefers the term "socialist humanism," see Vitale (*Martí*, 200).

31. Valdés Paz's epilogue, "Notas para un epílogo," to Monereo, *Con su propia cabeza*, 123.

32. T. B. Bottomore, introduction to *Karl Marx Early Writings*, trans. and ed. by T. B. Bottomore (New York: McGraw-Hill, 1964), viii. Marx identifies communism with humanism in *Manuscripts of 1844*, 296 and 341–42. Eugene Kamenka's "Marxian Humanism and the Crisis in Socialist Ethics" (in Erich Fromm, ed., *Socialist Humanism* [London: Allen Lane, the Penguin Press, 1967]) is still useful as a brief overview of Marxist humanism.

33. Karl Marx, "Contribution to the Critique of Hegel's Philosophy of Law. Introduction," in *Marx and Engels Collected Works* (New York: International Publishers, 1975), 3:182.

34. "En la primera reunión nacional de producción," in Guevara, *El Che en la Revolución cubana*, 3:433.

35. Ibid., 393.

36. "Volunteer Labor," found in Guevara, *Che: Selected Works*, 310; "Notes for the Study of the Ideology of the Cuban Revolution," found in ibid.,123.

37. "Reunión bimestral, diciembre 5 de 1964," found in Guevara, *El Che en la Revolución cubana*, 6:562. "Informe de la Empresa Consolidada del Petroleo," in ibid., 6:74.

38. "Acto conmemorativo del asesinato de Antonio Guiteras," found in ibid., 3:192.

39. "Create Two, Three, Many Vietnams (Message to the Tricontinental)," found in Guevara, *Che Guevara Reader*, 356.

40. Löwy suggests that this may be the case (*Marxism*, 8; see also 14). I have analyzed Ponce's views on humanism in Renzo Llorente, "El aporte de Aníbal Ponce a la crítica del humanismo moderno," *Utopía y Praxis Latinoamericana*, no. 60 (2013).

41. Fromm, *Socialist Humanism*. To my knowledge, Guevara himself only uses the term "socialist humanism" once, and in an almost parenthetical manner; see "Entrega de premios a ganadores en la emulación de Círculo de Estudios," found in Guevara, *El Che en la Revolución cubana*, 4:79.

42. Michael Löwy's "O humanismo do Che," found in Koutzii and Corrêa Leite, *Che 20 anos depois*, 97.

43. Ibid., 97; 106–10.

44. Castro, "In Tribute," 24; Alasdair MacIntyre, "Marxism of the Will," in *Alasdair MacIntyre's Engagement with Marxism: Selected Writings 1953–1974*, ed. Paul Blackledge and Neil Davidson (Leiden and Boston, Brill, 2008), 378.

45. See, for example, Alonso Aguilar Monteverde's "Mi imagen del Che," found in Almeida et al., *Che siempre*, 42; María del Carmen Ariet García, *El pensamiento político*, 185; Hart Dávalos's "El Che," found in Almeida et al., *Che siempre*, 15; Gadea, "A Ernesto Che Guevara," found in ibid., 173; and Eduardo Galeano and Tomás Borge, "Eduardo y Tomás, robles de raíz milenaria," interview by Iosu Perales, in Perales, *Querido Che*, 49.

46. "The Role of Morality in Communist Production," found in Lukács, *Tactics and Ethics*, 48.

47. Even so, Steven Lukes never mentions Guevara in his comprehensive survey *Marxism and Morality* (Oxford and New York: Oxford University Press, 1985).

48. "En el salón teatro de la Universidad de La Habana," in Guevara, *El Che en la Revolución cubana*, 2:61.

49. Sáenz, *El Che ministro*, 142.

50. Juan Valdés Paz, "Todo es según el color del cristal con que se mira (Comentarios a *La vida en rojo* de Jorge Castañeda)," in *Che: El hombre del siglo XXI* (Havana: University of Havana and Editorial Félix Varela, 2001), 112.

51. Monereo rightly emphasizes this fact (*Con su propia cabeza*, 107).

52. Elster, *Making Sense*, 531; emphasis in the original.

53. Fernández Buey, "Ernesto 'Che' Guevara," 17; Bonachea and Valdés's introduction to Guevara, *Che: Selected Works*, 27–28 (emphasis in the original). See also MacIntyre, "Marxism": "In Guevara . . . it is the voluntarist component of Leninism which is appealed to as never before" (377).

54. Farber, *Politics*, xviii; 118. See also 19ff.

55. See for example, Monereo, *Con su propia cabeza*, 45; and see also González, *Che Guevara*, 168 and 149–50. Lukács also seems to believe that Guevara was guilty of voluntarism (*Record*, 171).

56. I say "generally" because some do take issue with the "moralization" discussed in the preceding section.

57. Bonachea and Valdés's introduction to Guevara, *Che: Selected Works*, 28; González, *Che Guevara*, 168.

58. "Entrega de premios," found in Guevara, *El Che en la Revolución cubana*, 5:71.

59. In addition to the passages cited in the text, see, for example, "Entrega de premios a los 45 obreros más destacados del Ministerio de Industrias," found in ibid., 4:142; and "On Party Militancy," found in Guevara, *Venceremos!*, 351.

60. Guevara's "The Meaning of Socialist Planning," found in Silverman, *Man and Socialism*, 103.

61. "On the Budgetary Finance System," found in Guevara, *Che Guevara Reader*, 194.

62. Guevara's "The Meaning of Socialist Planning," found in Silverman, *Man and Socialism*, 102.

63. Ibid., 103.

64. "On the Budgetary Finance System," found in Guevara, *Che Guevara Reader*, 195; Guevara's "The Meaning of Socialist Planning," found in Silverman, *Man and Socialism*, 103.

65. Guevara, "Conferencia ofrecida," 165; Guevara's "The Meaning of Socialist Planning," found in Silverman, *Man and Socialism*, 103 and 101.

66. Marx, "Critique of Hegel's Philosophy," 182.

67. "On the Budgetary Finance System," found in Guevara, *Che Guevara Reader*, 195.

68. Guevara's contention that, while "the contradictions between the development of the productive forces and the relationships [that is, "relations"] of production that would make a

revolution imperative or possible (viewing the country as a whole, unique and isolated) might not exist objectively," these contradictions do exist on a world scale (Guevara's "The Meaning of Socialist Planning," found in Silverman, *Man and Socialism*, 103) is also relevant to the charge of voluntarism: the attempt to carry out a revolution in circumstances in which a contradiction between the forces and relations of production has yet to occur is surely a less "voluntaristic" enterprise if these circumstances are embedded within a larger system in which such a contradiction does exist and makes a revolution necessary and unavoidable. In short, assuming that there is some organic relationship between the larger (macro) system and the local (micro) conditions, one is at least appealing to objective circumstances on some level.

69. "La necesidad de este libro," found in Guevara, *Apuntes críticos*, 31. Two of the letters containing Engels's arguments are Frederick Engels to W. Borgius, January 25, 1894, in *Marx and Engels Collected Works* (New York: International Publishers, 2004), 50:264–67; and Frederick Engels to Conrad Schmidt, October 27, 1890, in *Marx and Engels Collected Works* (New York: International Publishers, 2001), 49:59–63.

70. "Memoria Anual 1961–1962," found in Guevara, *El Che en la Revolución cubana*, 6:676. This text is undated but appears to have been written in 1962.

71. For one passage in which Guevara *does* insist that what is decisive is the workers' level of enthusiasm, and a passage that also evokes the notion of "permanent revolution," see "A los ganadores de la emulación de alfabetización," found in ibid., 3:500.

72. "A los compañeros argentinos," found in ibid., 4:218; see also Guevara's "The Meaning of Socialist Planning," found in Silverman, *Man and Socialism*, 101.

73. "Graduación del curso de administradores," found in Guevara, *El Che en la Revolución cubana*, 3:559.

74. "Clausura del Consejo de la CTC," found in ibid., 4:131.

75. "Reunión bimestral, julio 11 de 1964," found in ibid., 6:491; see also "Acto homenaje a Camilo," in ibid., 5:260.

76. Guevara's "Meaning of Socialist Planning," found in Silverman, *Man and Socialism*, 109. More generally, "The miscroscopic [sic] correlations he [Charles Bettelheim] attempts to establish between the level of development of the productive forces and legal property relations in every region or situation are impossible" (ibid., 104).

77. Ernest Mandel's "Mercantile Categories in the Period of Transition," in Silverman, *Man and Socialism*, 90; emphasis in the original.

78. "Reunión bimestral, enero 20 de 1962," found in Guevara, *El Che en la Revolución cubana*, 6:148.

79. "Technology and Society," found in Guevara, *Che: Selected Works*, 302.

80. Trotsky's *Results and Prospects*, found in *"Permanent Revolution,"* 99.

81. Mandel, "El debate económico," 315. The passage cited in the previous note also serves to illustrate Guevara's rejection of a mechanistic Marxism.

82. The words quoted are from González, *Che Guevara*, 149.

83. "Interview with *Libération*," found in Ernesto Che Guevara, *Che Guevara Speaks* (New York: Pathfinder Press, 2000), 140.

84. For brief discussion of some parties' rejection of revolutionary initiatives, see Anderson, *Revolutionary*, 596 and 678–79.

85. Martínez Heredia, "El Che Guevara," 256–57.

86. Pedro Vuskovic and Belarmino Elgueta, *Che Guevara en el presente de la América Latina* (Havana: Ediciones Casa de las Américas, 1987), 36.

87. "Fragmento de la entrevista concedida al periódico *El-Taliah* (*La Vanguardia*) de El Cairo, abril de 1965," found in Guevara, *Apuntes críticos*, 427.

88. Valdés Paz, "Todo es según el color," 115.

89. See, for example, "Inauguración fábrica de bujías," found in Guevara, *El Che en la Revolución cubana*, 5:155; "Fidel's trip to New York," found in Guevara, *Che Guevara Speaks*, 23; "The OAS Conference at Punta del Este," found in Guevara, *Che Guevara Reader*, 253; "At the United Nations," found in ibid., 337; Borrego, *Recuerdos*, 113; and the interview with Ulises Estrada Lescaille found in Barrio and Jenkins, *The Che Handbook*, 344.

90. Taibo, *Ernesto*, 358. "Superfluous" is Taibo's word.

91. Vitale, *Martí*, 191.

92. Guevara, *Apuntes filosóficos*, 300–1.

93. Besancenot and Löwy, *Che Guevara*, 61.

94. See Ulises Estrada's brief remarks in the interview with him found in Barrio and Jenkins, *Che Handbook*, 344.

95. "Conferencia televisada," found in Guevara, *El Che en la Revolución cubana*, 3:45.

96. "Clausura de la Asamblea de Producción de la Gran Habana," found in ibid., 3:447.

97. Besancenot and Löwy, *Che Guevara*, 72.

98. Löwy's prologue to Pericás, *Che*, 9–10; and Löwy, *Marxism*, xxvi–xxvii.

99. See, for example, Monereo, *Con su propia cabeza*, 116; Farber, *Politics*, xviii, 84, and 117. See also Juan Valdés Paz's "Notas para un epílogo," the epilogue to that book, 124.

100. "On Economic Planning in Cuba," found in Guevara, *Venceremos!*, 222.

101. Besancenot and Löwy, *Che Guevara*, 76–77.

102. See, for example, "On Economic Planning," found in Guevara, *Venceremos!*, 224.

103. Castro, "In Tribute," 26.

104. Randall, *Che*, 17.

105. For the story of Guevara's continuing education in mathematics, see Héctor Hernández Pardo, "¿ . . . Cuándo empezamos?," in *Testimonios sobre el Che*, ed. Marta Rojas (Havana: Editorial Pablo de la Torriente and Ediciones Aurelia, 2006).

Bibliography

WORKS BY ERNESTO CHE GUEVARA

Guevara, Ernesto Che. *Apuntes críticos a la economía política.* Edited by María del Carmen Ariet García. Melbourne: Ocean Sur, 2006.

———. *Apuntes filosóficos.* Edited by María del Carmen Ariet García. Mexico City: Ocean Sur, 2012.

———. *The Bolivian Diary.* Melbourne and New York: Ocean Press, 2006.

———. Carta a Miguel A. Quevedo, Director de la Revista *Bohemia*, 23 de mayo de 1959. In *Che desde la memoria*, edited by Víctor Casaus, 210. Havana, Melbourne, and New York: Centro de Estudios Che Guevara and Ocean Press, 2004.

———. *Che Guevara Reader.* Edited by David Deutschmann. Melbourne: Ocean Press, 2003.

———. *Che Guevara Speaks.* New York: Pathfinder Press, 2000.

———. *Che Guevara Talks to Young People.* Edited by Mary-Alice Waters. New York: Pathfinder Press, 2000.

———. *Che: Selected Works of Ernesto Guevara.* Edited by Rolando E. Bonachea and Nelson P. Valdés. Cambridge, MA, and London: The MIT Press, 1969.

———. "Conferencia ofrecida por el Comandante Guevara a los estudiantes de la carrera de Economía de la Universidad de Oriente." *Utopías, Nuestra Bandera* 184, no. 1 (2000): 153-81.

———. *Congo Diary: Episodes of the Revolutionary War in the Congo.* North Melbourne, Au.: Ocean Press, 2011.

———. "Cuba and the U.S." Interview by Leo Huberman. *Monthly Review* 13, no. 5 (1961). http://monthlyreview.org/1961/09/01/cuba-and-the-u-s/.

———. "Cuba Will Continue to Call Things by Their Right Names. Reply to General Assembly Debate, December 11, 1964." In *To Speak the Truth: Why Washington's "Cold War" against Cuba Doesn't End*, Fidel Castro and Ernesto Che Guevara, 145–58. New York: Pathfinder Press, 1992.

———. *El Che en la Revolución cubana.* 7 volumes. Havana: Editorial Ministerio del Azúcar, 1966.

———. *Escritos y discursos.* 9 volumes. Havana: Editorial de Ciencias Sociales, 1977.

———. *Guerrilla Warfare.* Translated by J. P. Morray. New York: Vintage Books, 1961.

———. "An Interview with 'Che' Guevara, Cuban Minister of Industries, 14 September 1961." Interview by Maurice Zeitlin. In *Cuba: An American Tragedy,* edited by Robert Scheer and Maurice Zeitlin, 337–46. Harmondsworth, UK: Penguin Books, Ltd., 1964.

———. Interview with *Face the Nation.* CBS Television Network. December 13, 1964. Transcript available online at https://guevaristas.org/2016/07/15/interview-of-che-guevara-on-cbs-face-the-nation-transcriptvideo/.

———. "La conferencia de prensa del nueve de agosto en el Playa Hotel." In *Para dar vuelta el mate: 1961, Ernesto Che Guevara en Uruguay,* 1:319–59. Edited by Asdrúbal Pereira Cabrera. Havana: Editora Política, 2012.

———. "'Pueblo de Bolivia; Pueblos de América': Una primera proclama inconclusa del Che." In *El Che en Bolivia: Documentos y testimonios; los otros diarios,* 2:188–89, edited by Carlos Soria Galvarro Terán. La Paz: La Razón, 2005.

———. "Qué es un 'guerrillero.'" In *Obras 1957–1967,* 1:153–56. Havana: Casa de Las Américas, 1970.

———. *Venceremos! The Speeches and Writings of Che Guevara.* Edited by John Gerassi. London: Panther Books Ltd., 1969.

OTHER WORKS CITED

Acosta Hechavarría, Roberto. "An Interview with Roberto Acosta Hechavarría." By Tano Nariño. Translated by Gary Tennant and John Sullivan. In "The Hidden Pearl of the Caribbean," *Revolutionary History* 7, no. 3 (2000): 243–51.

Ainsworth, Kelly. "Ernesto (Che) Guevara de la Serna." In *Biographical Dictionary of Marxism,* edited by Robert A. Gorman, 124–26. Westport, CT: Greenwood Press, 1986.

Almeida, Juan, et al. *Che siempre.* Donostia (San Sebastián), Sp.: Tercera Prensa-Hirugarren Prentsa, S.L., 1997.

Alonso, Aurelio. "El pensamiento revolucionario es invariablemente crítico." Interview with Pedro de La Hoz. In *Como el primer día,* edited by Pedro de La Hoz, 21–27. Havana: Editorial Letras Cubanas, 2008.

Álvarez Batista, Gerónimo. *Che: Una nueva batalla.* Havana: Editorial Pablo de la Torriente, 1994.

Anderson, Jon Lee. *Che Guevara: A Revolutionary Life.* London: Bantam Books, 1997.

Arboleya Cervera, Jesús. *El otro terrorismo: Medio siglo de política de los Estados Unidos hacia Cuba.* Havana: Editorial de Ciencias Sociales, 2009.

Arcos Bergnes, Ángel. *Evocando al Che.* Havana: Editorial de Ciencias Sociales, 2007.

Ariet García, María del Carmen. *El pensamiento político de Ernesto Che Guevara.* Mexico City: Ocean Sur, 2010.

Arneson, Richard J. "Is Work Special? Justice and the Distribution of Employment." *American Political Science Review* 84, no. 4 (1990): 1127–47.

Arrosagaray, Enrique. *Rodolfo Walsh en Cuba: Agencia Prensa Latina, militancia, ron y criptografía.* Buenos Aires: Catálogos, 2004.

Báez, Luis. Más esperanza que fe: Revelaciones de Roberto Fernández Retamar. Havana: Casa Editora Abril, 2006.

———. "No te puedes separar de Fidel." Interview by Pedro de La Hoz. In *Como el primer día*, edited by Pedro de La Hoz, 43–50. Havana: Editorial Letras Cubanas, 2008.

Barker, Ronald. "Internationalism." In *Dictionary of Theories*, edited by Jennifer Bothamley, 282–83. London, Detroit, and Washington, DC: Gale Research International Ltd., 1993.

Barrio, Hilda, and Gareth Jenkins. *The Che Handbook*. London: MQ Publications, Ltd., 2003.

Benn, Stanley I. "Egalitarianism and the Equal Consideration of Interests." In *Equality* (Nomos IX), edited by J. Roland Pennock and John W. Chapman, 61–78. New York: Atherton Press, 1967.

Besancenot, Oliver, and Michael Löwy. *Che Guevara: His Revolutionary Legacy*. Translated by James Membrez. New York: Monthly Review Press, 2009.

Black, George. *The Good Neighbor: How the United States Wrote the History of Central America and the Caribbean*. New York: Pantheon Books, 1988.

Bolender, Keith. *Voices from the Other Side: An Oral History of Terrorism against Cuba*. London and New York: Pluto Press, 2010.

Borrego, Orlando. "Álvaro Vargas Llosa Jr.: Un vástago al descubierto." *Rebelión*, November 21, 2005. http://www.rebelion.org/noticia.php?id=23017.

———. *Che: El camino del fuego*. 2nd ed. Havana: Imagen Contemporánea, 2011.

———. *Che: Recuerdos en ráfaga*. Havana: Editorial de Ciencias Sociales, 2004.

———. Preface to Guevara, *El Che en la Revolución cubana*, vol. 1. Havana: Editorial Ministerio del Azúcar, 1966.

Bottomore, T. B. Introduction to *Karl Marx: Early Writings*, translated and edited by T. B. Bottomore, vii–xix. New York: McGraw-Hill, 1964.

Bottomore, Tom, ed. *A Dictionary of Marxist Thought*. 2nd ed. Oxford and Malden, MA: Blackwell Publishers, Ltd., 1991.

Bullock Alan. "Guevara de la Serna, Ernesto (Che)." In *Twentieth-Century Culture: A Biographical Companion*, edited by Alan Bullock and R. B. Woodings, 293–94. New York: Harper and Row Publishers, 1983.

Bychkova, N., R. Lavrov, and V. Lubisheva, eds. *Communist Morality*. Moscow: Progress Publishers, n.d.

Carens, Joseph H. *Equality, Moral Incentives, and the Market: An Essay in Utopian Politico-Economic Theory*. Chicago and London: The University of Chicago Press, 1981.

Castañeda, Jorge G. *Compañero: The Life and Death of Che Guevara*. Translated by Marina Castañeda. New York: Vintage Books, 1998.

Castro, Fidel. "Discurso pronunciado como conclusión de las reuniones con los intelectuales cubanos, Biblioteca Nacional 'José Martí.'" In *Habla Fidel: 25 discursos en la Revolución*, edited by Pedro Álvarez Tabío, 195–229. Havana: Oficina de Publicaciones del Consejo de Estado, 2008.

———. "Discurso pronunciado por el Comandante Fidel Castro Ruz, primer ministro del Gobierno Revolucionario y primer secretario del PCC, en el Acto Clausura." In *Tricontinental/ 1966*, 149–61. Havana: Secretaría General de la O.S.P.A.A.A.L., 1966.

———. "In Tribute to Che." In *Reminiscences of the Cuban Revolutionary War*, by Ernesto Che Guevara, translated by Victoria Ortiz, 15–27. Harmondsworth, UK: Penguin Books, 1969.

———. "Las ideas del Che son de una vigencia absolua y total." In *El pensamiento económico de Ernesto Che Guevara*, by Carlos Tablada, 77–103. Panama City: Ruth Casa Editorial, 2005.

Cohen, G. A. *Self-Ownership, Freedom, and Equality*. New York and Cambridge: Cambridge University Press, 1995.

Cushion, Stephen. *A Hidden History of the Cuban Revolution: How the Working Class Shaped the Guerrillas' Victory*. New York: Monthly Review Press, 2016.

Del Río, Eugenio. "Influencia de Che Guevara en la Europa occidental de los años setenta." In *Disentir, resistir: Entre dos épocas*, 21–31. Madrid: Talasa Ediciones, S.L., 2001.

Deutscher, Isaac. "On Socialist Man." In *Marxism in Our Time*, edited by Tamara Deutscher, 227–54. London: Jonathan Cape Ltd., 1971.

Díaz, Elena, and Delia Luisa López. "Ernesto Che Guevara: Aspectos de su pensamiento ético." In *Pensar al Che*, 2:135–96, edited by Alfredo Prieto González. Havana: Editorial José Martí, 1989.

Draper, Hal. *The "Dictatorship of the Proletariat" from Marx to Lenin*. New York: Monthly Review Press, 1987.

Elster, Jon. *Making Sense of Marx*. Cambridge: Cambridge University Press, 1985.

Engels, Frederick. *Anti-Dühring*. In *Marx and Engels Collected Works*, 25:5–309. New York: International Publishers, 1987.

———. Frederick Engels to Conrad Schmidt, October 27, 1890. In *Marx and Engels Collected Works*, 49:57–65. New York: International Publishers, 2001.

———. Frederick Engels to W. Borgius, January 25, 1894. In *Marx and Engels Collected Works*, 50:264–67. New York: International Publishers, 2004.

———. "Introduction to Karl Marx's *Wage Labour and Capital*." In *Marx and Engels Collected Works*, 27:194–201. New York: International Publishers, 1990.

———. "Karl Marx's Funeral." In *Marx and Engels Collected Works*, 24:467–71. New York: International Publishers, 1989.

———. *Ludwig Feuerbach and the End of Classical German Philosophy*. In *Marx and Engels Collected Works*, 26:357–98. New York: International Publishers, 1990.

———. "Principles of Communism." In *Marx and Engels Collected Works*, 6:341–57. New York: International Publishers, 1976.

Escalante Font, Fabián. *Operación exterminio: 50 años de agresiones contra Cuba*. Havana: Editorial de Ciencias Sociales, 2010.

Farber, Samuel. *The Politics of Che Guevara: Theory and Practice*. Chicago: Haymarket Books, 2016.

Fernández Buey, Francisco. "Ernesto 'Che' Guevara, ayer y hoy." Introduction to *Escritos revolucionarios*, by Ernesto Che Guevara, edited by Francisco Fernández Buey, 7–22. Madrid: Libros de la Catarata, 1999.

Fernández Retamar, Roberto. *Cuba defendida*. Buenos Aires: Nuestra América Editorial, 2004.

———. *Entrevisto*. Havana: Ediciones Unión, 1982.

Fornet, Ambrosio. "La década prodigiosa: Un testimonio personal." In *Narrar la nación: Ensayos en blanco y negro*, 353–63. Havana: Letras Cubanas, 2011.

Fromm, Erich, ed. *Socialist Humanism*. London: Allen Lane, the Penguin Press, 1967.

Galeano, Eduardo. "El Che Guevara: Cuba como vitrina o catapulta." In *Nosotros decimos no: Crónicas (1963/1988)*, 53–63. Madrid: Siglo XXI de España Editores, S.A., 1989.

Galeano, Eduardo, and Tomás Borge. "Eduardo y Tomás, robles de raíz milenaria."

Gálvez Rodríguez, William. *Che en Cuba: El guerrillero*. Havana: Editorial de Ciencias Sociales, 2007.

———. *El guerrillero heroico: Che en Bolivia*. Arrigorriaga, Spain: Status Ediciones, S.L.: 2003.

———. "Um exemplo superior." Interview by Viriato Teles. In *A utopia segundo Che Guevara*, by Viriato Teles, 157–69. Porto: Campo das Letras, 2005.

Geras, Norman. *Marx and Human Nature*. London: Verso, 1983.

González, Mike. *Che Guevara and the Cuban Revolution*. London and Sydney: Bookmarks, 2004.

Guerra, Sergio, and Alejo Maldonado. *Historia de la Revolución cubana*. Tafalla, Sp.: Txalaparta, 2009.

Habel, Janette. "Guevara: La ética en el combate político." *El Viejo Topo* 110 (1997): 14–23.

Halperin, Maurice. *The Taming of Fidel Castro*. Berkeley, Los Angeles, and London: University of California Press, 1981.

Hernández Pardo, Héctor. "¿ . . . Cúando empezamos?" In *Testimonios sobre el Che*, edited by Marta Rojas, 173–79. Havana: Editorial Pablo de la Torriente and Ediciones Aurelia, 2006.

Hernández, Rafael, Marta Gloria Morales, Omar Everleny Pérez, Manuel Pérez Paredes, and Manuel Yepe. "1968: Una mirada retrospectiva." In Último jueves: Los debates de Temas, 4:91–109. Havana: Ediciones ICAIC and Revista *Temas*, 2010.

Hodges, Donald C. *The Bureaucratization of Socialism*. Amherst: The University of Massachusetts Press, 1981.

———. *The Latin American Revolution: Politics and Strategy from Apro-Marxism to Guevarism*. New York: W. Morrow, 1974.

Karol, K. S. "Cuba's Road to Communism." *New Statesman*, May 19, 1961, 778–79.

———. *Guerrillas in Power: The Course of the Cuban Revolution*. Translated by Arnold Pomerans. New York: Hill and Wang, 1970.

———. "Why Quadros Fell." *New Statesman*, September 1, 1961, 265.

Kohan, Néstor. *De Ingenieros al Che: Ensayos sobre el marxismo argentino y latinoamericano*. Buenos Aires: Editorial Biblos, 2000.

———. "Por la revolución mundial." *Rebelión* (website). March 20, 2011. http://www.rebelion.org/noticia.php?id=124579.

Kohn, Melvin L., and Carmi Schooler. *Work and Personality: An Inquiry Into the Impact of Social Stratification*. Norwood, NJ: Ablex Publishing Corporation, 1983.

Korda [Alberto Díaz Gutiérrez]. "La foto que ha recorrido el mundo." Interview by Alicia Elizundia. In *Bajo la piel del Che*, edited by Alicia Elizundia, 136–40. Havana: Ediciones *La Memoria*, Centro Cultural *Pablo de la Torriente Brau*, 2005.

Koutzii, Flávio, and José Corrêa Leite. *Che 20 anos depois*. São Paulo: Editora Busca Vida, Ltda., 1987.

Kronenberg, Clive W. "Manifestations of Humanism in Revolutionary Cuba: Che and the Principle of Universality." *Latin American Perspectives* 36, no. 2 (2009): 66–80.

Lamrani, Salim. *The Economic War against Cuba*. Translated by Larry Oberg. New York: Monthly Review Press, 2013.

———, ed. *Superpower Principles: U.S. Terrorism against Cuba*. Monroe, ME: Common Courage Press, 2005.

Lane, Robert E. *The Market Experience*. Cambridge: Cambridge University Press, 1991.

Laski, Harold J. *Harold J. Laski on the Communist Manifesto*. New York: New American Library, 1967.

Lenin, Vladimir I. "From the Destruction of the Old Social System to the Creation of the New." In *Collected Works*, 30:516–18. Moscow: Progress Publishers, 1965.

———. "A Great Beginning: Heroism of the Workers in the Rear; 'Communist Subbotniks.'" In *Collected Works*, 29:409–34. Moscow: Progress Publishers, 1965.

———. "How to Organise Competition." In *Collected Works*, 26:404–15. Moscow: Progress Publishers, 1972.

———. "Imperialism and the Split in Socialism." In *Collected Works*, 23:105–20. Moscow: Progress Publishers, 1964.

———. *Imperialism, the Highest Stage of Capitalism: A Popular Outline*. In *Collected Works*, 22:185–304. Moscow: Progress Publishers, 1964.

———. *"Left-Wing" Communism: An Infantile Disorder*. In *Collected Works*, 31:17–118. Moscow: Progress Publishers, 1966.

———. "A Little Picture in Illustration of Big Problems." In *Collected Works*, 28:386–89. Moscow: Progress Publishers, 1965.

———. "The Petrograd City Conference of the R.S.D.L.P. (Bolsheviks)." In *Collected Works*, 24:139–66. Moscow: Progress Publishers, 1964.

———. "Preliminary Draft Theses on the National and the Colonial Questions (For the Second Congress of the Communist International)." In *Collected Works*, 31:144–51. Moscow: Progress Publishers, 1966.

———. "Report on Subbotniks Delivered to a Moscow City Conference of the R.C.P. (B.), December 20, 1919." In *Collected Works*, 30:283–88. Moscow: Progress Publishers, 1965.

———. "The Socialist Revolution and the Right of Nations to Self-Determination." In *Collected Works*, 22:143–56. Moscow: Progress Publishers, 1964.

———. "The Tasks of the Proletariat in Our Revolution (Draft Platform for the Proletarian Party)." In *Collected Works*, 24:55–88. Moscow: Progress Publishers, 1964.

———. "Theses on the Fundamental Tasks of the Second Congress of the Communist International." In *Collected Works*, 31:184–201. Moscow: Progress Publishers, 1966.

———. *What Is to Be Done? Burning Questions of Our Movement*. In *Collected Works*, 5:347–529. London: Lawrence and Wishart, 1961.

Levine, Andrew. *The End of the State*. London: Verso, 1987.

Llorente, Renzo. "El aporte de Aníbal Ponce a la crítica del humanismo moderno." *Utopía y Praxis Latinoamericana*, no. 60 (2013): 119–26.

———. Review of *The Politics of Che Guevara: Theory and Practice*, by Sam Farber. *International Journal of Cuban Studies* 9, no. 1 (2017): 155–57.

———. "'Socialism and Man in Cuba' Revisited." *International Critical Thought* 5, no. 3 (2015): 401–11.

López García, Delia Luisa. "Che Guevara: Una aproximación a su ideario." In *Che: El hombre del siglo XXI*, 118–25. Havana: University of Havana and Editorial Félix Varela, 2001.

López Muiño, Fernando. "Vivencias con el Che: Viaje desde Cuba a Punta del Este." Interview by Carlos González Torres. In *El debut continental de un estadista: Ernesto Che Guevara en Punta del Este, 1961*, edited by Carlos D. González Torres, 33–55. Havana: Editora Política, 2001.

Löwy, Michael. *The Marxism of Che Guevara: Philosophy, Economics, Revolutionary Warfare*. 2nd ed. Lanham, MD, and Boulder: Rowman & Littlefield Publishers, 2007.

Lukács, Georg. "The Moral Mission of the Communist Party." In Lukács, *Tactics and Ethics*, 64–70.

———. *The Process of Democratization*. Translated by Susanne Bernhardt and Norman Levine. Albany: State University of New York Press, 1991.

———. *Record of a Life*. Edited by István Eörsi. Translated by Rodney Livingstone. London: Verso Editions, 1983.

———. *Tactics and Ethics, 1919–1929*. Translated by Michael McColgan. London and New York: Verso, 2014.

Lukes, Steven. *Marxism and Morality*. Oxford and New York: Oxford University Press, 1985.

Luxemburg, Rosa. *The Rosa Luxemburg Reader*. Edited by Peter Hudis and Kevin B. Anderson. New York: Monthly Review Press, 2004.

———. *The Russian Revolution*. In Luxemburg, *The Rosa Luxemburg Reader*, 281–310.

MacIntyre, Alasdair. "Marxism of the Will." In *Alasdair MacIntyre's Engagement with Marxism: Selected Writings, 1953–1974*, edited by Paul Blackledge and Neil Davidson, 373–79. Leiden and Boston: Brill, 2008.

Macpherson, C. B. "Elegant Tombstones: A Note on Friedman's Freedom." In *Democratic Theory: Essays in Retrieval*, 143–56. Oxford: Clarendon Press, 1973.

———. *The Political Theory of Possessive Individualism: Hobbes to Locke*. Oxford and New York: Oxford University Press, 1962.

Mandel, Ernest. "El debate económico en Cuba durante el periodo 1963–1964." In *El Gran Debate*, edited by David Deutschmann and Javier Salado, 309–318. Melbourne and New York: Ocean Press, 2006.

Marcuse, Herbert. *Counterrevolution and Revolt*. Boston: Beacon Press, 1972.

———. *An Essay on Liberation*. Boston: Beacon Press, 1969.

Mariátegui, José Carlos. *Ideología y política*. In *Mariátegui total*, 1:159–276. Lima: Empresa Editora Amauta S.A., 1994.

Martí, José. "Discurso en el *Liceo Cubano*, Tampa (Con todos y para el bien de todos)." In *Obras Completas*, 2nd ed., 4:269–79. Havana: Editorial de Ciencias Sociales, 1975.

Martínez Heredia, Fernando. *A viva voz*. Havana: Editorial de Ciencias Sociales, 2010.

———. "El Che Guevara: Los sesenta y los noventa." In *El corrimiento hacia el rojo*, 244–59. Havana: Editorial Letras Cubanas, 2001.

———. *Las ideas y la batalla del Che*. Havana: Ciencias Sociales and Ruth Casa Editorial, 2010.

Martínez Llebrez, Vicente R., and Luis. A. Sabadí Castillo. *Concepción de la calidad en el pensamiento del Che*. Havana: Editorial de Ciencias Sociales, 2006.

Martinez-Saenz, Miguel. "Che Guevara's New Man: Embodying a Communitarian Attitude." *Latin American Perspectives* 31, no. 6 (2004): 15–30.

Marx, Karl. *Capital: A Critique of Political Economy, Vol. 1*. In *Marx and Engels Collected Works*, vol. 35. New York: International Publishers, 1996.

———. *Capital: A Critique of Political Economy, Vol. 3*. In *Marx and Engels Collected Works*, vol. 37. New York: International Publishers, 1998.

———. *The Civil War in France*. In *Marx and Engels Collected Works*, 22:311–59. New York: International Publishers, 1986.

———. "Comments on James Mill, Élémens d'économie politique." In *Marx and Engels Collected Works*, 3:211–28. New York: International Publishers, 1975.

———. "Contribution to the Critique of Hegel's Philosophy of Law. Introduction." In *Marx and Engels Collected Works*. 3:175–87. New York: International Publishers, 1975.

———. *A Contribution to the Critique of Political Economy, Part One*. In *Marx and Engels Collected Works*, 29:261–417. New York: International Publishers, 1987.

———. "Critical Marginal Notes on the Article 'The King of Prussia and Social Reform, by a Prussian.'" In *Marx and Engels Collected Works*, 3:189–206. New York: International Publishers, 1975.

———. "Critique of the Gotha Programme." In *Marx and Engels Collected Works*, 24:81–99. New York: International Publishers, 1989.

———. "Draft of an Article on Friedrich List's Book *Das Nationale System der Politischen Oekonomie.*" In *Marx and Engels Collected Works*, 4:265–93. New York: International Publishers, 1975.

———. *Economic and Philosophic Manuscripts of 1844.* In *Marx and Engels Collected Works*, 3:229–346. New York: International Publishers, 1975.

———. *Economic Manuscript of 1861–1863.* In *Marx and Engels Collected Works*, vol. 30. New York: International Publishers, 1988.

———. *The Eighteenth Brumaire of Louis Bonaparte.* In *Marx and Engels Collected Works*, 11:103–197. New York: International Publishers, 1979.

———. "Inaugural Address of the Working Men's International Association." In *Marx and Engels Collected Works*, 20:5–13. New York: International Publishers, 1985.

———. "Moralising Criticism and Critical Morality: A Contribution to German Cultural History; Contra Karl Heinzen." In *Marx and Engels Collected Works*, 6:312–40. New York: International Publishers, 1976.

———. "On the Hague Congress." In *Marx and Engels Collected Works*, 23:254–56. New York: International Publishers, 1988.

———. *Outlines of the Critique of Political Economy (Rough Draft of 1857–1858).* In *Marx and Engels Collected Works*, 29:7–255. New York: International Publishers, 1987.

———. *Outlines of the Critique of Political Economy (Rough Draft of 1857–1858).* In *Marx and Engels Collected Works*, 28:51–537. New York: International Publishers, 1986.

———. *The Poverty of Philosophy.* In *Marx and Engels Collected Works*, 6:109–212. New York: International Publishers, 1976.

———. "Provisional Rules of the Association." In *Marx and Engels Collected Works*, 20:14–16. New York: International Publishers, 1985.

———. "Theses on Feuerbach." In *Marx and Engels Collected Works*, 5:3–5. New York: International Publishers, 1976.

Marx, Karl, and Frederick Engels. "Circular Letter to August Bebel, Wilhelm Liebknecht, Wilhelm Bracke and Others." In *Marx and Engels Collected Works*, 24:253–69. New York: International Publishers, 1989.

———. *The German Ideology.* In *Marx and Engels Collected Works*, 5:22–539. New York: International Publishers, 1976.

———. *The Holy Family; or Critique of Critical Criticism.* In *Marx and Engels Collected Works*, 4:7–211. New York: International Publishers, 1975.

———. *Manifesto of the Communist Party.* In *Marx and Engels Collected Works*, 6:477–519. New York: International Publishers, 1976.

Masetti, Jorge Ricardo. *Los que luchan y los que lloran, y otros escritos inéditos.* Buenos Aires: Nuestra América, 2006.

Massari, Roberto. *Che Guevara: Grandeza y riesgo de la utopía.* 2nd ed. Translated by José María Pérez. Tafalla, Sp.: Txalaparta, 1992.

McLellan, David. *Marxism after Marx.* 4th ed. Basingstoke, UK: Palgrave Macmillan, 2007.

Mendoza Gil, Mayra, ed. *Para vivir como tú vives: Anecdotario del Che.* Havana: Editora Política, 2006.

Mikoyan, Anastas. "Más vale ver una vez que escuchar cien." Interview by Norberto Fuentes. In *Posición uno*, by Norberto Fuentes, 162–75. Havana: Ediciones Unión, 1982.

Miliband, Ralph. *Socialism for a Sceptical Age.* London and New York: Verso, 1995.

Mill, John Stuart. *Principles of Political Economy.* In *Collected Works of John Stuart Mill*, vol. 2. Edited by J. M. Robson. Toronto: University of Toronto Press, 1965.

Miller, David, ed. *Blackwell Encyclopedia of Political Thought*. Oxford and Cambridge, MA: Blackwell Publishers, Ltd., 1991.

Mills, C. Wright, ed. *The Marxists*. New York: Dell Publishing Co., Inc., 1962.

Minogue, Kenneth. "Che Guevara." In *The New Left: Six Critical Essays*, edited by Maurice Cranston, 17–48. London, Sydney, and Toronto: The Bodley Head, Ltd., 1970.

Monereo, Manuel. *Con su propia cabeza: El socialismo en la obra y la vida del Che*. Barcelona: El ViejoTopo, 2001.

Muñoz-Unsain, Alfredo. "Cuba, sociedad anónima: Memorias parciales de un corresponsal in La Habana." Unpublished manuscript. Accessed April 18, 2017. http://www.juangasparini.com/libros-especiales/cuba-sociedad-anonima/.

Napurí, Ricardo. "Thirty Years since the Death of Ernesto Guevara: An Interview with Ricardo Napurí." Interview with José Bermúdez and Luis Castelli. Translated by Alejandra Ríos and Philip Marchant. In "The Hidden Pearl of the Caribbean," *Revolutionary History* 7, no. 3 (2000): 262–77.

Nielsen, Kai. *Equality and Liberty*. Totowa, NJ: Rowman and Allanheld, 1985.

O'Donnell, Pacho. *Che: La vida por un mundo mejor*. Barcelona: Plaza y Janés, 2003.

Pannekoek, Anton. "World Revolution and Communist Tactics." In *Pannekoek and Gorter's Marxism*, edited by D. A. Smart, 93–141. London: Pluto Press, 1978.

Perales, Iosu, ed. *Querido Che*. Madrid: Editorial Revolución, S.A.L., 1987.

Pérez-Rolo, Martha, Juan Antonio Blanco, Miguel Limia, Delia Luisa López, and Jonathán Quirós. "El socialismo y el hombre en Cuba: Una mirada en los 90." *Temas* 11 (1997): 105–19.

Pericás, Luiz Bernardo. *Che Guevara y el debate económico en Cuba*. Translated by Rodolfo Alpízar Castillo. Buenos Aires: Ediciones Corregidor, 2011.

Piñeiro Losada, Manuel. *Barbarroja: Selección de testimonios y discursos del Comandante Manuel Piñeiro Losada*. Edited by Luis Suárez Salazar. Havana: Ediciones Tricontinental-Simar S.A., 1999.

Quatrième Internationale. "Entrevue avec 'Che' Guevara." *Quatrième Internationale* 14 (1961): 94–95.

Randall, Margaret. *Che on My Mind*. Durham and London: Duke University Press, 2013.

Rodríguez, Carlos Rafael. "Sobre el hombre nuevo." In *Letra con filo*, 2:566–67. Havana: Editorial de Ciencias Sociales, 1983.

Rodríguez Cruz, Juan Carlos, ed. *Cuba, la historia no contada*. Havana: Editorial Capitán San Luis, 2003.

Roemer, John E. *A Future for Socialism*. Cambridge, MA: Harvard University Press, 1994.

Russell, Bertrand. "Peace through Resistance to U.S. Imperialism." In *Readings in U.S. Imperialism*, edited by K. T. Fann and Donald C. Hodges, xi–xvii. Boston: Porter Sargent Publisher, 1971.

Russell, Sam. "The Americans Still Want to Come Here." *Daily Worker*, December 4, 1962, 2.

Sacristán Luzón, Manuel. *Sobre Marx y marxismo: Panfletos y materiales*. Edited by Juan-Ramón Capella. Barcelona: Icaria Editorial, S.A., 1983.

Sáenz, Tirso W. *El Che ministro: Testimonio de un colaborador*. Havana: Ciencias Sociales, 2005.

Salazar Bondy, Augusto. "La quiebra del capitalismo." In *Entre escila y Caribdis*, 155–58. Lima: Instituto Nacional de Cultura, 1973.

Sánchez, Germán. *Che sin enigmas*. Mexico City: Ocean Sur, 2007.

Sánchez Vázquez, Adolfo. "El socialismo y el Che." In *Filosofía, praxis y socialismo*, 115–19. Buenos Aires: Tesis 11 Grupo Editor, 1998.

Schoultz, Lars. *That Infernal Little Cuban Republic: The United States and the Cuban Revolution*. Chapel Hill: The University of North Carolina Press, 2009.

Silva, Ludovico. "El hombre del siglo XXI: La memoria futura del Che Guevara." In *En busca del socialismo perdido: Las bases de la Perestroika y la Glasnost*, 93–102. Caracas: Editorial Pomaire Venezuela, S.A., 1991.

Silverman, Bertram, ed. *Man and Socialism in Cuba: The Great Debate*. New York: Atheneum, 1973.

Sinclair, Andrew, ed. *Viva Che! The Strange Death and Life of Che Guevara*. Stroud, UK: Sutton Publishing Limited, 2006.

Singer, Peter. *How Are We to Live? Ethics in an Age of Self-Interest*. Melbourne: The Text Publishing Company, 1993.

Stryker, Deena. *Cuba 1964: When the Revolution Was Young*. Lexington, KY: Big Picture Publishers, 2013.

Suárez Ramos, Felipa de las Mercedes. "Tribunales revolucionarios: Monumento a la justicia." *Trabajadores*, January 19, 2014. http://www.trabajadores.cu/20140119/tribunales-revolucionarios-monumento-la-justicia/.

Suárez Salazar, Luis. "Che: Artista de la lucha revolucionaria." In *Pensar al Che*, vol. 1, edited by Alfredo Prieto González, 135–92. Havana: Editorial José Martí, 1989.

Sweezy, Paul M., and Leo Huberman, eds. *Paul A. Baran (1910–1964): A Collective Portrait*. New York: Monthly Review Press, 1965.

Taibo II, Paco Ignacio. *Ernesto Guevara, también conocido come el Che*. 4th ed. Barcelona: Editorial Planeta, 1997.

Tennant, Gary. "The Reorganised Partido Obrero Revolucionario (Trotskista) and the 1959 Revolution." In "The Hidden Pearl of the Caribbean," *Revolutionary History* 7, no. 3 (2000): 175–216.

Trotsky, Leon. *Literature and Revolution*. Translated by Rose Strunsky. Ann Arbor: University of Michigan Press, 1960.

———. *"The Permanent Revolution" and "Results and Prospects"*. Translated by Brian Pearce New York: Pathfinder Press, 1970.

———. *Problems of Everyday Life and Other Writings on Culture and Science*. New York: Monad Press, 1973.

———. *Terrorism and Communism*. Ann Arbor: The University of Michigan Press, 1961.

Valdés Paz, Juan. "Todo es según el color del cristal con que se mira (Comentarios a *La vida en rojo* de Jorge Castañeda)." In *Che: El hombre del siglo XXI*, 110–17. Havana: University of Havana and Editorial Félix Varela, 2001.

Venable, Vernon. *Human Nature: The Marxian View*. London: Dennis Dobson Ltd., 1946.

Vitale, Luis. *De Martí a Chiapas: Balance de un siglo*. Santiago, Cl.: Ed. Síntesis y CELA, 1995.

Vuskovic, Pedro, and Belarmino Elgueta. *Che Guevara en el presente de la América Latina*. Havana: Ediciones Casa de las Américas, 1987.

Weale, Albert. "Needs and Interests." In *Concise Routledge Encyclopedia of Philosophy*, 620. London and New York: Routledge, 2000.

Weber, Max. "Politics as a Vocation." In *From Max Weber: Essays in Sociology*, translated and edited by H. H. Gerth and C. Wright Mills, 77–128. New York: Oxford University Press, 1946.

Wilczynski, Jozef. *An Encyclopedic Dictionary of Marxism, Socialism and Communism*. Berlin and New York: De Gruyter, 1981.

Yaffe, Helen. *Che Guevara: The Economics of Revolution*. Basingstoke, UK: Palgrave Macmillan, 2009.

Index

About the Author

Renzo Llorente teaches philosophy on Saint Louis University's Madrid Campus. He is the author of *Beyond the Pale: Exercises in Provocation* (2010) and many articles on topics in moral, social, and political philosophy. He is also the translator and editor of *The Marxism of Manuel Sacristán: From Communism to the New Social Movements* (2014).

TV
366

Lightning Source UK Ltd.
Milton Keynes UK
UKOW01f1028210218
318253UK00001B/254/P